The Apple Personal Computer for Beginners

The Apple Personal Computer for Beginners

Seamus Dunn and Valerie Morgan
(New University of Ulster)

Englewood Cliffs, New Jersey London New Delhi
Singapore Sydney Tokyo Toronto Wellington

Library of Congress Cataloging in Publication Data

Dunn, Seamus, 1939–
The Apple personal computer for beginners.

Bibliography: p.
Includes index.
1. Apple computer. I. Morgan, Valerie, 1943–
II. Title.
QA76.8.A66D86 001.64 82-618
ISBN 0-13-039149-2 AACR2
ISBN 0-13-039131-X (pbk.)

British Library Cataloging in Publication Data

Dunn, Seamus
The Apple personal computer for beginners.
1. Apple computer
I. Title II. Morgan, Valerie
001.64′04 QA76.8.A/

ISBN 0-13-039149-2
ISBN 0-13-039131-X Pbk

PRENTICE-HALL INTERNATIONAL, INC., *London*
PRENTICE-HALL OF AUSTRALIA PTY. LTD., *Sydney*
PRENTICE-HALL CANADA, INC., *Toronto*
PRENTICE-HALL OF INDIA PRIVATE LIMITED, *New Delhi*
PRENTICE-HALL OF JAPAN, INC., *Tokyo*
PRENTICE-HALL OF SOUTHEAST ASIA PTE., LTD., *Singapore*
PRENTICE-HALL, INC., *Englewood Cliffs, New Jersey*
WHITEHALL BOOKS LIMITED, *Wellington, New Zealand*

10 9 8 7 6 5 4 3

Printed in the United States of America

This book is dedicated to the memory of
Vincent McGeown
colleague and friend

Contents

Preface

This book relies very heavily on learning by doing. It can be used most successfully if the reader is sitting in front of an Apple computer. At all stages it is necessary to test on the machine the ideas and suggestions proposed in the book. Many of the techniques will, in fact, only make sense when they have been typed in and tried.

The book is intended for beginners, in the first instance. It is not necessary to have had any experience at all with computers, nor is it necessary to have a teacher available. Anyone who has bought an Apple, or who has access to one, can begin immediately. The pace is deliberately slow and careful, especially in the early chapters, and all the materials have been tried out by a number of beginners.

We have not set out to write an introduction to programming or to the language BASIC. Any user of the book will certainly learn quite a lot of BASIC, incidentally; but in order to get the very best possible value from this work, we recommend that an introductory book on BASIC be used for reference purposes, and a list is provided in Appendix H. As well as this the *Applesoft BASIC Programming Manual*, produced by Apple Computers, is a useful supplementary book and we recommend all readers to use this book as well.

There is a mistaken assumption in the minds of many that computers can be successfully used only by mathematicians. We wish to make it clear that, although those with a background in mathematics could learn a great deal about programming on Apple from this book, it was written with a very general readership in mind. In other words those who are worried about mathematics need not be afraid of this book.

The book is divided into 11 chapters each of which deals with a different Apple facility. New words and new ideas are always introduced with references to an example or series of examples which are meant to be tested at once on the computer. Ideally the book should be read from the beginning, and worked through sequentially since some thought has gone into the ordering of the various ideas. However, a reader with some experience who wished to find information about a specific problem would be able to read the relevant section as a unit in itself.

We have written the book about the basic machine and about its general operation and have assumed that the user has a floppy disk system available for off-line storage. We have not referred to printers, or any other peripheral devices, except in appendices. Nor have we attempted to cover machine-code programing in any exhaustive way. We have, however, included a chapter which should make the basic necessities of machine-code programing available to the user.

At the back there are reference tables of data showing sets of special numbers associated with Apple. The importance of these is carefully explained in the text. There are also a number of Appendices which list and describe a number of other Apple facilities, including hardware, software, various configurations, Integer BASIC and other languages.

We hope that the book will also serve as a reference book for all Apple users, including experienced ones. The index is meant to be comprehensive so that anyone with a query about a particular Apple facility or routine ought to be able to find a suitable explanation or example.

We would like to express our thanks to Alex Parke of the Industrial Unit at the New University of Ulster, and Brian Keating of C.E.M. Microcomputer Services, Belfast, for help with equipment, resources and advice. Finally, our thanks are also due to our typist, Maxine Pickering, who had the unenviable job of typing the manuscript.

1

Beginning with Apple

LOOKING AT APPLE

A photograph of the Apple is shown on page 3. There are three main parts: the first part is a light-coloured box with the words Apple II written on it. At the front there is a keyboard rather like a typewriter, but with some extra keys. This is the actual computer. The second part is a television or monitor of some sort. This monitor and the Apple are connected together by a cable at the back. These two parts have separate power lines which are plugged into normal power sockets (that is normal AC circuits) and each is switched on with a rocker-switch. The third part is two small boxes with Disk II written on the front. Above this is a red light with the words "in use" beside it. These boxes are Disk Drives, and they are connected to the Apple by a multicolored flat flex. In some cases there will be only one of these disk drives.

There are a number of different versions of the Apple available, but this book will be concerned with the Apple II and the Apple II plus personal computer. Appendix A, at the back of this book (page 172), describes the various versions, and also indicates what the differences in operation are. However, it is important to say here that the differences are very small and almost everything that we describe will be usable on all Apples. Some machines may have a tape recorder instead of a disk drive and the operation of this is described on page 177.

Make sure that the monitor is properly attached to the computer and that the disk drive has been fitted carefully. A careful description of how to do these is given in the Apple manuals. When you are sure that they are properly fitted, plug in the two power lines and switch on the monitor. Do not switch on the Apple as yet.

Among the diskettes that accompany the Apple there is one labelled *System Master DOS* 3.3. (If your system uses DOS 3.2.1, turn to the description of this on page 173). Put this diskette into the disk drive and close the door. Now turn on the switch at the back of Apple. If you have two drives, watch to see where the light goes on and label this number one. This is the one that we will be referring to in this book.

As soon as you switch on the Apple II the word Apple II will appear at the top of the screen. If all is well, the light on the disk drive will go on, it will whirr and make clicking sounds, and after a while a square bracket (]) will appear on the screen. Shortly after this some words will appear and the screen should then look like this:

```
DOS VERSION 3.3    (DATE)
APPLE II PLUS OR ROMCARD     SYSTEM MASTER
]□
```

If this does not happen, try switching off at the back and then switching on again. You should also try to tune the screen of the monitor. If none of these work you should seek help.

When you press any key on the keyboard with single letters or numbers on it, the corresponding letter or number appears on the screen. This does not work for the unusual keys, for example the ones with **ESC** and **CTRL** written on them. These have special functions which will be explained later. The little flashing white square is called the *cursor,* and it moves about the screen indicating where the next letter, number or symbol will appear when you press an appropriate key. To demonstrate this, type in the word "NEW" and then press the key marked **RETURN** . This also clears out Apple's memory so that we can begin right at the beginning.

It is impossible to damage the internal workings of Apple by pressing keys on the keyboard, so do not worry about this and do not be afraid to experiment. What follows is a line-by-line demonstration of one approach.

The Apple II, with monitor and two disk drives. (*This photograph is reproduced with the permission of Apple Computers UK Ltd.*)

COMMUNICATION WITH APPLE

In order to use Apple you have to communicate with it, and to do this you must learn the kinds of words that it can respond to. It has a vocabulary of about 98 words. Begin by using trial and error.

Type words on the screen as shown:

```
]MICKEY MOUSE []
```

Notice that, although the cursor on the screen is white, we must represent it as black on the written page.

The kind of diagram that we have just used to contain the words "MICKEY MOUSE" is one of two kinds that we will use in this book to distinguish two kinds of presentation. It is intended to represent what actually appears on the Apple screen. This can result from your typing or from a computer response, or from a mixture of these.

When you write a phrase like this, nothing else happens because the machine has received no instructions about how to react (unless you have chosen an instruction by accident). You must always indicate to Apple when you are finished for the moment, and wish for a response from it. This is done by pressing the key marked **RETURN** . Press it now.

When you do, a bleep will sound, and the screen will look like this:

```
] MICKEY MOUSE
? SYNTAX ERROR
]▯
```

This means two things. Firstly, the words SYNTAX ERROR indicate that Apple does not recognize MICKEY MOUSE as a command meaning anything it can respond to. Secondly, Apple has ignored this command which it cannot respond to, and is ready to go on to your next try at communication. Try typing in other words and pressing **RETURN** when you have finished, to see what happens.

Now type in the number 47, using the calculator keys, on the top row, and then press **RETURN** . This is a number, rather than a word. Apple responds as shown:

```
] 47
]▯
```

This response is different. There is no SYNTAX ERROR message. The cursor merely moves down a line and continues flashing. It seems as if it doesn't reject the number, but it doesn't do much with it either.

Perhaps it works like some calculators and performs direct calculations. Type in:

4+7

Then press **RETURN** . Now type in:

4+7+

Again press **RETURN** . None of those produce very much response. The cursor merely moves down a line and goes on flashing, waiting for further instructions. The reasons for these different responses will become clear as we go along.

Now look at the key marked ← . Although it will be looked at in more detail later, it is so useful that it ought to be tried at once.

First type in "MICKY" and then press this key once. The cursor will move back one step on top of the Y of MICKY. Now type in EY to complete and correct the word. You can now proceed as before, with the knowledge that if you make a typing error you can use this key (often called the "delete" key) to go back and correct it.

FIRST WORD

So far we do not seem to have typed in any words that Apple recognizes: we have not learned how to talk to it. The first word to learn is PRINT. Type in PRINT 47 and press **RETURN** . Apple responds like this:

```
]PRINT 47
 47
]□
```

Earlier, we indicated that we would use two kinds of displays in this book. We have already used the way in which we will represent the screen a number of times. The second kind of display indicates that you are meant to type in the expressions or set of expressions contained within it. These will, as a result, appear on the screen. In the first few chapters of this book we will use the expression **CR** where we wish you to press the key marked **RETURN** , in order to get you into the habit of doing so after every line. CR is short for "carriage return", and referred originally to typewriters, where the carriage did in fact return after each line.

To make this clear, when we write:

PRINT 47 **CR**

this means that you should type in the word PRINT, and then the number 47 and then press the **RETURN** key.

When we write:

we mean this to represent what the screen should look like. Try some others like these:

```
PRINT 1426      CR
PRINT 7+3       CR
PRINT 10-4      CR
```

From now on you will not always be told to press **RETURN** after each input. However, you must remember always to do so. If you don't, Apple will just stay blinking at you.

We must also make a distinction between *pressing* a key and *holding* a key. When we say *press* a key, we mean push it with a finger and let it go again at once. The alternative to this is to be told to *hold* a key, which means push it with a finger and keep it pushed until something else is done.

For example, if you press the key marked 4 on the top row, the numeral 4 appears: but holding the **SHIFT** key and pressing the key marked 4 produces a dollar sign. When this has happened you then release both keys.

One other small point. Apple does not care a great deal whether or not you leave spaces between words and numbers. That is to say, it will treat PRINT 4 + 3 the same as PRINT4 + 3.

The symbols for addition, subtraction, multiplication and division are shown below:

\+ (add)
− (subtract)
* (multiply)
/ (divide)

Unlike algebra, you should never leave out any of these symbols. The order in which they are performed by the computer is very important and is now described.

(a) Any operations put inside brackets are done first: example (6 + 2)*3 becomes 24.

(b) If there are brackets within brackets, the inside ones are done first:

example $(2+(3\times 4))-7$ becomes

$(2+12)-7$, and this becomes

$14-7$.

(c) The four arithmetical operations are then performed in this order:

multiplication, division, addition, and substraction.

(d) If you wish to change this order, then you must indicate the new order using brackets.

Now try these:

```
PRINT 5*3        CR
PRINT 16/4       CR
PRINT 7*6/4      CR
```

PRINT is probably the word in Apple's vocabulary that is used most often, so it can usually be shortened to ?. Try a couple of examples:

```
? 16*3/4+10      CR
? 8+3+4+2–7      CR
? 147+452–124    CR
```

PRINT WITH WORDS

Now try to use PRINT (or ?) with letters of the alphabet. Some examples are:—

For each word or single letter Apple responds with zero or nought. (The circle with a line across it on your screen is used by Apple to represent the *number* zero. It must not be confused with the letter of the alphabet O. This is represented by a simple circle.)

So, when asked to PRINT a letter or a word Apple responds with zero. This is because all letters represent variables for Apple, and they are all assumed to be equal to zero unless specifically made equal to some different number. More about this comes later. Now try printing letters or words with quotation marks around them, as shown below. Remember to press **RETURN** .

```
]?"A.D."
A.D.

]?"MONDAY"
MONDAY

]□
```

Try putting any of the possible Apple keyboard symbols inside quotation marks. Here is an example:

```
] ?" * IS A 6 POINT STAR"
* IS A 6 POINT STAR

] □
```

The rule is that Apple always prints exactly the sequence of symbols, letters or numbers that it finds inside quotation marks. In fact it does not even need the second set of quotation marks.

```
]?"TUESDAY
TUESDAY

]□
```

However, there will be occasions later on when leaving out the second set of quotation marks causes problems, so, at this stage, both sets of quotation marks will always be used.

SPECIAL KEYS

In addition to the normal keys with letters and numbers on them, there are some special keys on the Apple keyboard. These are shown below and are then discussed one by one.

[SHIFT]	(There are two of these.)
[REPT]	This is short for "repeat"
[←]	Arrow left.
[→]	Arrow right.
[CTRL]	This is short for "control"
[ESC]	This is short for "escape"
[RESET]	

(a) The [SHIFT] keys. First press the key with the number 4 on it. A figure 4 will appear on the screen. Then hold the [SHIFT] key, that is put a finger on this and keep it there. Then press the key with 4 on it again. This time a dollar sign will appear on the screen. There are two of these [SHIFT] keys and either can be used to print, on the screen, the character written on the upper half of some of the normal typewriter keys.

(b) The [REPT] key. This stands for "repeat" and is easy to demonstrate. Put one finger on the key with the letter z on it, and another on the [REPT] key. Hold both of them. The letter z will be printed repeatedly across the screen.

(c) The "arrow left" and "arrow right" keys. As a result of (b) above, you will have a couple of rows of zs across the screen. Press the key which looks like this [←] : that is, the "arrow left" key, a few times. The result is that the cursor moves back to the left along the row of zs but without changing them or doing anything to them. Now do the same with the "arrow right" key.

(d) The [CTRL] key. This stands for "control" and is used mainly in programming and need not concern us much here. However, hold it with one finger and press the letter G. A bell-like sound will be made. See also paragraph (f).

(e) The [ESC] key. This stands for "escape". Unlike the others this one should not be held down but should simply be pressed once. Doing this puts the machine into "escape mode". A number of things can now be done. First, suppose we wish to clear the screen. Press the [ESC] key once, then hold the [SHIFT] key and press the key [P]. The result should be a clear screen with the cursor at the top left-hand corner.

Now press [ESC] again, and then press the key [K] a few times. The cursor should move to the right. Then try the letter *M*. This time the cursor will move down the screen. Now try the letter *I* a few times. This moves the cursor back up the screen. Finally, try the letter *J*. This moves it back to the left.

Notice that these four letters form a cross on the keyboard pointing in these four directions:

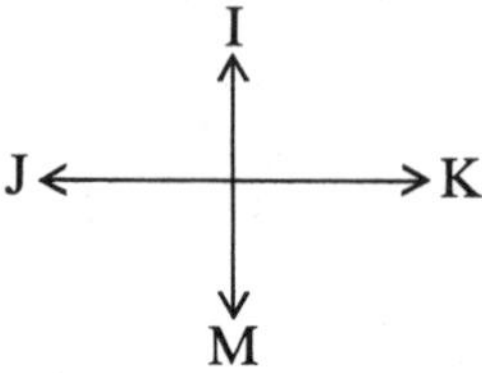

All of these four keys work over and over again while Apple is in *escape mode*. To get out of this mode, press the space bar (or almost any other key). Do this now and try pressing *I, J, K* or *M*. Now press ESC again, then try pressing any of the four keys *A, B, C* or *D*. These will move the cursor one place only and then immediately Apple will be out of escape mode. So if you wish to use *A, B, C* and *D* instead of *I, J, K* or *M* you have to press ESC for each single movement.

(f) The RESET key. The behavior of this key varies a little depending on your machine. On most machines, pressing it returns Apple to the ordinary direct mode with the square bracket and the cursor. On some machines, you must hold the CTRL key and press RESET. It is useful if you get stuck, lose the cursor, or do not know what to do next.

SPECIAL WORDS

We now consider four special words briefly. They are discussed in greater detail later on in this book.

(a) HOME. Type in "HOME" and press RETURN . This is another way of clearing the screen.

(b) INVERSE. Type this in and press RETURN . Now type in PRINT "EVERYTHING IS REVERSED", and press RETURN . The effect is to print the words as black lines against a white background.

(c) NORMAL. Type this word in and press RETURN . This turns the inverse facility off.

(d) FLASH. Type in this word and press RETURN . Now type in PRINT "ON AND OFF" and press RETURN . The words ON AND OFF will flash on and off the screen. Again, you can turn this facility off by typing in NORMAL and pressing RETURN.

MORE COMMUNICATION

The word PRINT, shortened to ?, was the first word of Apple's language that we met.

The next word to be considered is LET. Oddly enough, the word LET is not essential and, later on, will be left out. However, it is useful at this stage because it helps to demonstrate a particular point.

Type in these two lines. Remember to press **RETURN** after each:

```
LET A=3          CR
PRINT A          CR
```

The result is that the number 3 is printed on the screen:

```
]LET A=3
]PRINT A
3

]□
```

To explain this, we must try to understand what happens inside Apple. The first line LET A = 3 chooses a unit of memory, labels it A, and stores the number 3 inside it. A is called a variable because any number could have been chosen, and 3 is called a constant. (The distinction between variables and constants is a well-known one, and a more detailed explanation can be found in any introductory book: see Appendix H, page 250).

Typing in a line enters it on the screen only, but pressing **RETURN** enters it in the memory. The next line, which is a request to PRINT A (written ?A) makes Apple take the number that is stored in the unit of memory called A (i.e. the number 3), and print it on the screen.

It is worth considering this for a moment longer. Any statement typed on the screen will be acted on by Apple (if it understands it), if the cursor passes over the line and then the **RETURN** key is pressed.

To demonstrate this use the last example. The screen looks like this:

```
]LET A=3
]?A
3

] □
```

Retype this with the 3 in the first line replaced by 7. The response to ?A will now be 7. Repeat this whole process a few times, using a different number for A each time.

Now type in ?B. The result will be as shown:

That is B = 0. This is because any variable is assumed to be zero unless another number is deliberately assigned to it, and no other number has yet been assigned by the user to the space in the memory labelled B. Now type in the following (remembering to press **RETURN** after each line):

```
LET A=5          CR
LET B=4          CR
LET C=A*B        CR
?C               CR
```

The result should be 20. It is possible to shorten this a little by putting all of these statements on one line, separated by colons.

```
LET A=5 : LET B=4 : LET C=A*B : ?C          CR
```

Notice that the key **RETURN** needs only to be pressed once, at the end of the line.

The colon is interpreted by Apple as meaning the end of a statement, as though the **RETURN** key had been pressed. The word LET can be left out, if it is desired, so that the last example could be shortened further to:

```
A=5 : B=4 : C=A*B : ?C          CR
```

STRINGS

The following are all examples of strings. They are always placed inside quotation marks.

(a) "HELLO THERE!"
(b) "ABC493ZYX"
(c) "A*48 + $2"

Any collection of letters, symbols or numbers, including recognizable words and spaces, represents a string. Type in some of these and type in PRINT (or ?) in front, like this:

```
? "Z4K9 IS NOT A WORD"                    CR
```

Now try this:

```
LET A$="HELLO"                            CR
?A$                                       CR
```

As with numbers, it is possible to choose a unit of memory to store strings in, but the letter used must be followed by a dollar sign, as above. This is read "A-DOLLAR" and the unit of memory labelled A$ has the word (or string) HELLO stored inside it. So the screen should look like this:

```
]LET A$="HELLO"
]?A$
HELLO
]□
```

Labels like A$ are called *string variables* because they can be used to represent any string.

Try the following:

```
A$="APPLE": ? A$                          CR
B$="PUNK ROCK": ?B$                       CR
C$="GOBBLEDEGOOK": ? C$                   CR
```

Strings can be added together to make longer strings using an ordinary plus sign.

```
A$="COM" : B$="PUTER" : C$=A$+B$ : ?C$    CR
```

The result is as follows:

```
]A$="COM":B$="PUTER":C$=A$+B$:?C$
COMPUTER
]□
```

Notice that there is no space left between the two strings "COM" and "PUTER" when they are added together. If you would like to have a space, there are two ways to do this:

```
A$="APPLE" : B$=" " : C$="BOOK"          CR
?A$+B$+C$                                CR
```

The result is APPLE BOOK. B$ is obtained by leaving a single space between the two quotation marks.

The second way to do this is as follows:

```
A$="APPLE" : B$="BOOK"                   CR
?A$+" "+B$                               CR
```

All of the work so far has involved you in direct communication with Apple. You have not yet begun to write programs. This kind of interaction is called being in *command* (or *immediate*) *mode*. In the next section we begin to learn how to make Apple act in *programming mode.*

PROBLEMS

1. Use Apple as a calculator, with the word "PRINT" to do some arithmetic problems, like the following:
   (a) 4.27 + 31.28 + 173.1.
   (b) My annual salary is $13452. How much do I get monthly?
   (c) What is 6½% of 73216?
   (d) What is the new price caused by a mark-up of 11% on 12345?
   (e) If I spend $1.34, $1.78 and $0.69, how much change do I get from $5?
2. To begin with a bill was $172. Therefore, on Apple I write: A = 172 and press **RETURN** . $13 is added to this each week, so on Apple I write B = 13 and press **RETURN** . I pay off $27 each week, so again, I write C = 27 and press **RETURN** . After one week, I still owe:

   ```
   D=A+B-C : ? D                          CR
   ```

   and the next week, I still owe:

   ```
   D=D+B-C : ? D                          CR
   ```

   and I keep repeating this last line. Try it and see.

Use Apple to solve this similar problem. A debt of $650 is increased by 2% each week and is decreased by $71 each week. Use Apple to write the debt on the screen for each week until it is paid off.

3. Try this. Type in line 1:

```
A$="A" : PRINT A$                              CR
```

Then type in line 2:

```
A$=A$+A$ : PRINT A$                            CR
```

Repeat this line a few times. Begin again with:

```
A$="12345" : PRINT A$                          CR
```

(Remember that **CR** means press the **RETURN** key.)

2

Programming

USING BASIC

Although Apple can use a number of programming languages, we will be concerned mainly with the language called BASIC. This is built into the machine and is available to be used as soon as Apple is switched on. You cannot harm or destroy the language because it is stored in Read-Only-Memory chips, called *ROM* chips. As the name suggests, these can be read from but cannot be written to.

Very occasionally, usually as a result of an unhappy accident, BASIC is lost, or "goes down". That is to say, the flashing cursor disappears and cannot be retrieved. When this happens, and it really is fairly rare, you have to switch off at the back, and begin again. This brings the cursor back, but it also means that you lose any program you may have had in Apple's memory before BASIC went down. It is not a good idea to be continually switching on and off, so try to avoid it. For example, try the **RESET** key, before switching off.

BASIC stands for "Beginners All-purpose Symbolic Instruction Code", and it is a fairly simple language which most people can learn with a little effort. It has the great advantage that it is an interactive language. That is, you use it and learn about it by sitting at the machine, typing in statements and commands, and getting an immediate response. You don't have to learn it all in a book, or write it all down first. You can do a little of each as you go along.

We intend this book to be an introduction to the Apple computer. It is not meant to be an introduction to the language BASIC. If both of these tasks were attempted the book would become impossibly long and there would be bound to be some confusion. However, it is inevitable that, in order to begin to interact with Apple, we will meet and consider in detail some of the more elementary aspects of BASIC.

It is necessary, though, to have a good introductory book on BASIC available to supplement the occasionally rather sketchy and hurried treatment that we must give to some of the less elementary aspects of BASIC. We have, therefore, compiled a short list of books on BASIC, any one of which could act as an introduction. The list appears in Appendix H.

One last point about BASIC. There are many different versions of this language available and, therefore, books written about it must select which version or versions they intend to describe. However, there is a large common core of words and ideas to be found in all dialects of BASIC and translation is not impossible, even for a beginner, if a good reference book is used. An encyclopedia of the language has been published called *The BASIC Handbook*, by D.A. Lien, published by Compusoft Publishing, and this tries to include enough detail to make translation always possible (see Appendix H).

Apple uses two versions of BASIC, but the one we will be concerned mainly with is called *Applesoft BASIC*. One of the main purposes of this book is to try and make clear how to use those aspects of *Applesoft BASIC* that are unique to Apple, or at least uncommon in other versions.

STORING IN MEMORY

In Chapter 1 we found out how to evoke a reaction from Apple by typing in lines like this:

```
A=3 : B=4 : ?A*B                                    CR
```

and then pressing **RETURN** . Try this now, just as a reminder. Now, suppose we wished to do this, or something similar, again. We would have to type it all in again, or move the cursor about. We have not held on to the line of instructions, or stored it for later use.

This facility to keep lines or sequences of instruction in the computer's memory, to be called up or used again and again, is made possible by what is called programming. This is done very simply by numbering each line that we type in. Here is an example:

```
1 ? "THE EDUCATION CENTER,"                         CR
2 ? "NEW UNIVERSITY OF ULSTER,"                     CR
3 ? "COLERAINE,"                                    CR
4 ? "20TH. SEPT."                                   CR
5 ? "DEAR SIR,"                                     CR
6 ? "           WRITING PROGRAMS IS EASY"           CR
```

Type this in, remembering to press **RETURN** at the end of each line. (If you make a mistake, use the ← key). Now type in an instruction without a line number, similar to the sort discussed in Chapter 1, like this:

```
? "THIS RESPONDS AT ONCE"                    CR
```

and press **RETURN** . The main difference between this and the set of lines suggested above is that, without a line number, Apple obeys the instruction, but when numbers are included, it doesn't appear to do anything. However, the program above with line numbers is all stored in memory, waiting to be used. To demonstrate this, we introduce a new word. Type in LIST and press **RETURN** .

As you can see, the program is still in the memory but the instruction without a line number has disappeared, Type in LIST again. You can list the program as often as you like. (Notice that Apple translates ? into PRINT).

So a program is a store of instructions in the form of a set of successive lines. It is retained in memory, waiting to be used. Now, another new word. Type in RUN and press **RETURN** . The screen should look like this (well actually there will be lots of other things written above it on the screen):

```
THE EDUCATION CENTER,
NEW UNIVERSITY OF ULSTER,
COLERAINE,
20TH SEPT.
DEAR SIR,
          WRITING PROGRAMS IS EASY
```

This time the program has been used. That is to say, Apple begins at line 1 and prints THE EDUCATION CENTER on the screen. It then moves to line 2, and so on. Try running it again: type in RUN and press **RETURN**. Now list it again. Think about the difference.

CHANGING LINE NUMBERS

If we now decide that the address for the letter being written in this program is faulty, how can it be changed? For example, suppose that we now wish to insert a new line after line 3 and before line 4 to indicate that the address is in Northern Ireland. At present line 4 is:

```
4 ? "20TH. SEPT."
```

Now type in:

```
4 ? "N. IRELAND,"                                    CR
```

and press RETURN . Now list the program, that is type in "LIST" and press RETURN. You will find that the new line 4 has replaced the old one. You can now retype line 5 as the date:

```
5 ? "20TH. SEPT."                                    CR
```

but this replaces the "DEAR SIR" line, so you must now retype this as line 6. And finally the first line of the letter must be retyped as line 7. The program is now correct again: list it and run it to check.

Obviously this sort of problem is likely to occur quite often, and with a long program putting in a line will be a time-consuming job. To make the program easier to handle, lines should never be numbered in succession, but in steps as shown below.

But first, some ways of removing a program from the memory so that the memory is clear and you can start again.

List the program already in the memory. Now type in 4 and press RETURN . Now list the program again. Both listings will now be on the screen, and if you examine them carefully you will find that the second one does not include a line 4. By typing in the line number 4, by itself, and pressing RETURN you remove that line from the program. Try another one. Type in 6 and press RETURN . Now list the program. Line 6 should now be gone.

List the program again. Now type in the word NEW (remember that we used it at the beginning). Remember to press RETURN . This wipes out the whole of any program in the memory. If you now type in LIST and press RETURN , nothing appears on the screen except] and the cursor. This is a very necessary and useful word because it allows us, at any time, to begin again with a completely free memory. However, be very careful not to use it unless you are sure you wish to remove everything that you have typed in. Once it has been used there is no way of recovering the program wiped out in this way.

There is one other way of removing a number of lines from a program without having either to remove them one at a time or to remove the whole program.

First type this in:

```
100 PRINT                                            CR
120 PRINT "A"                                        CR
140 PRINT "B"                                        CR
160 PRINT "C"                                        CR
```

This is just an example program to make the point. Now type in DEL 100, 140 and press **RETURN**. This DEL is short for DELETE and is used with a comma between the numbers as shown. Now type in LIST and press **RETURN**. Line 160 only will be left. To remove this type in 160 and press **RETURN**.

Now type in this:

```
10 ? "THE EDUCATION CENTER,"                                CR
20 ? "NEW UNIVERSITY OF ULSTER,"                            CR
30 ? "COLERAINE,"                                           CR
40 ? "20TH. SEPT."                                          CR
50 ? "DEAR SIR,"                                            CR
60 ? "                WRITING PROGRAMS IS EASY"             CR
```

It is now possible to insert missing lines by using intermediate line numbers. First list the above program. Then type in:

```
35 ? "N. IRELAND,"                                          CR
```

Now list the program again. You will find that the new line, numbered 35, has been correctly placed by the computer between lines 30 and 40. This will always happen and makes it much easier to edit programs.

Because of this it is possible to begin a program with any line number you choose, and use any size of gap between line numbers. It is not necessary to begin at line 10 or go up in jumps of 10. Many people begin at line 100 and go up in jumps of 20. The decision is your own. In this book all program examples will begin at line 100 and go up in 20s. (The largest possible line number on Apple is 63999.)

INPUT

The program that we have just used allowed us to write an address, a date and the beginnings of a letter. These are all fixed or specified within the program. If we would like to be able to vary them we must learn how they can be put in from the keyboard as the program is being run. To do this we introduce another new word, INPUT.

This allows us to feed numbers or words into a program. Here is an example (remember, first, to type in NEW, in order to clear the old program out of memory):

```
100 INPUT A                                                 CR
120 B=4*A                                                   CR
140 ? B                                                     CR
```

We will examine this line by line. An attempt has been made in the diagram to picture the process that is now described, so keep your eye on it as well.

First, type in RUN and press **RETURN**. Apple will now go to the first numbered line, i.e. line 100. The instruction there means, first label a unit of memory A, and then invite the person using the machine to feed in a number. It does the inviting by printing a question mark on the screen and stopping there. So, assuming you have typed in RUN, there should now be a question mark on the screen.

Type in 7 (or any number) and press **RETURN**. Apple now stores 7 in the memory unit labelled A, and goes to the next line, numbered 120. It now labels a new unit of memory B, and stores in it a number which is four times the number in A, that is 4 times 7, or 28. It then moves to the next line, line 140, and obeys the instruction there which is to print the number stored in B on the screen. All of this happens very quickly indeed.

This process is shown in the diagram below:

program	*inside memory*	*Apple screen*
100 INPUT A	A [ ]	? □
		the user inputs 7
	A [7]	? 7 □
120 B=4*A	A [7] B [28]	? 7 □
140 ? B	A [7] B [28]	? 7 □ 28] □

Now type in RUN again, and this time respond to the question mark with a different number, say 9. Try it a few more times with different numbers. Now add this line to the program:

```
90 ? "WHAT NUMBER DO YOU WANT"          CR
```

and run it again.

Later on we will discuss at some length ways in which programs can be written so that they make sense on the screen to the user. This is one example of how to begin to do this.

SCREEN FORMAT

Keep the same program, but add the new lines 130 and 135 and change line 140.

```
 90 ? "WHAT NUMBER DO YOU WANT"     CR
100 INPUT A                         CR
120 B=4*A                           CR
130 C =5*A                          CR
135 D =6*A                          CR
140 ? B, C, D                       CR
```

Now run the program, and input 2 for A. Apple responds as shown below.

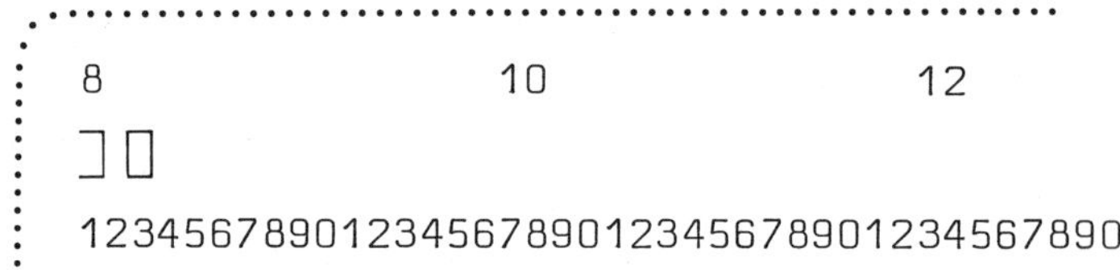

In order to demonstrate the spacing of these numbers, we have written the numbers 1 to 9, and then 0 for 10, repeatedly across the bottom of the diagram. These numbers will not, of course, appear on the screen of your Apple. First notice that the Apple screen is 40 spaces or columns wide. Then notice that the three numbers 8, 10 and 12 are written with the first digit on the columns numbered 1, 17 and 33.

This spacing was caused by the commas. In programs which involve printing numbers on the screen, using commas will always produce this kind of format.

Now rewrite line 140 as follows (remember that, when we type in a new line numbered 140, it simply replaces the old one):

```
140 ? B ; C ; D                     CR
```

That is, replace the commas by semicolons. Now run the program, and again input 2 for A. The response is shown below where, again, numbers are written along the bottom to demonstrate the spacing.

The use of semicolons pushes the written responses together with no spaces at all.

SCREEN FORMAT WITH STRINGS

Remove the last program by typing in NEW. Now copy the following program:

```
100 A$="TOM"                CR
120 B$="DICK"               CR
140 C$="HARRY"              CR
160 ? A$, B$, C$            CR
```

and then run it. The screen will look like this, where again we have used the row of reference numbers along the bottom:

```
TOM             DICK            HARRY
]□
1234567890123456789012345678901234567890
```

The three names are spaced quite like the three numbers, i.e. the first letter of each begins on the columns 1, 17, 33.

Now replace line 160 as follows:

```
160 ? A$ ; B$ ; C$          CR
```

and run the program again. The result is shown below.

This time no spaces are left at all. If we wished to have a space (or more than one) between each name, these should be put in beside the names when they are declared (in lines 100, 120, and 140). For example, change line 100 to:

```
100 A$="TOM  "                                  CR
```

A space has been left between the M of TOM and the closing quotation marks. Now run the program again.

INPUT WITH A STRING

We will now return to the letter program to look at how it might be made more general. First type in NEW and press **RETURN** .

Now we will rewrite the program so that it invites the user to input each line of the address in turn, and then the date, and then the name of the person who is receiving the letter. Begin as follows, with two instructions and an input.

```
100 ? "PUT IN THE ADDRESS IN FOUR LINES."           CR
120 ? "FIRST, LINE ONE:-"                           CR
140 INPUT A$                                        CR
```

Remember to press **RETURN** after each line. Now run this to see what it does so far. The screen will look like this:

```
PUT IN THE ADDRESS IN FOUR LINES.
FIRST, LINE ONE:-
?▯
```

The question mark is the invitation to type in the first line of the address. This will then be stored in the unit of memory labelled A$.

Now type in the rest of the program, as follows.

```
160 ? "NOW, LINE TWO:-"                             CR
180 INPUT B$                                        CR
200 ? "NOW, LINE THREE:-"                           CR
220 INPUT C$                                        CR
240 ? "NOW, LINE FOUR:-"                            CR
260 INPUT D$                                        CR
280 ? "NOW THE DATE:-"                              CR
300 INPUT E$                                        CR
320 ? "NOW THE NAME OF LETTER RECIPIENT:-"          CR
340 INPUT F$                                        CR
360 ? A$ : ? B$ : ? C$ : ? D$ : ? E$                CR
380 ? "DEAR MR. " F$                                CR
400 ? "            WRITING PROGRAMS IS EASY "       CR
```

This program, which is quite long, is divided into two parts. The lines numbered from 100 to 340 are to do with input: successively the user is invited to type in the four address lines, the date, and the name of the letter recipient. These are stored in A$, B$, C$, D$, E$, F$. The second part of the program runs from line 360 to 400. These lines print the information that has been input onto the screen.

Three special points to notice:

(a) In line 360, the instructions to print the four letters of the address and the date are all typed on one line with colons between them. This procedure has been described in Chapter 1.

(b) In line 380 the question mark, meaning "print", refers both to the words DEAR MR. (with a space after them), and to the variable F$, which is the label of the unit of memory containing the name of the letter recipient. Thus both of these are printed.

(c) Do not use either a comma or a colon as part of any of the INPUTS A$ to F$.

The letter has not been taken beyond the first line, but it should be obvious even from this simple example how it would be possible to use the Apple to produce well-formatted letters, if a printer were attached.

Try running the program. When requested on the screen, type in your own address and then today's date, and then a surname. Try it a few times. Then list it again and make sure you understand how it works.

You will notice that, with a long program, the listing happens so quickly that you cannot read it while it is happening. To stop a listing, hold the control key and press S , and then press any other key to start it again.

REM

If you wished to make this program easy to read and understand when listed, you could now add some REM lines. REM is short for "remark" and it allows you to annotate or write explanatory comments into a program. This is because Apple ignores all lines beginning with REM when it is running a program in BASIC. It acknowledges their existence only when listing a program. Here are some examples of REM statements attached to the letter program just completed:

```
80 REM LETTER PROGRAM ALLOWS              CR
81 REM INPUT OF NAME, ADDRESS, DATE       CR
82 REM AND LETTER RECIPIENT               CR
```

(continued overleaf)

```
350 REM ROUTINE FOR PRINTING                    CR
351 REM LETTER FOLLOWS                          CR
```

We have attached two sets of REM statements, one corresponding to each of the two parts of the program already described: that is, the input part and the print part. There is, of course, no limit on the number of REM statements you can make, except memory limitations, and these are now described.

BYTES OF MEMORY

The number of units of memory available to the Apple user is measured in *bytes*, and this depends on the number of Kilobytes in the machine which you have bought. This could be 16 or 32 or 48 or 64 Kilobytes and is normally referred to as 16K or 32K and so on. One K means 1024 bytes, and so 32K means 32768 bytes.

In general terms, a byte is a unit of memory so that when you type a line of BASIC each character pressed uses a byte of memory. We can check on the number of free bytes at any time by using the built-in special function FRE(0). (The zero is not significant, and any number will do). This can be done in direct mode, as follows:

```
? FRE(0)                                        CR
```

Apple responds at once with a number which is the number of free bytes. However, if you have more than 32K, that is more than 32768 bytes, Apple will respond with a negative number. In this case write:

```
? 65536+FRE(0)                                  CR
```

This function FRE(0) can also be used as a statement within a program to indicate at specific times how much memory still remains. Later on in this book we will use it in this way on a number of occasions. Here is a short example which can be used to show that each character typed into Apple uses exactly one byte of memory. First type in NEW and then this program:

```
100 INPUT A$                                    CR
120 PRINT 65536+FRE(0)                          CR
```

Type RUN and press **RETURN**. Apple prints a question mark, so type in one letter, say A, and press **RETURN**. An Apple with 64K of memory should then print 47069, which means that this program and the single letter A, between them, reduce the available memory to 47069. Now run it again, and this time respond to the question mark with two letters, say AB. Apple prints 47068, which shows that the extra letter B has used one extra byte of memory.

Although it is generally true that each character uses a single byte of memory, there are exceptions. The word PRINT, for example, uses one byte altogether instead of five.

VARIABLE NAMES

So far we have simply used single letters like A, B, C to represent variables, and A$, B$, C$ to represent string variables. However we can extend the range of variable names by using two characters for each. The second character can be any letter or any number. Possible examples are AP or AT$ or A3. Note that the first character must be a letter.

As well as this it is permissible to use much longer strings as variable names, and this can be most useful if you are not short of memory. But remember that only the first two characters are used for recognition purposes by Apple. To demonstrate this, type in this program.

```
100 PRENTICE=9          CR
120 PRACTICE=99         CR
140 PRINT PRENTICE      CR
160 PRINT PRACTICE      CR
180 PRINT PR            CR
```

When this is run, each of the lines 140 to 180 prints 99. When the program is listed it should appear as above. So, although the variable names PRENTICE and PRACTICE are acceptable to Apple, and look different, they are both stored in memory as PR, and line 120 changes the value of PRENTICE to 99. It is also necessary to be careful not to include within a variable name any word that Apple uses for a special purpose, such as “PRINT” or “INPUT”.

PROBLEMS

1. Write a program which allows you to enter a set of six names and an amount of money for each name. It should be written in such a way that:

(a) Apple invites you, with a message on the screen, to put in the information.
(b) When it has all been entered, Apple lists the names and amounts of money on the screen.
Use the words PRINT, INPUT, REM and FRE.

2. This problem is quite similar to the last one. The program should allow you to enter a set of four names and addresses where each address is to be three lines long. That is, a total of 16 inputs will be demanded. The program should be written so that:
(a) Apple invites you to put in the information;
(b) When it has all been entered, Apple displays the names and addresses on the screen.
Use the words PRINT, INPUT, REM and FRE, and use A1$, A2$, A3$ and A4$ for the names. Similarly, use B1$ to B4$ for the first lines of the addresses. Then use C1$ to C4$, and D1$ to D4$ for the other two lines.

3. Complete the letter program on pages 17 and 18 of the text. It should, at the end, produce a standard letter to a client, as shown below. The words in capitals, however, will change with each run of the program and these should be input at the beginning of the program. So the program should begin by inviting the input of the following data:—
(a) Date (Use A$).
(b) Person to whom the letter is addressed (B$).
(c) Reason for meeting (C$).
(d) Date when writer will be available (D$).
(e) Time when writer will be available (E$).
(f) Where the writer will be available (F$).

Education Center,
New University of Ulster,
Coleraine, N. Ireland.
TODAY'S DATE

Dear MR JONES

I would like to arrange a meeting to discuss:
YOUR RECENT ORDER
I would be available on MONDAY 14TH JAN. in MY OFFICE AT HALF PAST TWO.
I would be grateful if you could come at this time.

Yours sincerely,

Brian McGarvey

3

Program Presentation

INTRODUCTION

When a program has been typed into Apple (or put in from disk) and you need to use it, you then type in RUN and press RETURN. If the program has been carefully written it ought then to be completely clear what the program is about, and what the machine (or the program) wants you to do. This level of well-organized explanation and presentation needs to be maintained all the way through the program, so that the user is never placed in the position of not knowing what to do next, or what the results mean.

This chapter is about this kind of presentation. The techniques used are very simple and easy to adapt, and some of them are unique to Apple. It begins with a short three-line program, and adds to this repeatedly until it ends up as a quite long but well-documented final program. It is absolutely essential that, at each stage in what follows, you type in the new lines, list the program to check its accuracy, and run it to see what it now does. Indeed the two commands LIST and RUN should be used often when writing in programs as they allow you to get instant feedback about what is going on.

USER PRESENTATION

We begin by typing in a short three-line program as shown. It is carrying out a simple arithmetical calculation involving three multiplications and two additions. However, don't worry if, to begin with, you do not understand what it is doing. Type it in in the usual way remembering to press the RETURN key after each line. The unusual line numbers are because this is going to be part of a longer program. The rest will be added as we go along. If you have already been using Apple remember to type in NEW before starting.

```
440 INPUT A, B, C                                  CR
460 T=15*A+24*B+13*C                               CR
500 ?T                                             CR
```

Now type in RUN and then press RETURN. Apple goes to the first line, 440 and, because it is an input, responds with ?. It has now labelled three units of memory A, B and C and is waiting for you to tell it what numbers to store in each of these. That is, it needs an input of three separate numbers.

Type in three numbers separated by commas to represent A, B and C, like this:

```
3,1,4                                              CR
```

Then press RETURN. Apple responds immediately with:

```
121
]□
```

If this does not work, check your program by typing in LIST.

All of this will be easy to do, but it may be difficult to understand what is going on. No attempt has been made to make the program understandable to the user in the way it appears on the screen when you type RUN.

So we will now try to improve this presentation so that it is self-explanatory and can be used by anyone.

PURPOSE OF PROGRAM

The object of this program is to provide a simple method of calculating a family's daily bill for milk and other dairy products. It is suggested that milk costs 15c per pint, cream costs 24c a carton and yoghurt costs 13c. The letters on line 440 stand for the number of pints of milk (A), the number of cartons of cream (B), and the number of yoghurts (C). Line 440 invites you to tell Apple what A, B and C are to be in a particular case by printing a question mark on the screen. You have to enter the numbers into Apple using the same punctuation pattern: i.e. 3, 1, 4. Line 460 does the sum:

```
3 PINTS OF MILK AT              15C
1 CARTON OF CREAM AT            24C
4 YOGHURTS AT                   13C
```

and calls the total T. Line 500 prints the answer on the screen.

STOP

At various stages in what follows you will want to run the program to see what is going on, but you may not want to go right through to the end each time. At any stage you can stop Apple in the middle of the program by holding the key marked CTRL and pressing C. It is sometimes also necessary to press RETURN.

LIST

It is also helpful to be able to look at the program, or any part of it, printed out on the Apple screen whenever you wish. As mentioned earlier this can be done by typing in LIST and then pressing RETURN . This will produce a display of the whole program, but there are also four variations on this which can be used when only part of a program is wanted. These make use of the subtract symbol.

This is thought of in this context as meaning "to".

Example 1. List 440 — 460
This lists all lines from 440 to 460.

Example 2. List — 500
This lists all lines from the beginning to line 500.

Example 3. List 460 —
This lists all lines from 460 to the end of program.

Example 4. List 460
This lists line 460 only.

Try all of these.

It is also possible, when the program is long and the listing is running off the screen, to stop it at any time by holding the key CTRL and pressing S.

CLEAR SCREEN

If you have been trying some of the things described above, the chances are that your Apple screen is covered with statements and print. The result is that when you input RUN followed by RETURN the question mark appears at the bottom of all this, scarcely visible.

Now type in this new line and press RETURN .

```
100 HOME                                          CR
```

This means that you have programmed the "clear-screen" command. As soon as Apple comes to line 100, after RUN has been typed in, the word HOME will clear the screen, and Apple will then go on to the next line. Try it now and see.

This "clear screen" line is most useful and is often used more than once, especially in long programs. If this is the case it is useful to put it in what is called a *subroutine,* which can be called up whenever necessary.

SUBROUTINES

The notion of a subroutine is very simple. In this case we are dealing with the simple routine for clearing the screen and believe that we may have to use it more than once within a program. So we place it in a separate, isolated part of the program, called a subroutine, and call it up whenever we need it. We put it at line 1000. Type this in:

```
1000 HOME                                  CR
```

and we wish to call it up at line 100, whose place it is now taking. To do this line 100 becomes this. Type it in:

```
100 GOSUB 1000                             CR
```

This means that, when Apple comes to line 100 the instruction GOSUB 1000 (short for "go to the subroutine at line 1000), sends it to line 1000. The instruction there makes Apple clear the screen. It will now go on to the line after line 1000, and if there is no line after it, it will stop. But we wish it to come back to the line after line 100 and continue with the program. So now add the line:

```
1010 RETURN                                CR
```

This has the desired effect of returning Apple to line 440 and allows it to continue with the calculation.

These two new words GOSUB and RETURN act as a pair. The program now looks like this:

```
 100 GOSUB 1000                            CR
 440 INPUT A, B, C                         CR
 460 T=15*A+24*B+13*C                      CR
 500 ? T                                   CR
 700 END                                   CR
1000 HOME                                  CR
1010 RETURN                                CR
```

Type in LIST and check that your program is the same. You will see that there is one other new line:

```
700 END                                        CR
```

This means that Apple will stop when it gets to that line. If it was not there Apple would go on to line 1000 again, and clear the screen, and so lose the answer. Apple now acts on these lines in this order:

first	line 100	start
then	line 1000	subroutine
then	line 1010	
then	line 440	
then	line 460	rest of
then	line 500	program
then	line 700	

It is worth mentioning that Apple does not normally need an "END" line where subroutines are not involved.

Notice also that the word RETURN is different from the key marked **RETURN** . The first has to be typed in like any other word and is an instruction within a program. The second is just a key to be pressed which enters a line of BASIC into the memory and moves the cursor onto a new line.

TITLE

It always helps to put a title on your programs. This can be done very simply, as follows:

```
120 ? "          ***DAILY MILK BILL***"          CR
140 ? "          ______________________"          CR
```

Type these two lines in and run the program. Remember that, if you wish to *centre* the title, there are 40 spaces across the Apple screen. Techniques for doing this will be shown later.

REVERSE FIELD

Letters and symbols are normally printed on the screen as white lines against a black background. It is possible to reverse this with words and lines on Apple so that they become black lines against a white background. This helps to draw attention to particular words and commands and is especially suitable for the title. The word which turns this reverse-field writing on is INVERSE, and the word that turns it off is NORMAL. Put in these two new lines:

```
110 INVERSE                                        CR
130 NORMAL                                         CR
```

Now run the program again. The title "***DAILY MILK BILL***" should now be in reverse field, but unfortunately so is the rest of the line starting on the left. One way to tidy this up is to put the whole line in reverse field, but there is an alternative. Retype the three lines 110 to 130 as below:

```
110 PRINT "              ";                        CR
120 INVERSE : PRINT "***DAILY MILK BILL***"        CR
130 NORMAL                                         CR
```

Now run it and this time, only the title should be in reverse field. In line 110 we print the space before the title, and put a semicolon after it to ensure that Apple goes on printing on the same line. In line 120 we turn on the reverse field with the word INVERSE and then print the title. In line 130 we turn it off again with the word NORMAL.

FLASHING TITLES

It is also possible to make the two forms of presentation, that is the normal and the reverse field appear alternatively in quicker succession so that the words flash on and off. The only difference between this and the format above is that the word INVERSE is replaced by the word FLASH. So rewrite line 120 as follows:

```
120 FLASH : PRINT "***DAILY MILK BILL***"          CR
```

Now run this program and try this.

DESCRIPTION

We now need a short description of what the program does.

Type this in:

```
180 ? "THIS PROGRAM CALCULATES A DAILY"          CR
200 ? "MILK BILL.              MILK COSTS 15C"   CR
220 ? "                        CREAM COSTS 24C"  CR
240 ? "                      YOGHURT COSTS 13C"  CR
260 ? "WHEN YOU SEE THE QUESTION MARK"           CR
280 ? "PUT IN THE NUMBER OF EACH"                CR
300 ? "BOUGHT FOR TODAY."                        CR
```

Try typing this in and running the program.

There are two problems now: (a) the instructions are very crowded; and (b) we are still not told exactly how to respond to the ? sign that Apple prints after them. So we must consider spacing and further instructions to the user.

SPACING

(a) A single space can be made by putting in an extra line containing just the word PRINT. For example, type in the line below and run the program.

```
190 PRINT                                        CR
```

There will be an extra space, that is, a line will be printed with nothing on it, as a result of the instruction in line 190. It is also possible to put an extra PRINT (or ?) at the beginning or the end of the appropriate existing lines. Here it is done at the end of the line, using a colon between the quotation marks and the ? sign to make Apple move on to a new line.

```
180 ? "THIS PROGRAM CALCULATES A DAILY" : ?      CR
200 ? "MILK BILL             MILK COSTS 15C" : ? CR
```

Do this for each of the lines 180 to 280 by retyping the lines and then run the program again. Remember also to remove the extra line 190 put in above. To do this just type in 190 and press **RETURN** .

(b) Large spaces. Obviously this can be done using a line like this:

```
160 ? : ? : ?                                    CR
```

In most programs such spacing is used quite often and is therefore best put into a subroutine, as shown.

```
2000 ? : ? : ?                                  CR
2010 RETURN                                     CR
```

Then we call it up whenever we wish to have a larger space between chunks of writing on the screen. This is done twice in our program, the current version of which is listed and annotated below. You should now list your own program and add the new lines to make it exactly like this one.

Notice that we have left out the CR reminders at the end of each line. From now on, when presenting programs, we will not include this reminder after each line, but you must remember to press the **RETURN** key at the end of each line.

```
A     100 GOSUB 1000

B     120 ? "       ***DAILY MILK BILL***"
      140 ? "       ______________________"

C     160 GOSUB 2000

D     180 ? "THIS PROGRAM CALCULATES A DAILY" : ?
      200 ? "MILK BILL.              MILK COSTS 15C" : ?
      220 ? "                       CREAM COSTS 24C" : ?
      240 ? "                     YOGHURT COSTS 13C" : ?
      260 ? "WHEN YOU SEE THE QUESTION MARK" : ?
      280 ? "PUT IN THE NUMBER OF EACH" : ?
      300 ? "BOUGHT FOR TODAY."

E     320 GOSUB 2000

F     440 INPUT A, B, C
      460 T=15*A+24*B+13*C
      500 PRINT T
      700 END

G    1000 HOME
     1010 RETURN
     2000 ? : ? : ?
     2010 RETURN
```

Section A. This clears the screen.
Section B. This creates the title.

Section C. This makes a three-line space.
Section D. This describes the program. Note the extra print signs at the end of each line except line 300.
Section E. This means a three-line space.
Section F. This solves the problems and prints the result.
Section G. Subroutines for clearing screen and making space.

INSTRUCTION TO USER

When this program is now run, the screen looks like this:

```
       ***DAILY MILK BILL***
       _____________________


 THIS PROGRAM CALCULATES A DAILY
 MILK BILL.     MILK COSTS 15C
               CREAM COSTS 24C
             YOGHURT COSTS 13C
 WHEN YOU SEE THE QUESTION MARK
 PUT IN THE NUMBER OF EACH
 BOUGHT FOR TODAY.



 ?
```

We must now consider the second problem mentioned above. That is, we have not yet given explicit instructions about how to input the numbers. This is done as follows. Type in the two lines:

```
380 ? "NOW INPUT THE 3 NUMBERS WITH" : ?
400 ? "COMMAS BETWEEN THEM."
```

Now run the program again.

We have now solved all the spacing and presentation problems but, as no doubt you will have noticed, when we run the program the last two lines push the title off the top of the screen. The next section shows you how to stop that happening.

PRESS ANY KEY

The press any key technique allows Apple to present information in chunks. This means that you can read some information on the screen, and then — by pressing any key — bring up the next chunk of information. Since the technique is normally used quite often in a long program we will once again put it in a subroutine. This is now shown below. Type it in.

```
3000 ? "              PRESS ANY KEY"
3010 GET A$
3020 RETURN
```

Line 3000 prints the words PRESS ANY KEY on the screen. Apple then moves down to the next line, line 3010. This uses a new word, GET. The statement is:

```
GET A$
```

This tells Apple to expect an input of one single character, which can be any character on the keyboard. When this happens it moves on to the next line, which is:

```
3020 RETURN
```

and so the subroutine ends. The subroutine is now typed in, so put a line calling it up as shown:

```
340 GOSUB 3000
```

Now run the program again.

This works very well except that the lines NOW INPUT THE THREE NUMBERS WITH COMMAS BETWEEN THEM are crowded up against the line PRESS ANY KEY, and the question mark is also crowded up against the last instruction line. So, to make this more legible, put in two further lines to make two more major blocks of space.

```
360 GOSUB 2000
420 GOSUB 2000
```

EXPLAINING THE ANSWERS

The response from Apple when the numbers have been put in, is to print the answer on the next line and stop. Some further lines of explanation and spacing are needed. Try typing these in:

```
480 GOSUB 2000
500 ? "THE TOTAL BILL FOR TODAY IS" : ?
520 ? T ; "            CENTS"
540 GOSUB 2000
```

now run the program.

Finally, it is useful to put some instructions at the end about what the user may wish to do next. Put in the lines shown:

```
560 ? "DO YOU WISH TO DO ANOTHER BILL?" : ?
580 ? "IF SO, INPUT YES. OTHERWISE NO." : ?
600 INPUT A$ : IF A$="YES" THEN 100
620 GOSUB 2000
640 ? "THANK YOU. IF YOU WISH TO START" : ?
660 ? "AGAIN, TYPE IN RUN AND PRESS" : ?
680 ? "RETURN. GOODBYE FOR NOW."
```

Line 600 may need a little explanation.

```
600 INPUT A$ : IF A$="YES" THEN 100
```

Apple responds to INPUT A$ by printing a question mark and waiting for a response from you. You type in a word and press **RETURN** . If the word is YES then Apple goes to line 100, which is the beginning of the program. If it is any word other than YES it goes on to the next line, i.e., line 620.

This complete program now follows. Check yours against this and try running it a few times.

```
100 GOSUB 1000
120 ? "          ***DAILY MILK BILL***"
140 ? "          ______________________"
160 GOSUB 2000
```

(continued overleaf)

```
180 ? "THIS PROGRAM CALCULATES A DAILY" : ?
200 ? "MILK BILL.                MILK COSTS 15C" : ?
220 ? "                         CREAM COSTS 24C" : ?
240 ? "                       YOGHURT COSTS 13C" : ?
260 ? "WHEN YOU SEE THE QUESTION MARK" : ?
280 ? "PUT IN THE NUMBER OF EACH" : ?
300 ? "BOUGHT FOR TODAY."
320 GOSUB 2000
340 GOSUB 3000
360 GOSUB 2000
380 ? "NOW INPUT THE 3 NUMBERS WITH" : ?
400 ? "COMMAS BETWEEN THEM."
420 GOSUB 2000
440 INPUT A, B, C
460 T=15*A+24*B+13*C
480 GOSUB 2000
500 ? "THE TOTAL BILL FOR TODAY IS" : ?
520 ? T ; "         CENTS"
540 GOSUB 2000
560 ? "DO YOU WISH TO DO ANOTHER BILL?" : ?
580 ? "IF SO, INPUT YES. OTHERWISE NO." : ?
600 INPUT A$ : IF A$="YES" THEN 100
620 GOSUB 2000
640 ? "THANK YOU. IF YOU WISH TO START" : ?
660 ? "AGAIN, TYPE IN RUN AND PRESS" : ?
680 ? "RETURN. GOODBYE FOR NOW."
700 END
1000 HOME
1010 RETURN
2000 ? : ? : ?
2010 RETURN
3000 ? "         PRESS ANY KEY"
3010 GET A$
3020 RETURN
```

PROBLEMS

1. This is a short program which translates pounds weight into grams.

```
200 INPUT A
210 B=A* 453.593
230 PRINT A, B
```

Type this in and then add as many other lines as are necessary to turn it into a self-explanatory, easily used conversion program. Try to use as many of the techniques discussed in Chapter 3 as possible.

2. Write another program of this sort which invites the user to put a small set of numbers one at a time. The program then calculates and presents the average of these. Again try to make sure the program is self-explanatory and easy to use.

3. Write a program which will convert any sum of money from one currency into four other currencies. The program should invite you to put in the names of the other four currencies and their current exchange rates. It will then calculate the exchange values and print all four of these on the screen.

4

Disk Management

INTRODUCTION

Your Apple has at least one disk drive attached to it. (See Chapter 1, page 1). If there are two drives then one is called drive 1 and the other is drive 2. You should establish by simple trial which is which and label them clearly. The disk drive is joined to the computer by a flat multi-colored cable. This can be attached to and removed from the computer quite easily and the procedure for doing this is described very clearly on pages 2 and 3 of the *Apple DOS Manual.*

It is also possible to use a tape recorder with Apple and there are some instructions about this given in Appendix B on page 177.

DISKETTES

If you have spent some time writing and typing in a program which you would like to keep and use on another occasion, it is very frustrating to lose it all when Apple is switched off. This problem can be solved using the disk drive and a storage device called a *floppy disk,* or a *diskette.* This looks like a small square envelope and you should read very carefully pages 5 and 6 of the *Apple DOS Manual,* if you do not know how to insert these into the drives or how to look after them. If the diskette is a new one, it must first be *initialized.* That is to say it must be formatted and made ready to be used with Apple.

INITIALIZING A DISKETTE

If your diskette is already initialized then this section can be skipped for now. Put the new diskette into disk drive 1, and close the door. Now type in a program which can be as long or as short as you wish and is required only to set the process of initialization in motion. The program is like a pump-primer. It is usually called the HELLO program and usually contains a line like line 5, and so this program can always be identified. Here is an example.

```
 5 HOME : PRINT "HELLO"
10 PRINT "INITIALIZED ON 20TH JULY"
20 PRINT "BY MICHAEL O HARA"
```

When you have written this, or something similar, then type in: INIT HELLO and press **RETURN**.

We have chosen to call our diskette and this program "HELLO" because, as described above, this is normally done. But you could choose to call it something else. When you press **RETURN** the red light on the front of the disk-drive will come on, and there will be a series of whirrings and small clacking noises. This will last for about two minutes, then the red light will go off and the cursor will reappear on the screen. The diskette is now initialized and ready for use.

CATALOG

Now type in CATALOG and press **RETURN** . The red light will come on again, the disk-drive will whirr and the following will appear on the screen:

```
DISK VOLUME 254
A002 HELLO
```

The volume number 254 will always be used by APPLE unless you specify a different volume number when initializing. The A means that your program was written in *Applesoft BASIC*, the 002 is a measure of the length of your program or of the amount of storage which it has taken up on the diskette.

The word CATALOG is a most useful command. Note the spelling carefully and use it with any diskette at any time if you want to know what programs are stored on it. It produces a list on the screen of all the programs on the diskette currently in the disk drive.

PROGRAM SAVING

We will now assume that you have typed in a program and that you wish to save it to use on another occasion. The procedure is as follows:

(a) Put a diskette in the disk drive 1.
(b) Decide on a name for the program: we will pretend that you have chosen "example".
(c) Type in SAVE EXAMPLE and press the **RETURN** key. Immediately the disk drive begins to whirr, the red light comes on, and the cursor disappears from the screen. When the operation is complete, the red light will go off, the whirring will stop and the cursor will re-appear. If you just type in SAVE and forget to put a name after it, and then press **RETURN**, the cursor will again disappear, but nothing else will happen. In this case Apple is responding to a command (i.e. SAVE by itself), to save the program on a cassette tape; but since your intention was to save the program on the diskette, there is a confusion. In this case, press the **RESET** key and try again.
(d) If you want to make sure that the program has in fact been saved type in VERIFY EXAMPLE. If all is well the cursor will reappear as before. If it has not worked properly, Apple will respond with FILE NOT FOUND.
(e) You can check if the file has been saved in another way. Type in CATALOG and press **RETURN**. The same signs will appear, but the list of the contents of the diskette will also appear on the screen. Somewhere among them, not necessarily at the end, the name EXAMPLE should appear. If it does not, then do it all again. (Note that if the diskette contains more than 18 files, the names of the first 18 only will appear on the screen. When you have looked at this list, press the space bar, and the rest will come up on the screen).

There are a number of other points to be noted about this procedure.

(a) If you have more than one disk drive and wish to specify which one you are going to use, this is done as follows. To save a program on drive 2, write: SAVE EXAMPLE, D2.
In this case the red light will appear on the second drive and the process continues as before. Similarly you can specify which drive you wish to see a catalog of, by writing CATALOG, D1 for drive 1. Once you have specified a drive

in this way, Apple will continue to refer to this one without a direct reference until you specify another.

(b) The name of the program which you choose can be up to 30 characters long. If it is more than this, Apple will remember the rest but will only write the first 30 on the catalog. It will thereafter accept either the original long name or the 30 character name. So, for example, the name:

THE APPLE PERSONAL COMPUTER FOR BEGINNERS

is 41 characters long. Note that we must count the spaces as characters. Apple will save this on the diskette as:

THE APPLE PERSONAL COMPUTER FO

which is 30 characters long.
There are two other small rules about names. They must start with a letter of the alphabet. After that any symbol can be used except a comma. So while 007 JAMES BOND is unacceptable, JAMES BOND 007 is acceptable: and MURPHY, B. is unacceptable while MURPHY B. is acceptable.

(c) A program saved in this way is called a *file* and these rules about names are really rules about *files*. All such rules continue to apply to files when, later on, we deal with files of information as well as program files.

PROGRAM RECOVERY

"Load" is the word used when you wish to recover a program already saved on a diskette. We load a program from the diskette into Apple's memory, where we can run it. The technique is very simple:

(a) Insert the diskette into the drive and close the door.
(b) Type in LOAD EXAMPLE. Put the name of the program which you wish to recover in place of EXAMPLE. Then press **RETURN** . Apple responds in the normal way. That is, the red light comes on, the disk drive whirrs and the cursor disappears from the screen. In a few seconds all of these will stop, the cursor will return and the program should now be in memory.
(c) To check this type in RUN (or LIST) and press **RETURN** .
(d) If an error occurs, then begin the process again. Remember

that the process of loading the program does not destroy or in any way change the copy of the program on the diskette.

(e) If errors persist use CATALOG to make sure that the program you want is actually on the diskette. The program EXAMPLE, if it exists, will appear on the CATALOG as: A 004 EXAMPLE. Ignore the A, which stands for Applesoft and the 004, and use just the word EXAMPLE. It is possible to combine the two commands LOAD and RUN so that the program begins to run as soon as it is loaded. To do this type in RUN EXAMPLE instead of LOAD EXAMPLE and then RUN.
Remember also that if you type in LOAD, by itself, and press **RETURN** , Apple will again go in search of a cassette tape file.

REMOVING A FILE

Since a program goes through a large number of stages in its development, it is very likely that you will end up with a whole series of files containing successive versions of your attempts to write a program. You will often want to remove or delete these earlier versions from your diskette since they are taking up space unnecessarily.

This is very easy to do. We will assume that you have a program on the diskette called EXAMPLE. Type in DELETE EXAMPLE and press return. You can then check that it has gone by typing in CATALOG and looking at the list of contents. Be very careful with this DELETE command, because once a file is removed it cannot be recovered again.

If you try to delete a file that is not on the catalog Apple will give you the message FILE NOT FOUND.

CHANGING FILE NAMES

Suppose you wish to call a file EXAMPLE, and make a typing error like this:

```
SAVE EXAMBLE
```

and then press **RETURN** . If you then type in CATALOG the list will contain the name wrongly spelt as above. It is easy to fix this. Type in:

```
RENAME EXAMBLE, EXAMPLE
```

and press **RETURN** . Now type in CATALOG and check if the file now has the correct title.

You can of course use this RENAME command to change any file name.

DATA SAVING

One of the most important uses of a computer is the storage and subsequent reuse of data such as lists of names, numbers, prices or book titles. For this reason many of the programs written for Apple will be used for generating, storing and allowing reuse of data by businessmen and teachers. The storage or saving of such data on diskette is almost as easy as the storage of programs, but it is done by routines written within programs rather than by typing direct commands (like SAVE or LOAD) onto the screen. The process is now illustrated by writing a full program.

We will begin with a short routine to input a set of four names and test marks to Apple's memory. It is called *Subprogram* 2 because, later on, we will put another subprogram before it.

Subprogram 2

```
200 REM INPUT ROUTINE
210 HOME
220 DIM A$(4), A(4)
240 FOR N=1 TO 4
260 PRINT : INPUT "INPUT NAME OF PUPIL   "; A$(N)
270 PRINT : PRINT : INPUT "NOW INPUT SCORE   "; A(N)
280 NEXT N
```

First type this program in, and we will consider it line by line.

(a) Line 210 clears the screen.

(b) Line 220 involves a new notion, that of declaring two data arrays. In very general terms this means that Apple reserves or books memory space for four strings and for four numbers. The word DIM tells it to reserve space. A$(4) tells it to book enough space for four strings, called A$(1), A$(2), A$(3) and A$(4). The number four can of course be much greater if necessary. (In fact, for numbers up to 10, line 220 is not needed, but it is included here so that you can use numbers greater than 10 if you wish, and to demonstrate the principle).

Similarly A(4) tells Apple to book enough space for four numbers. (Actually, since A$(0) and A(0) are also counted by Apple, there is in fact another unit of memory reserved which we are ignoring in this case to avoid confusion).

(c) Lines 240 and 280, together, make a loop which Apple cycles through four times.

(d) Line 260 allows you to input the four names, one during each cycle of the loop created by lines 240 and 280. These four names are stored in A$(1), A$(2), A$(3) and A$(4).

(e) Line 270 does exactly the same for the four scores which are stored in A(1), A(2), A(3) and A(4).

Now, type in RUN and follow instructions as they appear on the screen. This is, of course, a practice exercise since we have yet to complete the program.

We now come to the program that will actually save these four names and data on the diskette. First type it in carefully and we will, as before, consider it line by line.

Subprogram 3

```
300 REM SAVE NAMES ON DISK
320 D$=CHR$(4)
340 PRINT D$ ; "OPEN NAMES"
360 PRINT D$ ; "WRITE NAMES"
380 FOR N=1 TO 4
400 PRINT A$(N)
420 NEXT N
440 PRINT D$ ; "CLOSE NAMES"
460 PRINT "NAMES NOW SAVED ON DISK"
```

(a) Line 320 involves some ideas which we have not yet discussed and must be taken to some extent on trust. CHR$(4) is a control command and is the equivalent of directly holding the control key and pressing the letter D. When it is printed, as in lines 340, 360 and 440, it alerts the computer to the fact that disk commands are about to be used within a program.

(b) Line 340 opens a file called NAMES. Later on this same file is closed. The file title NAMES is chosen by the user and can be any legitimate file title (see page 45).

(c) Line 360 prepares the computer to *write* a file called NAMES. This is in contrast with a later situation where it will be asked to *read* a file. The file title must be the same as that used in line 340, in this case NAMES.

(d) Lines 380 and 420, together, make a loop which Apple cycles through four times.
(e) Line 400 prints the data, that is the names or strings entered earlier into A$(N), onto the diskette.
(f) Line 440 closes the file and again the same file title must be used as in lines 340 and 360.
(g) The last line, 460, lets us know when the job is finished.

Subprogram 4

The next piece of the program saves the four scores on diskette and uses almost exactly the same routine. First type it in.

```
500 REM SAVE SCORES ON DISK
520 D$=CHR$(4)
540 PRINT D$ ; "OPEN SCORES"
560 PRINT D$ ; "WRITE SCORES"
580 FOR N=1 TO 4
600 PRINT A(N)
620 NEXT N
640 PRINT D$ ; "CLOSE SCORES"
660 PRINT "SCORES NOW SAVED ON DISK"
```

The only differences are in lines 540, 560, and 640, where the file title is SCORES this time rather than NAMES; and in line 600 where A(N), the store for numbers, has replaced A$(N), the store for strings.

Make sure that there is a diskette in the drive ready to receive the data. Then type in RUN and press **RETURN** and follow instructions as they appear on the screen. This means that we first enter the four names and scores into Apple's memory, and then save them on the diskette.

DATA RECOVERY

We must now enter some routines for retreiving this data. First, the names. Type this in:

Subprogram 5

```
700 REM RECOVER NAMES FROM DISK
720 D$=CHR$(4)
740 PRINT D$ ; "OPEN NAMES"
```

(continued overleaf)

```
760 PRINT D$ ; "READ NAMES"
780 FOR N=1 TO 4
800 INPUT A$(N)
820 NEXT N
840 PRINT D$ ; "CLOSE NAMES"
860 PRINT "NAMES NOW RECOVERED"
```

This routine is almost identical to the routine starting on line 300 for saving NAMES on disk. The differences are as follows:

(a) Line 760. In this case the word READ has replaced the word WRITE. That is to say we are now reading from disk rather than writing to disk.

(b) Line 800 replaces the word PRINT with INPUT. That is, instead of printing data to the disk file we are inputting data from the file.

Finally the scores are recovered using an almost identical routine. Type this in:

Subprogram 6

```
900 REM RECOVER SCORES FROM DISK
920 D$=CHR$(4)
940 PRINT D$ ; "OPEN SCORES"
960 PRINT D$ ; "READ SCORES"
980 FOR N=1 TO 4
1000 INPUT A(N)
1020 NEXT N
1040 PRINT D$ ; "CLOSE SCORES"
1060 PRINT "SCORES NOW RECOVERED"
```

The only differences are where the word SCORES replaces NAMES and in line 1000 where A(N) for scores replaces A$(N) for names.

PROGRAM ORGANIZATION

This program is now almost complete in that it allows you to do three things:

(a) To enter data into Apple (lines 200 to 280).

(b) To save this data on disk (lines 300 to 660).

(c) To recover this data from disk (lines 700 to 1000).

The only difficulty is that it always follows this order exactly, which is something of a problem if, for example, you wish *only* to recover data or *only* to save data. This program, as it stands, does not allow you to choose. Since we have already saved some data on disk, how can we go directly to the data recovery part of the program? To be able to choose which of the three processes we wish to use we must now enter a new subroutine which organizes the rest of the program. It will come first and will offer the user a choice of three possible routines, that is, entering data, saving data and recovering data. Type this in and we will then discuss it:

Subprogram 1

```
100 PRINT : PRINT "WHICH ROUTINE DO YOU WISH TO USE"
110 PRINT : PRINT "        DATA ENTRY . . .E"
120 PRINT : PRINT "      DATA SAVING . . .S"
130 PRINT : PRINT " DATA RECOVERY . . .R"
140 PRINT : PRINT "CHOOSE ONE OF THE 3 LETTERS"
150 INPUT B$
160 IF B$="E" GOTO 200
170 IF B$="S" GOTO 300
180 IF B$="R" GOTO 700
190 GOTO 100
```

(a) The lines 100 to 140 are straightforward print statements which give the user instructions. The list of options is sometimes called a *menu.*

(b) Line 150 prints a question mark on the screen and waits for an input from the user. This input is stored in Apple's memory **B$.**

(c) Line 160. If the user chooses the data entry option and presses the letter E, Apple then goes to that part of the program which starts at line 200. If the user chooses some letter other than E, Apple goes on to line 170.

(d) Lines 170 and 180 do similar jobs for the other two options, in each case sending Apple to the appropriate part of the program.

(e) Line 190 is a fail-safe line. If the user chooses any letter other than the three correct ones, the program goes back to line 100 again.

(f) Finally, it is necessary to put a line at the end of each of the three possible routines which will in each case return the user to subprogram 1 when that routine is complete. These lines are:

```
 290 GOTO 100
 680 GOTO 100
1080 GOTO 100
```

Type them in now as they are very important.

The program is now complete except for a print routine, and an escape routine: i.e. a routine to print the data on the screen and a routine to allow you to stop. The inclusion of these is left as an exercise for the reader. Apart from that the program is now complete, and is shown in total. List your own program and compare it with this one. It will be necessary to list it in parts since the screen will not hold it all.

```
 80 DIM A$(4), A(4)
100 PRINT : PRINT "WHICH ROUTINE DO YOU WISH TO USE"
110 PRINT : PRINT "          DATA ENTRY . . .E"
120 PRINT : PRINT "        DATA SAVING . . .S"
130 PRINT : PRINT "  DATA RECOVERY . . .R"
140 PRINT : PRINT "CHOOSE ONE OF THE 3 LETTERS"
150 INPUT B$
160 IF B$="E" GOTO 200
170 IF B$="S" GOTO 300
180 IF B$="R" GOTO 700
190 GOTO 100
200 REM INPUT ROUTINE
210 HOME
240 FOR N=1 TO 4
260 PRINT : INPUT "INPUT NAME OF PUPIL    " ; AS (N)
270 PRINT : PRINT : INPUT "NOW INPUT SCORE    " ; A(N)
280 NEXT N
290 GOTO 100
300 REM SAVE NAMES ON DISK
320 D$=CHR$(4)
340 PRINT D$ ; "OPEN NAMES"
360 PRINT D$ ; "WRITE NAMES"
380 FOR N=1 TO 4
400 PRINT A$(N)
420 NEXT N
440 PRINT D$ ; "CLOSE NAMES"
460 PRINT "NAMES NOW SAVED ON DISK"
500 REM SAVE SCORES ON DISK
520 D$=CHR$(4)
540 PRINT D$ ; "OPEN SCORES"
```

```
560 PRINT D$ ; "WRITE SCORES"
580 FOR N=1 TO 4
600 PRINT A(N)
620 NEXT N
640 PRINT D$ ; "CLOSE SCORES"
660 PRINT "SCORES NOW SAVED ON DISK"
680 GOTO 100
700 REM RECOVER NAMES FROM DISK
720 D$=CHR$(4)
740 PRINT D$ ; "OPEN NAMES"
760 PRINT D$ ; "READ NAMES"
780 FOR N=1 TO 4
800 INPUT A$(N)
820 NEXT N
840 PRINT D$ ; "CLOSE NAMES"
860 PRINT "NAMES NOW RECOVERED"
900 REM RECOVER SCORES FROM DISK
920 D$=CHR$(4)
940 PRINT D$ ; "OPEN SCORES"
960 PRINT D$ ; "READ SCORES"
980 FOR N=1 TO 4
1000 INPUT A(N)
1020 NEXT N
1040 PRINT D$ ; "CLOSE SCORES"
1060 PRINT "SCORES NOW RECOVERED"
1080 GOTO 100
```

FINAL POINTS

There are two last points to be made about data files. First, in the example just completed it would have been possible to have combined the two save routines, at lines 300 and 500, into one routine. To do this it is necessary only to put the line:

```
410 PRINT A(N)
```

after the current line 400. Then the whole routine from 500 to 680 can be deleted. The difference is that in this case the two files previously used, i.e. NAMES and SCORES, are now amalgamated into one file. Certainly this is more economical of effort, although there will be occasions when you will want to use separate files as was shown originally.

In this new pattern, it is now necessary also to amalgamate the two recovery routines. Again it is only necessary to put in the line:

```
810 INPUT A(N)
```

and then delete the whole routine from 900 to 1080.

The second point is about the use of file names. In the program just described, the two file titles, NAMES and SCORES, are part of the program so that every time this program is used it will create files with those titles and those titles only. It is easy however to adapt the program so that you can choose a different file name each time. This will now be done for the first "SAVE" routine, starting on line 300, but remember that if you do this you will also have to change the corresponding "RECOVERY" routine.

First type in the line:

```
330 INPUT "WHAT FILE NAME   "; N$
```

Then change lines 340, 360 and 440 as follows:

```
340 PRINT D$; "OPEN"; N$
360 PRINT D$; "WRITE"; N$
440 PRINT D$; "CLOSE"; N$
```

In line 330 you choose a file title. This is stored by Apple in N$. Then in lines 340, 360 and 440 this title is used to name the data file.

PROBLEMS

1. Write a program that will store the numbers 1 to 100 on a diskette file, and will then recover them. Make sure you have a menu (see page 51) which allows you to choose whether to store data or to recover data.
2. Write a mailing list program which allows you to input, save and recover a list of names and addresses.

5

Graphics

INTRODUCTION

The graphics facility is simply a way of making it possible to put dots or lines on the Apple screen. There are two forms of this facility, called *low resolution graphics* and *high resolution graphics.*

LOW RESOLUTION

There are a number of new words that must be used each time you wish to have low resolution graphics. The first is simply GR, which is clearly a shorthand for the full word GRAPHICS. To see the effect of this best we will use an example.

First type in NEW and press **RETURN** to clear out any program that may be in Apple's memory. Then type in HOME and press **RETURN**. This clears the screen and moves the cursor up to the top left-hand corner of the screen.

Now type in any short one-line program. This is a dummy program and is going to be used only as a way of showing how the word GR affects the screen. This would do:

```
100 PRINT "WHERE IS THE TOP"
```

Type this in and list it a couple of times just to fill the screen up. Then type in GR, directly, and press **RETURN**. The whole of the top part of the screen will, as a result, be cleared and the cursor will appear down near the bottom of the screen.

The effect of this is still not clear, so now type in list and press **RETURN** . Then type in RUN and press **RETURN**. Type LIST and RUN a number of times. The screen will look like this:

```
]RUN
WHERE IS THE TOP
]
```

So it is now impossible to put lines of print anywhere except on the bottom four lines of the screen. The top 20 lines have been reserved for graphics or drawings. It is as if the top of the screen had been moved down 20 lines. This is the effect of the command GR.

Another way to make this clear is as follows. Press the letter A and the **REPT** keys, and hold these two for a while. Eventually there will be four rows made up entirely of As, but never more than four. Try it and see.

The word TEXT is used to turn this screen arrangement off. Type it in now and press **RETURN**. The effect is a bit strange, in that the top 20 lines are now covered with a pattern, but the important point is that it is again possible to use the full screen for text. If you don't like the screen like this, type in HOME and press **RETURN** and this will clear it.

DRAWING ON THE SCREEN

The second new word is COLOR. For the moment we will deal only with black and white, but later in this chapter we will consider the 16 colors that are available. The colors are numbered 0 to 15, but for black and white work we will use only the number 5. So now type in COLOR=5 and press **RETURN**. Nothing obvious happens, but Apple will remember this and anything that you draw will be coloured white.

Another new word is PLOT. Type in PLOT 20, 20 and press **RETURN**. The result should be that a white rectangle appears in approximately the middle of the graphics part of the screen. (You can now use the control knobs on your TV or monitor to carefully focus this 'rectangle'. If you do you will see that the rectangle is in fact made up of four rows of eight dots).

Now try some other examples, like these:

```
PLOT 10, 10
PLOT 0, 0
PLOT 0, 15
```

Now try these three in succession. Remember to press **RETURN** after each.

```
PLOT 3, 6
PLOT 4, 6
PLOT 5, 6
```

Clearly the first number represents the column number going from left to right. That is to say, if we now try PLOT 6, 6 another bar will be added to the right end of the line.

To look at the other direction, try these:

```
PLOT 5, 12
PLOT 5, 13
PLOT 5, 14
```

In this case it is the second number that changes and these represent points moving down the screen from top to bottom.

In fact, the graphics part of the screen is made up of 40 rows and 40 columns, numbered like this, with the example PLOT 2, 3 shown.

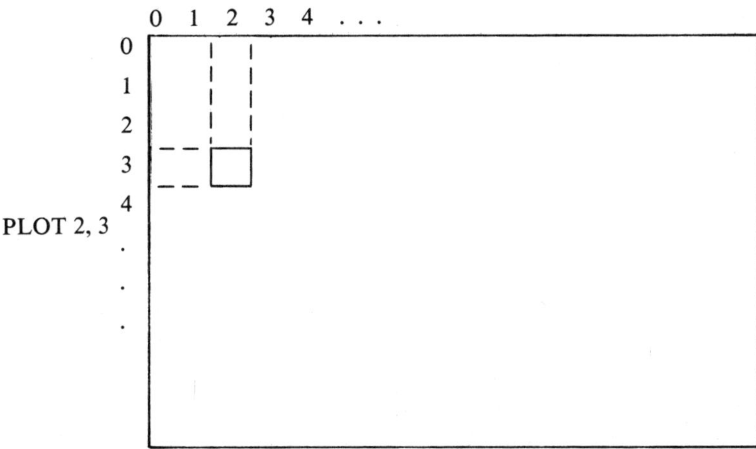

To test this, try PLOT 40, 8. The result is ? ILLEGAL QUANTITY ERROR because the first number cannot be larger than 39.

The rows are also limited to the number 0 to 39 as shown, but there is a complication here. Remember that the screen contains 24 rows altogether and that the top 20 of these are reserved for graphics and the bottom four for writing of text. Each of these top twenty is divided into two narrower rows for graphics to make the necessary total of 40 (numbered 0 to 39). However, if you try to use numbers greater than 39 for rows, Apple will accept them up to 47. This is because the screen has 24 rows, and twice this is 48 and so Apple counts from 0 to 47. However, even though the machine will not give you any error message until you use 48 you must remember not to use numbers greater than 39. Later on when we write a program we will put in a detection routine for this problem (see page 62).

We can summarize these new words as follows:

GR	Turns on graphics mode.
TEXT	Turns on text mode.
COLOR=5	For black and white work, color 5 is white.
PLOT X, Y	Places a rectangle on column X, row Y.

A WHITE SCREEN

We will now use these words all together in a short program to make the whole graphics screen white. The program begins as follows: (it is numbered rather oddly because it is part of a longer program).

```
100 GR
120 COLOR=5
180 FOR B=0 TO 39
200 PLOT B, 0
220 NEXT B
500 PRINT "   PRESS ANY KEY"
520 GET A$
540 TEXT
```

Lines 100 and 120 establish graphics mode and set the colour at white. Lines 180 to 220 generate a loop which puts a white line across the top of the screen. Lines 500 and 520 hold the screen until the user presses a key. Line 540 then uses the word TEXT to return the screen to text mode. Type this program in and run it.

Now add two more lines and change line 200 as follows:

```
160 FOR A=0 TO 39
200 PLOT B, A
240 NEXT A
```

Now run this, and the screen should rapidly fill up with white lines.

COLORED SCREENS

If you do not have a color TV or color monitor this section should be left out since it simply repeats the above experiment but uses it to demonstrate the various possible colors that Apple can produce. Do not type in NEW as we will be making use of the previous program, which so far looks like this:

```
100 GR
120 COLOR=5
160 FOR A=0 TO 39
180 FOR B=0 TO 39
200 PLOT B, A
220 NEXT B
240 NEXT A
500 PRINT "   PRESS ANY KEY"
520 GET A$
540 TEXT
```

Now change line 120 and put in four new lines

```
120 FOR N=1 TO 15
140 COLOR=N
150 PRINT "COLOR IS NUMBER        " N
260 GET A$
280 NEXT N
```

Now run this program. First the screen will fill up with a green color. At least that's what it does on our TV set. Yours may be different and at this stage it is wise to try to tune the set so that the color is as clear and well-balanced as possible. The message at the bottom of the screen will read "COLOR IS NUMBER 1". We left out number 0 in line 120 because it represents black and so nothing would show on the screen.

The screen is being held there by line 260 so press a key and Apple will, from line 280, go on to the next color, which on our TV set is a violet color. Each time the screen is filled up with a color, press a key and go on to the next color. If you run the program a few times you will get to know the color numbers that work well with your monitor or TV set.

A FACE ON THE SCREEN

We now return to a black and white television and remember that we had filled the screen with white lines (see the program on page 58).

We can now draw on this white screen using black lines. To get black we must use color number 0. Then we use two simple loops to draw a rectangle as shown. Type this in:

```
250 COLOR=0
260 FOR A=15 TO 25
280 PLOT A, 10 : PLOT A, 30
300 NEXT A
320 FOR A=10 TO 30
340 PLOT 15, A : PLOT 25, A
360 NEXT A
```

The lines 260 to 300 make the top and bottom lines of a rectangle. The lines 320 to 360 make the left and right lines. Run it and see if it works.

Finally add these lines, and run the whole program. If you do it correctly it should produce a smiling rectangle face.

```
380 PLOT 19, 17 : PLOT 21, 17
400 PLOT 20, 20
420 PLOT 18, 23 : PLOT 22, 23
440 FOR A=18 TO 22
460 PLOT A, 24
480 NEXT A
```

If you are using a color set, put in these lines:

```
120 COLOR=11
240 COLOR=3
370 COLOR=9
```

SCREEN ARTIST

The program that we will now produce allows the user to draw a picture directly on the screen. Only the bones of the program are presented here and it would be necessary to produce a great deal of description and introduction, as shown in Chapter 3, if you wished to make it clear to others how to use the program.

We can begin to draw on the screen at any point and we will call this point (X, Y) — that is X columns across from top left and Y rows down from the top left.

The first few lines of the program are like this:

```
100 GR
110 COLOR=5
120 PRINT "REMEMBER THAT THE TOP LEFT IS 0, 0"
140 INPUT "WHAT IS X CO-ORD OF START  "; X
160 INPUT "WHAT IS Y CO-ORD OF START  "; Y
180 REM PLOT POINTS
260 PLOT X, Y
```

This allows you to decide on your starting point and to plot a point there. We now need a routine to move this point about the screen. We will use the set of letters grouped on the left of the keyboard as shown below:

```
Q  W  E
A  S  D
Z  X  C
```

It would be reasonable to assume that pressing W means to move up, pressing X means to move down, A means left, D means right, Q means up and left, and so on. The effect of these on the values of X and Y are summarized below. For example, pressing W and moving up means that X does not change but Y changes to $Y-1$. So, corresponding to W we have $(X, Y-1)$.

Q	W	E
A	S	D
Z	X	C

$X-1, Y-1$	$X, Y-1$	$X+1, Y-1$
$X-1, Y$	X, Y	$X+1, Y$
$X-1, Y+1$	$X, Y+1$	$X+1, Y+1$

This can be programmed as follows. We will first show in detail what happens if you press W, and then we will write in the rest of the program.

```
300 GET A$
320 IF A$="W" THEN Y=Y-1 : GOTO 180
```

In line 300 Apple is told to expect an input of one character. If this character is W, line 320 changes the numbers from (X, Y) to $(X, Y-1)$ and then goes back to line 180 where this new point is plotted and the circuit begins again at 300.

The rest of the lines look like this:

```
340 IF A$="E" THEN X=X+1 : Y=Y-1 : GOTO 180
360 IF A$="D" THEN X=X+1 : GOTO 180
380 IF A$="C" THEN X=X+1 : Y=Y+1 : GOTO 180
400 IF A$="X" THEN Y=Y+1 : GOTO 180
420 IF A$="Z" THEN X=X-1 : Y=Y+1 : GOTO 180
440 IF A$="A" THEN X=X-1 : GOTO 180
460 IF A$="Q" THEN X=X-1 : Y=Y-1 : GOTO 180
480 IF A$="S" THEN 180
520 GOTO 180
```

Type this in and try it.

There are many further refinements possible, and two small ones are now shown. The values of both X and Y must not be smaller than 0 and must not be larger than 39. In order to avoid getting an error message and an aborted program, put in this routine:

```
180 IF X < 0 THEN X=0
200 IF X > 39 THEN X=39
220 IF Y < 0 THEN Y=0
240 IF Y > 39 THEN Y=39
```

Finally you may wish at any stage to stop drawing and escape from the program. To do this, add this routine:

```
500 IF A$="F" THEN 540
540 PRINT "PRESS ANY KEY"
560 GET A$
580 TEXT : HOME
600 PRINT "THE END FOR NOW"
```

You should now save this program on your diskette for future use.

As usual it is possible to put color into the picture. Suppose for example that you wished at any stage to change the color being used. First type in the following two lines:

```
490 IF A$="L" THEN 530
530 INPUT "INPUT THE NEW COLOR NUMBER  "; C :
535 COLOR=C : GOTO 180
```

This means that when you wish to change the color you press the letter L. Line 530 then invites you to enter the new color and eventually returns the program, as usual, to line 180.

HLIN AND VLIN

These two words allow you to draw horizontal lines and vertical lines. Begin with HLIN, and type in this example. (Remember to type in NEW before you start).

```
100 GR : COLOR=5
120 HLIN 10, 30 AT 20
```

Then run this. The result will be a horizontal line across the screen, like this:

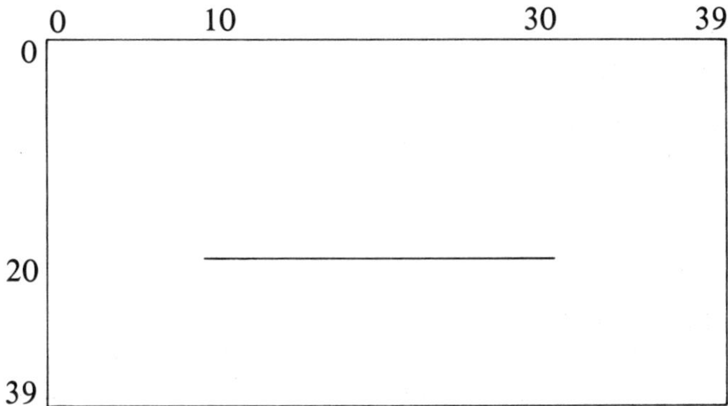

That is to say, the statement:

```
HLIN 10, 30
```

indicates to Apple where the horizontal line should start (i.e. at 10) and where it should end (i.e. at 30). The rest of the statement, that is AT 20, indicates which horizontal row to draw the line on. Now type in NEW and TEXT and then this program:

```
100 GR : COLOR=5
120 INPUT "STARTING POINT ?" ; S
140 INPUT "END POINT ?" ; E
160 INPUT "HORIZONTAL LINE ?" ; H
180 HLIN S, E AT H
200 PRINT "PRESS A KEY"
220 GET A$
240 TEXT
```

Now run the program. First line 120 will ask you to input where the line should start. Suppose you input 2 and then press **RETURN**. Then line 140 will ask you to input where it should end. Put in 25. Then line 160 will ask you to input which horizontal line you wish to draw on: remember that 0 means the top row and 39 means the bottom row. Suppose you input 5. So you have asked for a horizontal line to be drawn from point 2 to point 25 at row number 5. The screen will look like this:

Lines 200 to 240 allow you to go back into text mode before ending the program.

To show how VLIN works, we need change one line only of this program. Type this in:

```
180 VLIN S, E AT H
```

Now run the program again, and try putting in some numbers.

BAR GRAPHS

Low resolution graphics are very suitable for drawing bar graphs, so we will look at one example. Here is the data that we wish to turn into a graph: "One hundred people were asked to choose their favourite color from a list of 6." Here are the results:

white	5
red	38
yellow	18
blue	10
green	26
black	3

Remember that the biggest number we can deal with is 39, so if another couple of people had chosen red we would have had to scale all the numbers down.

Here is the first part of a first attempt at this program. It allows you to put the data into Apple's memory.

```
 10 DIM A(20)
100 GR : COLOR=5
120 INPUT "HOW MANY BARS WILL THE GRAPH HAVE" ; N
140 PRINT "WHEN YOU SEE THE QUESTION MARK PUT IN"
160 PRINT "THE NUMBERS FOR THE BARS, ONE AT A TIME"
180 FOR C=1 TO N
200 INPUT A(C)
220 NEXT C
```

Line 120 stores the number of bars in the variable *N*. Lines 140 and 160 give instructions to the user, and lines 180 to 220 use a loop to put in the *N* numbers. These are stored in A(C): that is, in A(1), A(2), A(3) and so on.

The next part draws the graph. Type it in.

```
240 FOR C=1 TO N
260 HLIN 0, A(C) AT C
280 NEXT C
```

Now run this program, put in the numbers and look at the result. A bar graph is drawn, but it's all a bit crowded. So we can now fiddle around with the program and make it work better. For example, change line 260 to:

```
260 HLIN 0, A(C) AT 4*C
```

Run this and think about the difference.

Now add the line

```
261 HLIN 0, A(C) AT 4*C+1
```

and run this.

Finally, on both lines 260 and 261 change the word HLIN to VLIN.

COLOR GRAPH

It is possible to choose a different color for each bar in the graph. First put in these lines:

```
170 PRINT "THEN PUT IN A NUMBER FOR THE BAR COLOR"
210 INPUT "NOW THE COLOR NUMBER " ; B(C)
250 COLOR=B(C)
```

Then change line 10 to:

```
10 DIM A(20), B(20)
```

Now run the program again and, when the message appears on the screen, put in a different color for each bar. These are then programmed in line 250.

HIGH RESOLUTION GRAPHICS

In low resolution graphics the top 20 rows of the screen are isolated using GR and it is then possible to draw lines and pictures on this. However, the number of points is only 40 by 40 so the lines seem at times a bit heavy and not really very good for drawing.

In high resolution graphics it is again possible to isolate the top 20 lines of the screen using the instruction HGR, but this time the number of points is greatly increased to 280 across (numbered 0 to 279) and 160 down (numbered 0 to 159). As well as this there are only two instructions used in drawing lines, that is the word HPLOT, and the word TO. This makes it very easy to draw quite complicated pictures very quickly. First we must try to imagine what the screen looks like and how the points are numbered.

The drawing opposite is an attempt to show this. The numbers along the top start at the extreme left at 0 and end on the extreme right at 279.

The numbers down the side start at the top 0 and end at the bottom of the graphics screen at 159. When referring to points, the number along the top is shown first, then, after the comma, the number along the side is given. The example shown is the point 200, 50: that is, move to 200 along the top, and then move down to 50.

There is a slight complication about the last downward number. We show it as 159, but Apple will accept numbers up to 191 here. This is because Apple numbers the whole screen including the text lines at the bottom. It is possible to remove the text lines altogether, and to use the whole screen for drawing. This will be done later, but, for the moment, it will be necessary in any program to put in a line to check if the downward number exceeds 159.

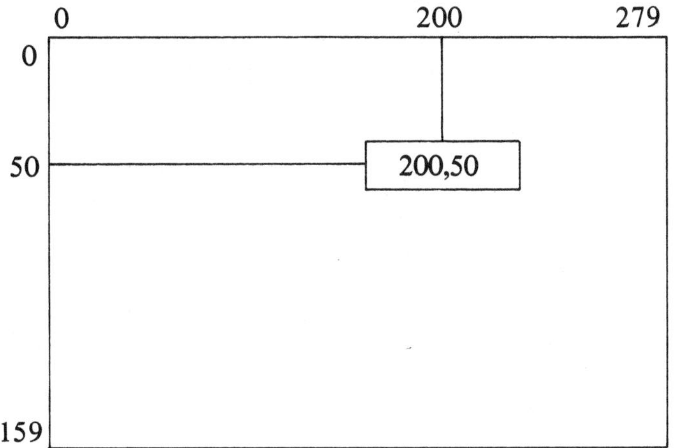

We will now write a short program to plot this point 200, 50.

```
100 HGR
120 HCOLOR=3
140 HPLOT 200, 50
160 PRINT "PRESS ANY KEY"
180 GET A$
200 TEXT
```

Type this in and run it: it is explained below, line by line.

(a) Line 100 uses HGR to put the screen into high-resolution graphics mode. So the top 20 lines are cleared and all text appears on the bottom four lines.

(b) Line 120 sets the color at 3. Notice that the word we now use is HCOLOR and the number for white is 3. Later on we will look at how to use high resolution graphics in color for those who have a color monitor.

(c) Line 140 plots the point. Notice how small it is compared to the large rectangle used in low resolution graphics.

(d) The last three lines are just a way of ensuring that the screen is returned to text mode at the end. They can be left out if you wish.

HPLOT AND TO

These two words allow us to draw lines on the screen joining any two points. This can be done directly, without a program. First type in HGR and press RETURN. This puts the screen in graphics mode. Then type in HCOLOR = 3. This makes the color white. Then type in:

```
HPLOT 1, 3 TO 130, 100
```

and press RETURN . Now type in:

```
HPLOT 4, 150 TO 260, 3
```

Now try as many others as you like, choosing whatever points you wish.

Now try this (first type in HGR and press RETURN , to clear the screen):

```
HPLOT 170, 10 TO 140, 140 TO 30, 70 TO 170, 10
```

and press RETURN . If you've done it properly the result should be a triangle on the screen. This demonstrates how to use the word TO to chain points together to make a sequence of lines joined end to end.

It is easy now to write a program to draw triangles. The one below is a simple example which could be much improved as shown in Chapter 3. First type in TEXT, and then NEW, to clear out any program in memory, and then type this:

```
100 HGR
120 HCOLOR=3
140 INPUT A, B
160 INPUT P, Q
180 INPUT Y, Z
```

This invites you to put in the co-ordinates of the three corners of the triangle. In each case put in the two numbers, with a comma between them. The rest of the program is just the HPLOT line:

```
200 HPLOT A, B TO P, Q TO Y, Z TO A, B
```

Now run it a few times.

DRAWING A CIRCLE

The program for drawing a circle is slightly more mathematical than usual and so a little bit of extra explanation is necessary; but even if you don't understand all of it you can type it in and see if it works. You can then change bits of the program to make the circle smaller or bigger, or with a different center.

To draw a circle we need to know the following things to start with.

(a) Where is its center? We can choose this: and because we want, on this occasion, to draw as big a circle as possible we will put the center of the circle near the center of the screen, so the first line to consider is:

```
160 XC=139 : YC=75
```

where *XC* is the number we go across and *YC* is the number we go down to get the center of the circle. This is not the first line of the program. We will add bits to this as we go along.

(b) What is the length of the radius? This, of course, depends on where we put the center. Remember that the screen is 160 units high so the maximum possible value for the radius is 80. To be on the safe side we will make it a bit smaller, using *R* for the radius:

```
180 R=75
```

(c) The line making up the actual outline of the circle will not be a continuous line, but a series of dots. We must choose the number of dots to use. This is a matter of trial and error, and for our large circle we chose 90, and call it *NP:*

```
140 NP=90
```

(d) We also need to declare π because we are going to use the fact that, in one complete circle or revolution there are 2 π radians. Use the letters PI to represent the Greek letter π.

```
200 PI=3.141593
```

With the usual introductory lines, the program so far looks like this:

```
100 HGR
120 HCOLOR=3
140 NP=90
160 XC=139 : YC=75
180 R=75
200 PI=3.141593
```

Make sure that your version on the screen looks like this. The next bit involves a bit of trigonometry. Each point on the circumference of a circle can be located with reference to the center of the circle as shown in this diagram:

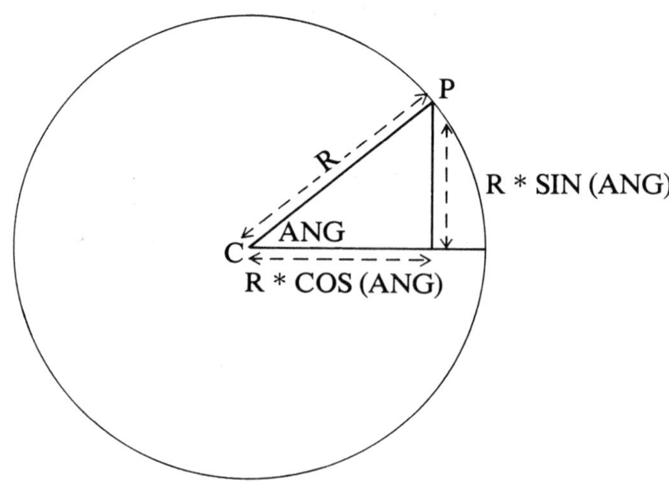

We have chosen the center C(139,75) in line 160, and the radius R(75) in line 180. The angle (ANG) will be different for each of the 90 points. The length of the two lines which determine the position of P from the center are shown, R*COS(ANG) and R*SIN(ANG). So if we can compute these two lengths for each of the 90 positions, and in each case add them to the center numbers, then we can use HPLOT to put a dot on each. Fortunately the computer does this for us.

The number of points, i.e. 90, has been stored in NP, so using C as the counter we can set up a loop:

```
220 FOR C=1 TO NP
```

Now we need the angle size (called ANG) which changes for each point. Since an angle of 2 π means one full revolution, then the angles we want will be first one ninetieth of this, and then two ninetieths of this, and then three ninetieths, and so on until ninety ninetieths (i.e. a full circle) have been calculated.

i.e. $(2*\pi)*(1/90)$
and $(2*\pi)*(2/90)$
and $(2*\pi)*(3/90)$

down to

$(2*\pi)*(90/90)$

Now since C runs from 1 to 90 (in line 220) and since NP is 90, we can express all this as:

```
240 ANG=(2*PI)*(C/NP)
```

We then compute the coordinates of the points corresponding to each angle.

```
260 X=R*SIN (ANG)
280 Y=R*COS(ANG)
```

Finally we plot each point, remembering to add the coordinates of the center of the circle (XC, YC) to each point.

```
300 HPLOT X+XC, Y+YC
```

Finally we close the loop:

```
320 NEXT C
```

So the second part of the program looks like this:

```
220 FOR C=1 TO NP
240 ANG=(2*PI)*(C/NP)
260 X=R*SIN(ANG)
280 Y=R*COS(ANG)
300 HPLOT X+XC, Y+YC
320 NEXT C
```

List your program and check it with this. Now run it to see if it works.

Remember that you can change the center, the radius and the number of points, but be careful with the numbers and remember that the screen is only 160 by 280 points.

COLORED CIRCLES

In high resolution graphics it is also possible to have color, but this time only 6 colors are available. There are, however, eight color numbers because 0 and 4 are alternative codes for black, and 3 and 7 are alternative codes for white. We can add a few lines to the circle program just completed which will demonstrate the available colors.

First remove line 120 by typing in 120 and pressing the **RETURN** key. Then type in these four new lines:

```
205 FOR N=1 TO 7
210 HCOLOR=N
340 GET A$
360 NEXT N
```

Then change line 300 as follows:

```
300 HPLOT XC, YC TO XC+X, YC+Y
```

Now run the program. The loop set up by lines 205 and 360 means that the colors used will range through those available, starting with HCOLOR = 1. We have deliberately left out 0 which is black, but 4 also represents black, so when it gets to that color, it will seem as if the circle is being removed. Line 340 stops the program when the circle is complete. When you press a key, it goes on to draw the circle again, but with a different color. The change in line 300 means that instead of simply plotting the points on the circumference of the circle we are joining the center to each point each time, so the circle is like a wheel with a great many spokes.

A MOVING SHAPE

We can now use HPLOT to draw a shape and make it move across the screen. To begin with the shape that will move must be drawn on squared paper. Here is an example.

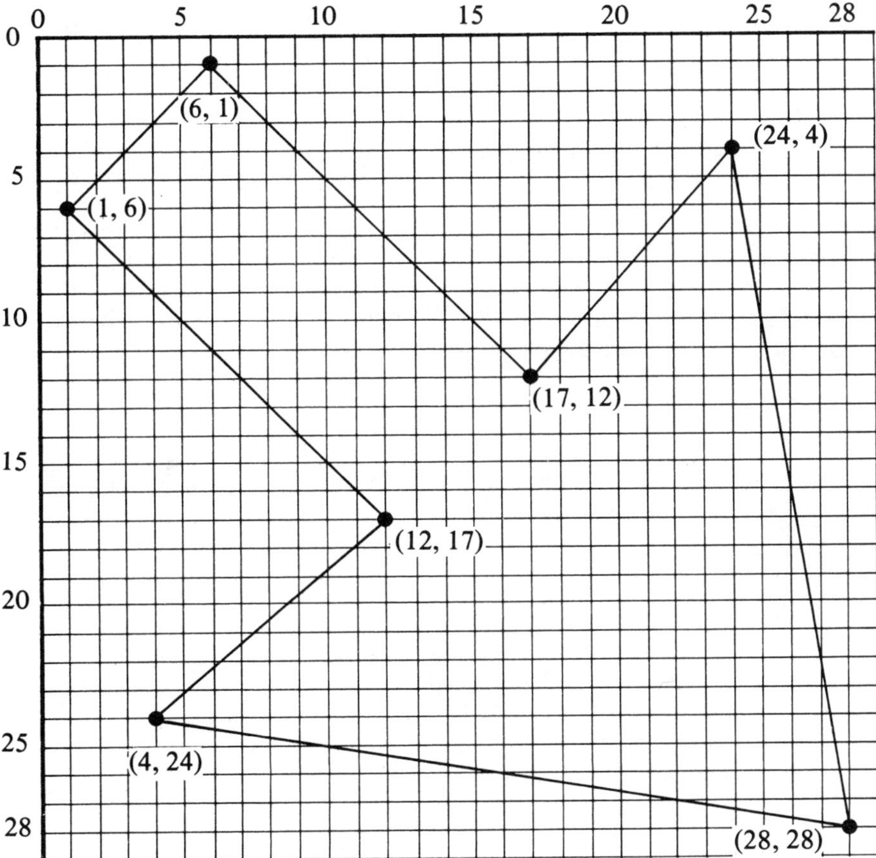

You can, of course, make up your own, but draw it carefully and find the coordinates of the points as shown.

We are now going to use HPLOT to draw and join these points in this order:

(6, 1) → (17, 12) → (24, 4) → (28, 28) → (4, 24) → (12, 17) →
(1, 6) → (6, 1)

Note that we put the first point in again at the end. The first thing we will do is put these numbers, in exactly the order they appear here, into a data statement, like this:

```
900 DATA 6, 1, 17, 12,24, 4, 28, 28, 4, 24, 12, 17, 1, 6, 6, 1
```

We will now read these numbers into two arrays, A and B, as follows. (Since the number of points is less than 10 we need not declare the arrays.) A is for the X numbers and B is for the Y numbers.

```
120 FOR C=1 TO 8
140 READ A(C), B(C)
160 NEXT C
```

We want to be able to draw and redraw the shape in a number of positions across the screen so we will have to use two variables to represent the changes in the position points. We will call them XS and YS and, to begin with, we will make them equal to zero.

```
180 XS=0 : YS=0
```

We now need a routine to actually draw the shape and, since we will be doing this over and over again, we will put it into a subroutine, starting at line 1000.

```
1000 REM DRAWS SHAPE
1020 HPLOT XS+A(1), YS+B(1)
1040 FOR C=2 TO 8
1060 HPLOT TO XS+A(C), YS+B(C)
1080 NEXT C
1100 RETURN
```

(a) In line 1020 we simply plot the first point.
(b) Then we set up a loop, lines 1040 and 1080, to join this point to the next one, i.e., using line 1060; and then that one to the next one, and so on to the end.

We now go to this subroutine for the first time, remembering to declare a color:

```
200 HCOLOR=3
220 GOSUB 1000
```

We then wish to move it and draw it again. So we change XS and YS as follows, and then go back to line 200 and draw it again.

```
320 XS=XS+3 : YS=YS+3
360 GOTO 200
```

We have added three to both XS and YS, but you can choose your own numbers. Two more lines are necessary and then you can run the program.

```
100 HGR
999 END
```

If you have copied all of this in correctly you will find that the program works quite well, but there are two further problems to solve. The first is that since XS and YS increase by three each cycle of the program, eventually they get too big and Apple gives you an error message, "ILLEGAL QUANTITY ERROR IN 1060". So we must write in a line to trap this error.

```
340 IF YS > 129 THEN 999
```

Type this in and run it again.

The second problem is that the shape does not disappear after it has been drawn. That is, it leaves a trace behind. The way to solve this is to remove the whole shape each time immediately after it has been drawn. The routine to do this is simple. We just change the HCOLOR to zero and draw it again. Since HCOLOR=0 means black, the shape will be erased.

```
280 HCOLOR=0
300 GOSUB 1000
```

Type these two lines in and try it again. This solves the problem. However, the whole process is perhaps a little too fast, so we can slow it down by putting in the following line. (This technique is described in full on page 88).

```
260 FOR Z=1 TO 200 : NEXT Z
```

One final refinement. Put in a line that gives you control over the movement, so that the shape only moves one step when you press a key.

```
240 GET A$
```

Try this. You may now find that you do not need line 260.

PROBLEMS

1. Write a program, using high resolution graphics, which will make a ball bounce repeatedly from the top of the screen to the bottom and, at the same time, move slowly across from left to right.
2. Write a program which draws a grid of hexagons on the screen, using high resolution graphics.
3. Write a program to draw each of the numerals on the high resolution graphics screen. The program should invite the user to input the coordinates of the top left-hand corner of the numeral and should then draw the requested numeral on the screen.

Routines and Useful Information

INTRODUCTION

This chapter is an attempt to put together in one place a number of techniques and sets of information that we have found very useful. None of these separate pieces is long enough to justify a full chapter, but each is of considerable importance and interest.

LEFT AND RIGHT ARROWS (← →)

Although use of these arrow keys has already been referred to on page 9, it is necessary, before the next section, to be quite sure about what they do. We will look at three examples.

(a) First type in this line and press **RETURN** .

```
100 PRINT "A B C D E F"
```

(b) Now type this in, but do not press **RETURN** as yet.

```
120 PRINT "A B C D E F"
```

Now use the *arrow-left* key (←) to move the cursor back five spaces until it is on top of the C. Now press **RETURN** .

(c) Finally type this in, and again do not press the **RETURN** key.

```
140 PRINT "A B C D E F"
```

Now use the *arrow-left* key to move the cursor back five spaces, as before. Now use the *arrow-right* key (→) to move the cursor three spaces to the right until it is on top of the letter F. Now press **RETURN** .

The result is as follows:

```
100 ? "A B C D E F"
120 ? "A B
140 ? "A B C D E
```

List it to check that this is exactly what was entered. The effect of the arrow-left key is to move the cursor to the left, so that when you press **RETURN** , anything to the right of the cursor, including the character it rests on, is wiped out. The effect of the arrow-right key is to enter anything it passes over into Apple's memory. (You must of course press **RETURN** at the end.) So that, in the third example above, the arrow-left wiped out the letters CDE, but the arrow-right reinstated them again.

SCREEN EDITING

If we have typed in a program and discover that one of the lines has been mistyped we then have two possible ways of correcting this mistake. One is to type in the whole line again, so replacing the mistaken line with a corrected version. The other way is shown in detail with an example. Suppose the line to be corrected is somewhere in the middle of a program, and is numbered 500.

First type in LIST 500, which places this specific line at the bottom of the screen close to the cursor and easily accessible.

```
500 PRINT "INPUP NAME OF BOK"
```

There are two mistakes on this line:

(a) INPUP should be INPUT.

(b) BOK should be BOOK.

To correct this we must first of all put Apple into escape mode. To do this simply press the **ESC** key once. To get out of escape mode again, just press the space bar once. (In fact, most other keys will do to get out of escape mode, but since there are a number of exceptions the safest thing to do is to use the space bar.)

Put Apple into escape mode now. Press the letter M a few times. The cursor will move down the screen in a straight line. Now press the letter I a few times. The cursor will move up the screen in a straight line. When you press the letter K the cursor will move to the right; and when you press the letter J the cursor will move to the left. These four keys are placed on the keyboard in a cross, each roughly pointing in the direction of movement associated with it, like this:

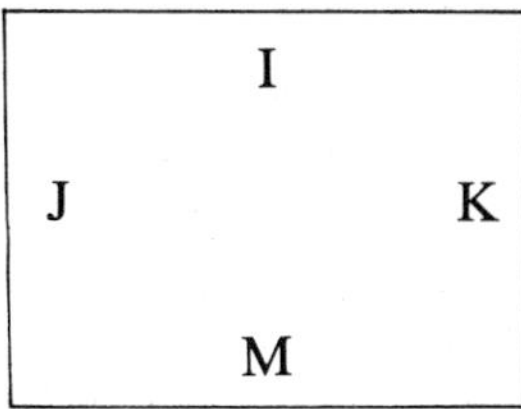

Experiment with these four keys, and move the cursor about the screen.

Now return to the line which we wished to correct. Type in LIST 500 and press **RETURN** .

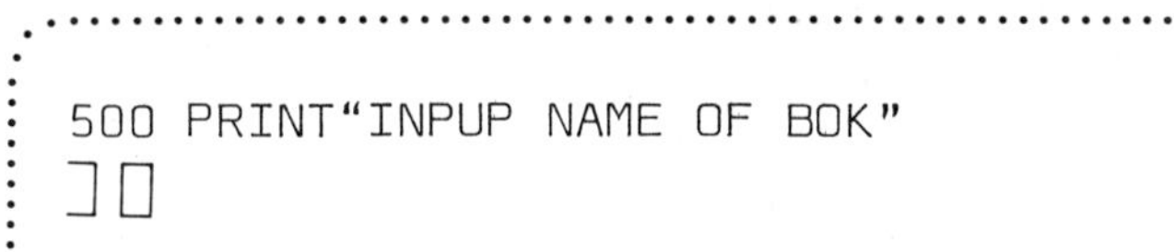

There are two stages in this editing process. In the first we use escape mode to move the cursor back up the screen to the correct position. In the second we get out of escape mode and actually edit the line using the arrow-left and arrow-right keys.

Stage 1

(a) Press the **ESC** key once.
(b) Press the letter I twice. This moves the cursor on top of the first zero of 500.
(c) Press the letter J once. This moves the cursor on top of the 5 of 500.
(d) Press the space bar once. This puts Apple out of ESCAPE mode. We are now ready to begin to edit the line.

Stage 2

(e) Use the arrow-right key to move the cursor across the line until it rests on top of the last letter of INPUP, i.e. the wrong P.
(f) Press the letter T. This changes the incorrect P into a correct T.
(g) Use the arrow-right key again to move the cursor over to the K of BOK.
(h) Then type the rest of the line correctly, i.e. O, then K, then quotation marks.

(i) Press **RETURN** .

(j) Now type in LIST 500 and see if it is correct.

There are a number of points to be made about this editing facility.

(a) When you wish to edit a line you must always move the cursor, in escape mode, to the very first symbol on the line, that is to the first digit of the line number. (Even when the line actually spills over onto the next row).

(b) When you press the space bar and begin to actually edit the line, the cursor must be moved by the arrow-right key to the very end of the line, even when it overflows into another line. If the mistake is near the beginning of a line, there is a tendency to correct it and then press **RETURN** immediately. If you do this you will wipe out the whole of the rest of the line.

(c) If the line is very long and overflows onto the next screen-row, another problem arises. This is best illustrated with another example. When you first type in the line it looks like this (including a deliberate mistake):

```
600 PRINT"THIS LANE IS GOING TO OVERFLOW INT
O THE NEXT LINE."
```

Then, when you type in LIST 600, and press **RETURN**, it looks like this:

```
600 PRINT "THIS LANE IS GOING TO
      OVERFLOW INTO THE NEXT LINE
      ."
```

If you count the characters and spaces carefully you will find that when you are typing material in Apple uses the full 40 spaces across the screen, but when you list it Apple uses only 33 spaces starting from the left.

Now type in LIST 600 and use the technique described above to edit this line and correct the misspelling, remembering to keep pressing the arrow-right key until you reach the end. Now list it again. This time there will be two large spaces in the line, after TO and after LINE. These have been caused by the fact that the cursor has been moved across these spaces by the arrow-right key during editing. If you are not clear about this, begin again and watch the screen carefully.

The problem is how to avoid making these spaces when editing. There are a number of solutions. One is to use the arrow-right key only as far as the end of the first row of the line and then simply to retype all the rest.

The second is to use the arrow-right key until you reach the end of the first row, then go back into escape mode and use the letter K to move the cursor until it reaches the first letter of the next line, then leave escape mode and use the right-arrow key again, and so on. The point is that while Apple is in escape mode, you are not using the right-arrow and so are not entering the 'spaces' into your line.

A third method involves the use of the *poke* command and this is described in the next chapter. This is probably the least troublesome solution.

THE ESC KEY

There are a number of other uses of the **ESC** key.

(a) First press **ESC** to put Apple into the escape mode. Then, hold the **SHIFT** key and press the letter P. This should have the effect of clearing the screen.

(b) Use the **ESC** key and the letters I, J and K to move the cursor to some point on the screen above where the writing on the screen ends. Then press F. Everything from the position of the cursor to the bottom of the screen should then disappear.

Do this again and then press E. This removes everything from the position of the cursor to the end of that particular line.

INSERTION OF MISSING WORDS

It is possible to use the escape mode to insert a missing word or words into a line. A well-known mistake is to leave out a word at the beginning of a line, such as INPUT. First type this in:

```
100 "WHAT IS THE NAME   "; A$
```

but do not press **RETURN** yet. You have noticed your mistake. First use the arrow-left key to move the cursor back to the first set of quotation marks, then press **ESC** once. Use the M key to move the cursor down a line (or more if necessary) to where there is nothing written. Now press the space bar to get out of **ESC** mode. Then type the missing word INPUT. Then immediately go back into ESC mode and use the letters I and J to move the cursor back on top of the first quotation marks. Press the space bar once, then use the arrow-right key to move the cursor out to the end of the line. Now press **RETURN**. The screen will look like this:

```
] 100"WHAT IS THE NAME";A$
      INPUT
]□
```

Now type in LIST, and the screen should look like this:

```
]LIST
100   INPUT"WHAT IS THE NAME";A$
]□
```

Do this sort of correction a few times and think about what is happening. The point is that while Apple is in escape mode you can move the cursor wherever you like but nothing is being entered into memory. Only when you press the space bar and come out of escape mode does Apple take in what you print or pass over.

CONTROL OPERATIONS

Below the **ESC** key on the keyboard is one with the letters CTRL on it. This is short for *control*. This key is used for a number of interesting operations such as the control of screen listings. To demonstrate these properly you will need a long program in memory. Put your *systems master* disk into disk drive 1, and type in CATALOG. Then choose a long program, that is one with a large number in front of it. A good example is LITTLE BRICK OUT. Load this in the usual way. (That is, type in LOAD LITTLE BRICK OUT, and press the **RETURN** key).

CONTROL AND C

Type in LIST and press **RETURN**. Suppose you wish to stop the listing completely, as soon as it has started. Type in LIST again and press **RETURN**. Then hold the **CTRL** key with one finger and press the letter C with another. The "bell" will ring and the listing will stop with the message BREAK, and the cursor will return. Now type in RUN and press **RETURN**. As soon as the program starts, hold **CTRL** and press C. The program will stop at once. (If it doesn't stop, press **RETURN** after **CTRL** and C. It may also be necessary, in this program, to type in TEXT to remove the graphics facility).

So, **CTRL** with C is a way of aborting the listing or running of a program at any time.

CONTROL AND S

Type in LIST again, then, as soon as the listing starts, put one finger on CTRL and the other on the letter S. This stops the listing at once. Pressing any key will start it again.

CONTROL AND X

Type in NEW to wipe out the previous program and then type in the line below, but don't press RETURN :

```
100 PRINT "THIS LINE IS WRONG
```

Suppose you suddenly realized that this line was indeed completely wrong and that you just wanted to abandon it and begin again. Hold the CTRL key and press the letter X. This will have the effect you want. The screen will look like this:

```
]100 ?"THIS LINE IS WRONG\
]□
```

The presence of the symbol "\" is an indication that you have abandoned this line. If you now type in LIST and press RETURN, nothing will appear.

CONTROL AND G

First, hold the CTRL key and press the letter G. Do this a few times. A sound something like a bell will be made. We can program this as follows: first type in the line below and then read the following instructions:

```
100 A$="
```

You have opened a set of quotation marks. Now hold the CTRL key and press G so that the bell sounds. (Nothing will appear on the screen, but you are nonetheless entering it into Apple's memory). Now close the quotation marks, and press RETURN. The line now looks like this:

```
100 A$="  "
```

And, although there is nothing visible between the quotes, there is in fact a programmed command there. Now type in:

```
120 PRINT A$
```

Now type in RUN and press **RETURN** . The result is that the bell sounds. This is caused by line 120 actually printing A$, which is the bell sound.

Now change line 120 as follows and add the rest:

```
120 FOR N=1 TO 20
140 PRINT A$
160 NEXT N
```

Now type in RUN and the bell will ring 20 times.

RANDOM NUMBERS

A routine to generate random numbers is frequently needed when writing games and simulation programs on Apple. This is done using Apple's built-in random number function, which is activated by the statement RND (short for random). First type in this program and then run it.

```
100 HOME
120 INPUT A
140 FOR N=1 TO 5
160 PRINT RND(A)
180 NEXT N
```

Apple responds by first clearing the screen (line 100) and then printing a question mark to indicate that it is waiting for you to input A (line 120). Lines 140 and 180 together create a loop which is cycled round five times. During each cycle RND(A), that is a random number linked in some way to the starting value A, is printed. So we can test the effects of using different values of A by running this program a number of times. First, type in 4 in response to the question mark. Then press **RETURN**. The result on one particular occasion is shown opposite. Your sequence will almost certainly be slightly different.

```
.748548247
.75659165
.613849493
.0841481608
.695520398
```

Now run this program again and put in 9. Make a note of the last number on the list. Now run it again and put in 0. Repeat this a few times. The effect of 0 in this program is to produce five copies of the last random number generated when 9 was input. Run it again and put in 3.7. Try a great variety of numbers. Then run it again and put in –2. The result is shown:

```
2.99205567E-08
2.99205567E-08
2.99205567E-08
2.99205567E-08
2.99205567E-08
```

The value of A is obviously important. If you wish to be sure to produce a different set of numbers each time, then you may use for A any number greater than 0.

Normally you will use positive numbers and in each case you will produce a positive decimal with a value of less than 1, and with up to 10 digits. In this form, these random numbers are not very useful, so we need ways of changing them to make them less cumbersome.

First type in NEW to remove the old program and then put in the following:

```
100 HOME
120 FOR N=1 TO 10
200 PRINT RND(7)
220 NEXT N
```

Run this to make sure that it produces a set of ten quite different numbers. Then use an auxiliary variable A, and change the program with the two lines:

```
140 A=RND(6)
200 PRINT A
```

Notice that, in order to show that any positive number will do, we keep changing the number in the brackets after RND.

If you now run this program you will find that changing line 200 and inserting line 140 does not change what the program does, but it makes it possible to manipulate this auxiliary variable A.

First type in these two lines, changing line 200 again in the process.

```
160 B=10*A
200 PRINT A, B
```

Now run this. This time not only are the random numbers printed, but each is multiplied by 10 and these are also printed. Then, add line 180 and change line 200 again. (We have used the statement TAB(35) to make the results easier to read. This is explained in detail in chapter 9: just type it in for now.)

```
180 C=INT(B)
200 PRINT A, B TAB(35) C
```

This time, the integral or whole-number part of each number is placed by line 180 in C. Then line 200 ensures that this whole number is also printed on the screen. Try running this program now.

Notice that the last column of numbers are all single-digit whole numbers. We now have a complete program and this is listed below. Note that there have been two small changes from the version worked out above. In line 120 we have replaced 10 by 100, and we have changed line 200 so that C (the whole number part of each random number) only is printed. Now run this program, which follows, a few times to make sure that you know what it is doing. We have ended up with a program that generates 100 single-digit random numbers each time.

```
100 HOME
120 FOR N=1 TO 100
140 A=RND(6)
160 B=10*A
180 C=INT(B)
200 PRINT C
220 NEXT N
```

Examine the results carefully, and notice that C can be any one of the 10 numbers 0-9. If you would like C to be one of the 10 numbers from 1 to 10, rather than from 0 to 9, then add 1 to C each time. One way to do this is to change line 200.

```
200 PRINT C+1
```

It is also possible to combine three of these lines (140, 160, 180) into one as follows:

```
140 C=INT(10*RND(2))
```

The definition of random numbers suggests that each of these numbers (0 to 9) comes out with equal regularity. The following program tests this. It simulates tossing a coin as follows. If the random number is less than 5 (i.e. 0, 1, 2, 3 or 4) then we record a head (lines 200 and 260). Otherwise (i.e. when the number is 5, 6, 7, 8 or 9) we record a tail. First, type in NEW, and then the new program below.

```
100 HOME : INPUT "HOW MANY TOSSES   " ; J
120 FOR N=1 TO J
140 A=RND(4)
160 B=10*A
180 C=INT(B)
200 IF C < 5 THEN 260
220 T=T+1
240 GOTO 280
260 H=H+1
280 NEXT N
300 PRINT "NO. OF HEADS" ; H
320 PRINT "NO. OF TAILS" ; T
```

Now type in RUN and press **RETURN**. When the question mark appears on the screen in response to line 100, input 100, which is the number of times we wish to simulate the coin-tossing. This is stored in J. Then press **RETURN**. Do this a number of times, and keep notes of the results. The number of heads and the number of tails should be close to 50 each time. Now run it again and put in 1000. This time it will take longer.

Some final points about random numbers. The two lines:

```
160 B=10*A
180 C=INT(B)
```

can be replaced by this line:

```
160 C%=10*A
```

and line 200 changed to:

```
200 IF C% < 5 THEN 260
```

A letter or variable followed by the percentage sign stands for a whole number or integer. This means that, no matter what 10*A looks like, only its integral part will be stored in the variable C%.

Suppose we wished only to have the numbers 0, 1 and 2 rather than the whole set up to 9. In this case we need only multiply the random number by 3. (The biggest posible random number will be less than 1, say about 0.999. When this is multiplied by three and the integral part taken, it cannot be bigger than 2).

Type in this program and try it.

```
100 HOME
120 FOR N=1 TO 100
140 A=RND(9)
160 B=3*A
180 C=INT(B)
200 PRINT C ;
220 NEXT N
```

It should produce only the numbers 0, 1 or 2.

Finally, suppose that you wished to have only the numbers 17, 18 and 19 in your set. In this case you would have to add 17 to each number produced by the above routine.

DELAYS

It is possible to delay or stop the running of a program for a few seconds when it is necessary to read something on the screen. The routine works as shown below, where it is put in a subroutine. Type it in and run it.

```
100 HOME
120 PRINT "NOW THERE WILL BE A DELAY"
140 GOSUB 1000
160 PRINT "THE DELAY IS NOW OVER"
180 END
.
.
.
1000 FOR N=1 TO 1000
1010 NEXT N
1020 RETURN
```

In this case Apple cycles round the loop in lines 1000 and 1010, one thousand times. This takes approximately one second.

NUMBERS IN APPLE

We will now consider the question of how Apple handles large numbers and the maximum size of number it can cope with. To test this, type in and run the program shown below:

```
100 HOME
120 FOR N=1 TO 10
140 PRINT 10 ∧ N
160 NEXT N
```

This prints out all the powers of 10 (the inverted v in line 140 means 'to the power of'). The screen looks like this:

```
10
100
1000
10000
100000
1000000
10000000
100000000
1E+09
1E+10


]□
```

The last number printed out in full is 1 followed by eight zeros. 1 followed by nine zeros is printed as

```
1E+09
```

which conventionally means 1 multiplied by 10, nine times. This is called scientific notation. Now subtract one from each of these numbers and print this by retyping line 140 like this:

```
140 PRINT 10∧N, 10∧N−1
```

This produces the same set of numbers as before, and, more-or-less beside them, the result of subtracting one from each of them. (The limitations on the accuracy of some numbers in Apple become clear from this example as well.) But the important thing, from our point of view, is that Apple prints 999 999 999 (i.e. nine times) in this form, but when one is added to this it prints it as 1E + 09, i.e. in scientific notation. In other words "nine nines" is the largest whole number that Apple can cope with. After that it gives you an estimate only.

Type in NEW and try this program:

```
100 HOME
120 FOR N=1 TO 10
140 PRINT 999 999 995+N
160 NEXT N
```

This asks Apple to print all the whole numbers, starting with 999 999 996 and up to 1 000 000 005. Run the program and see what happens.

We will now try to see how Apple handles decimals. First type in this program:

```
100 HOME
120 INPUT A
140 PRINT 1/A
160 GOTO 120
```

Notice that line 160 sends the program back to the INPUT line, line 120. This means that you can go on inputting numbers for A and then examining the decimal caused by dividing A into 1. (When you wish to leave the program, press CTRL and C and then press the RETURN key). That is, you can look at 1/3 or 1/7 or 1/103 as decimals. Run the program. Line 120 will make Apple put a question mark on the screen. Type in 3 and press RETURN. Then type in 7; then 53; then 179. Try as many numbers as you like. Remember that our problem is to try to understand how Apple writes decimals.

Here are four responses from this program when the numbers shown are typed in:

```
? 7
 .142857143
? 23
 .0434782609
? 107
 9.34579439E-03
? 231
 4.32900433E-03

?□
```

Obviously some fractions, like 1/23, produce straightforward decimals, but with a maximum of nine significant figures. (That is, it does not count the zero after the decimal point as a significant figure.) But other decimals like 1/231 produce less accurate answers in the scientific notation form. At what stage does the changeover take place? That is, when are decimals too small to be written normally?

Run this program again, and put in 100. The response is, not surprisingly, .01. Now put in 101. This number will be smaller than .01 and the response is in scientific notation. In fact Apple will translate any number smaller than .01 into scientific notation, and at the other extreme any number greater than 999 999 999 into scientific notation.

The conclusions then are as follows:

(a) Any number numerically less than .01 is changed into scientific notation.
(b) Any number numerically greater than 999 999 999 is changed into scientific notation.
(c) Any number between these two limits is written as an ordinary number or decimal.
(d) If this number or decimal has more than nine digits, only the first nine are recorded. If the 10th digit is 6, 7, 8 or 9, then the ninth digit has 1 added to it.

TRACE/NOTRACE

This is a useful facility which can help to find a mistake in programming. The example that follows is a simple program which is designed to test whether an input number is smaller or larger than 6. To show the value of the TRACE facility this program has a mistake in its logic. First type it in:

```
100 HOME
120 INPUT "CHOOSE A NUMBER    "; A
140 IF A < 6 THEN 200
160 PRINT "A IS EQUAL TO OR LARGER THAN 6"
200 PRINT "A IS SMALLER THAN 6"
220 END
```

Now run it a few times. The idea is that at line 140 we test the input number. If it is less then 6 we send the program to line 200 where it prints "A IS SMALLER THAN 6". If A is not less than 6, then the program goes on to the next line (line 160) and prints "A IS EQUAL TO OR LARGER THAN 6".

But this does not work properly. When A is less than 6, say 4, it works. But when A is greater than 6, say 9, both messages apear on the screen. Now type in the word TRACE, press **RETURN** and run the program. Then put in 9 and press **RETURN**. The screen looks like this:

```
#120 ?9
#140 #160 A IS EQUAL TO OR LARGER THAN 6
#200 A IS SMALLER THAN 6
#220
]▯
```

This means that the program has first gone to line 120, and waited there for an input (in this case 9). Note the hash sign (#). This stands for the word "number", so #120 means number 120. It appears here to indicate that a trace is being carried out.

List the program, and examine this sequence. Lines 120 and 140 make sense. Since A is not less than 6, then line 160 makes sense. But then there is nothing to stop the program going on to line 200, which it should not do. So we have discovered the mistake and now put in a new line:

```
180 GOTO 220
```

Now run the program, and this time it works. One final point: it is always necessary to turn the trace facility off at the end of the routine, by typing in NOTRACE. It is, of course, possible to use the words TRACE and NOTRACE as parts of a program, rather than typing them in directly as we have just demonstrated.

PROBLEMS

1. Using the random number function, write a program to simulate the tossing of a single dice.
2. Write a program that will present in sequence the verses of the Christmas song *The Twelve Days of Christmas*. The words are:
   "On the twelfth day of Christmas
   My true love sent to me:
   Twelve lords a-leaping
   Eleven ladies dancing
   Ten pipers piping
   Nine drummers drumming
   Eight maids a-milking
   Seven swans a-swimming
   Six geese a-laying
   Five gold rings
   Four colly birds
   Three French hens
   Two turtle-doves
   And a partridge in a pear tree."

7

The Use of Machine Code

INTRODUCTION

Writing programs in machine-code is not easy and it would be impossible in one short chapter to do anything more than demonstrate how to use machine code programs written by others. In doing this, however, it is hoped that those interested in learning how to write machine-code will begin to understand the elements of the process.

We normally write programs in the BASIC language and there are two main reasons why we might want to use machine-code. Firstly, a routine written in machine-code will work a great deal more quickly, and there are occasions when we want things to happen as quickly as possible. Secondly, a routine written in machine-code is more economical in its use of memory, and, although this is not a great problem for us now, if we wished later on to write a very long and complex program it might become necessary to write at least parts of it in machine-code.

Both of these reasons suggest that normally it is not necessary to write a whole program in machine code. It is more likely that most of a program will be written in BASIC and machine-code will be used for a small part of it, perhaps one single routine which needs to work fast. This means that there must be some way of incorporating machine-code within BASIC. This is done using three BASIC words, POKE, PEEK and CALL.

We will consider each of these words in detail in what follows. The rest of this chapter has four sections:

(*a*) *The Screen RAM.* This part deals with that section of the memory associated with the screen. This is called the screen RAM, and we write about it first because it allows us to deal directly with memory in a way that is immediately visible to the eye.

(*b*) *Music.* This second part shows how to use Apple to make music. This process allows us to introduce and use a machine-code program without necessarily understanding the detail of how it works.

(*c*) *A Machine-Code Program.* The third section uses a short and simple piece of machine-code as an introduction to an understanding of the processes involved in the construction of such code. This also allows for a demonstration of one method of actually getting the program into Apple's memory.

(*d*) *Poke as a Switch.* This fourth and last section shows how changing the contents of units of memory can act as a sort of switch with respect to certain aspects of Apple's functioning.

THE SCREEN RAM

Poke

This mysterious word is rarely met in BASIC texts and yet it turns up unheralded in many programs. Perhaps the best way to begin to understand it is to do some examples.

Try this:

```
100 HOME
120 POKE 1724, 170
```

Then type in RUN and press **RETURN** . The result is not very dramatic. The star (*) graphic appears about the middle of the screen which has been cleared by line 100.

Look at line 120 again:

```
120 POKE 1724, 170
```

The star graphic (*) has the number 170 associated with it. The location, that is the center of the screen, has the rather unwieldy number 1724 associated with it. So the line can be read, "poke, into space number 1724, the symbol 170".

Symbol Numbers

In fact each letter, number and symbol on the Apple keyboard has a *poke number* associated with it. As well as this the reverse field and flash version of each of these characters has a different number associated with it. These characters and their associated numbers are all shown in Tables D1 and D2, pages 194 and 195. Notice that the numbers run from 0 to 255.

In Table D1 there is a copy of the Apple keyboard. Above each normal key are written four code numbers which are associated with that key. They are, starting with the bottom and lowest of the four numbers and moving up, the following:

(a) The number representing the symbol in reverse field. Remember that, normally you must type in INVERSE and press **RETURN** to be able to access this symbol.
(b) The number representing the symbol in flash mode. Again, normally you must type in FLASH and press **RETURN** to be able to make use of this symbol.
(c) The number representing the symbol.
(d) Another number representing the symbol.

For example, look at the key S. The poke numbers and the symbols associated with them are:

S (in reverse field) 19
S (in flashing mode) 83
S (normal) .... 147 or 211

In this way the poke number associated with each symbol can be found. However, if the number is known, but not the symbol, Table D2 provides an opposite-way dictionary.

Screen numbers

The Apple screen can be thought of as a rectangle 40 spaces wide by 24 spaces high. That is, it is made up of 960 small squares. Each of these is given a number starting at the top left-hand corner with 1024 and finishing at the bottom right-hand corner with 2039. (Actually the units are not squares but rectangles, but the difference need not concern us here. See page 56.)

If you now add 960 to 1024, you will find that the total is not 2039, so that some numbers in the sequence are left out. In fact, the way in which the Apple screen is numbered is a bit strange and needs some explanation. It is as if the screen were divided into three equal sections, A, B and C by lines across from left to right, like this:

A
B
C

These are then placed side by side like this:

A	B	C	D

and a little extra is placed at the end. Each little square is then numbered in sequence right across each row of this long thin rectangle, starting at the top with 1024 and going on as follows:

Section A	1024 – 1063
Section B	1064 – 1103
Section C	1104 – 1143
Section D	1144 – 1151

The second row then starts at 1152 and each row has the same pattern. Since section D is not in fact part of the screen, this means that eight numbers are lost off each row. On the first row these are, as shown above, numbers 1144 to 1151. An attempt to show the whole pattern is given in Table D3.

Lines and movement

Now try this program. First type it in, and then look at the explanation that follows.

```
100 HOME
120 FOR A=1704 TO 1743
140 POKE A, 171
160 NEXT A
```

Line 100 clears the screen. Lines 120 and 160 together create a loop that allows A to run successively from 1704 to 1743. These numbers represent one full line of locations across the Apple screen (see Table D3). Line 140 pokes the symbol represented by 171, i.e. the plus sign, into each of these locations. The result, when you run the program, is that a line of plus signs appears across the screen. The whole thing happens very quickly, so we slow it down by adding:

```
150 FOR B=1 TO 20 : NEXT B
```

Now run it again. Suppose we wish to create an illusion of movement. We do this by removing each plus immediately after it has been placed.

Put in the line:

```
145 POKE A-1, 160
```

160 is the symbol for a space and the result of line 145 is that a space, i.e. nothing, replaces the plus sign placed last time round in space A, (now space A – 1). Now run the program again. Finally there is the problem that the very last plus is not removed by the loop: because the last circuit of the loop put in the last plus and removed the second last plus. In order to remove this last plus add the final line, as follows:

```
170 POKE A-1, 160
```

Now run the program again.

Obviously this technique has enormous scope for experiment. Try making diagonal runs, vertical runs, or simultaneous runs. Of course, with Apple we can do this sort of thing a good deal more easily using the graphics techniques, but there are two important points to be made about this way of doing it.

(a) These screen numbers shown above and in Table 3 are in fact the addresses of units of memory. So that when we use a line like:

```
POKE 1704, 171
```

we are putting the number 171 into the unit of memory numbered 1704. That is we are dealing directly with units of memory, in that we are choosing which units of memory to deal with and we are choosing what numbers to put in them. This essentially is what machine-code programming is about, the direct placement of numbers in chosen memory units. The numbers we place can mean many things. Here they represent characters used by Apple, but they can also mean commands which Apple understands, or the addresses of other memory units, and so on.

(b) The second important point is that when we use this technique we can use any character and not just the lines used in graphics. In the example above we used the plus sign. But if we changed the number 171 to 157 we would then be using the closing square bracket. Try it and see.

In the next section we show how to examine these characters.

Symbol listing

The three programs that follow use the poke technique to show the full set of Apple symbols on the screen in various ways. First type in NEW to remove the old program and then type in this program.

```
100 HOME
120 FOR N=0 TO 255
140 POKE 1980, N
160 NEXT N
```

Now run this program. This prints in succession each of the symbols to be found on the Apple keyboard in the centre of the screen. This is location 1980. However it does this so quickly that the numbers cannot be read. So add this slowing down line:

```
150 FOR J=1 TO 400 : NEXT J
```

Now try running the program again. Here, each symbol replaces the previous one, so if we want to display all the symbols at once, a new program (like this one in many ways) has to be devised. Type in NEW and then this program:

```
100 HOME
120 N=1024
140 FOR A=0 TO 255
160 POKE N, A
200 N=N+1
220 NEXT A
```

Now type in RUN and press **RETURN** . This demonstrates at once the problem with the screen numbering and, as well, some of the symbols are missing because of the unused numbers at the end of the bottom row.

Screen number conversion

To solve these two problems we have written a subroutine which allows us to treat the screen as though it was numbered from 1 to 960. Change lines 120 and 160 as shown and put in lines 180 and 240.

```
120 N=1
160 GOSUB 1000
180 POKE P, A : REM N IS CONVERTED TO P BY SUBROUTINE
240 END
```

Line 120 uses N = 1 to represent the first, i.e. the top left-hand corner of the screen as 1. Line 160 sends the program to the following subroutine, which translates N into the correct number, i.e. 1024 which is here called P, and then line 180 pokes the first symbol into this memory unit. In the next circuit of the program, N has become 2 and again the subroutine translates this into the correct number. In fact the subroutine translates each of the numbers from 1 to 960 into the correct memory-unit-number for the corresponding screen-location. Don't worry too much if you don't understand how it works. Just type it in and try using it.

```
 999 REM N IS SCREEN NUMBER 1 TO 960
1000  M=INT (N / 40)+1
1020  R=N-40 * (M-1)
1040 R=R-1
1060 IF M < 9 THEN 1120
1080 IF M < 17 THEN 1140
1100 X=56 : Y=M-24 : GOTO 2000
1120 X=0 : Y=M-1 : GOTO 2000
1140 X=72 : Y=M-13 : GOTO 2000
1999 REM P IS PROPER SCREEN NUMBER FOR POKE
2000 P=984+M * 40+X+Y * 88+R
2020 RETURN
```

Random pictures

The next example uses poke and this subroutine to draw a random picture on the screen, made up of the four symbols #, *, + and $, all in reverse field. (You can, of course, choose your own symbols.) Table D1 shows that the numbers corresponding to these are:

#	35
$	36
*	42
+	43

First we choose one of the four numbers 0, 1, 2 or 3 randomly.

```
100 HOME
120 B=INT (4*RND(7))
```

Then we use this to choose one of our four symbols.

```
160 IF B=0 THEN A=35
180 IF B=1 THEN A=36
200 IF B=2 THEN A=42
220 IF B=3 THEN A=43
```

We also choose one of the 960 screen locations randomly.

```
140 N=INT(960*RND(3))+1
```

Then we poke the number representing the symbol, that is A, into the chosen screen location, after going to the subroutine described above.

```
240 GOSUB 1000
260 POKE P, A
```

We then put in a loop to make it repeat over and over again:

```
280 GOTO 120
```

Now run it and watch what happens. When you want it to stop, hold the **CTRL** key and press C. If that doesn't work then press **RETURN**.

Don't type in NEW because we will use the subroutine at line 1000 for the next section. Type in DEL 100, 280 and press **RETURN**.

Introduction to peek

The *peek* statement makes use of the same set of symbol and screen location numbers as have already been used by poke, that is those in Tables D2 and D3. It is a way of checking whether or not a memory location is empty or has a number stored in it.

Notice that characters such as A or ? cannot be stored directly in a unit of memory. Only numbers can be stored, and so when you wish to store A or ?, you actually store the numbers corresponding to them shown in Tables D2 and D3. A method must then be devised for translating the numbers back into characters.

We will now try to illustrate this process. First we must place a number in a known memory location using poke. Then we will use peek to test for its existence. The routine below places the question mark (poke number 191) in the screen location 461.

```
100 HOME
120 A=191 : REM QUESTION MARK
140 N=461 : REM SCREEN LOCATION
160 GOSUB 1000: REM TRANSLATES N INTO P
180 POKE P, A
999 END
```

Type this in and run it. A question mark should appear on the screen.

Suppose we now wish to check this screen row for the presence of a symbol of any kind. This sort of checking is often necessary and useful, in games for example. The numbers associated with the screen locations on this row are 441 to 480. (On Table D3 these are 1448–1487.)

Add these lines to the programs

```
200 FOR N=441 TO 480
220 GOSUB 1000
240 B=PEEK (P)
260 VTAB 1 : PRINT N, B
280 NEXT N
```

Lines 200 and 280 together create a loop which allows N successively to take up the values 441, 442 and so on to 480. Line 220 translates these into P and line 160 peeks at each of these locations in turn and stores the number found there in B.

It is to be expected that most of these locations will have nothing stored in them, and the number corresponding to nothing is 160.

Line 260 prints, for each cycle of the loop, the values of N and B at the top of the screen, using VTAB1 (for an explanation of this facility, see Chapter 9). These are the location numbers and the content numbers.

Try running this. The results are printed on the screen very quickly, but if you watch the number on the right very carefully you will see that although it stays as 160 most of the time it does change to 191 at one point. You can check this by putting in a slow-down line as follows:

```
270 FOR Z=1 TO 500 : NEXT Z
```

Now run the program again and watch the screen carefully. At 461, the number 160 changes to 191, the number for a question mark, and immediately changes back. Now put in the line:

```
150 IF B=160 THEN 280
```

and remove line 270. Now run the program again. This time when nothing is encountered, that is, when B = 160, that answer is excluded, so only the result survives.

```
461     191
```

However, we poked a question mark into the space, and the peek routine has produced the number 191. We can translate this using the table of peek and poke numbers but often it would be more useful to have a direct translation by the machine. We can use another Applesoft-BASIC function to achieve this. The function is CHR$. CHR is short for character, and the dollar sign indicates that it represents a string. It is used to translate code numbers like those on Tables D1 and D2 back into symbols. This function is described in more detail in the chapter on string functions, where some difficulties associated with its use are described, but in this case there is no problem. Put in the line:

```
255 A$=CHR$(B)
```

and change line 260 to:

```
260 PRINT N, B, A$
```

This sets A$ equal to the string associated with the number B, and prints this, i.e. A$, beside the two numbers N and B. The complete program now looks like this:

```
100 HOME
120 A=191 : REM QUESTION MARK
140 N=461 : REM SCREEN LOCATION
160 GOSUB 1000 : REM TRANSLATION
180 POKE P, A
200 FOR N=441 TO 480
220 GOSUB 1000
240 B=PEEK(P)
250 IF B=160 THEN 280
255 A$=CHR$(B)
260 PRINT N, B, A$
280 NEXT N
999 END
```

(*continued overleaf*)

```
1000 M=INT (N / 40) + 1
1020 R=N−40 * (M−1)
1040 R=R−1
1060 IF M < 9 THEN 1120
1080 IF M < 17 THEN 1140
1100 X=56 : Y=M−24 : GOTO 2000
1120 X=0 : Y=M−1 : GOTO 2000
1140 X=72 : Y=M−13 : GOTO 2000
1999 REM P IS PROPER SCREEN NUMBER FOR POKE
2000 P=984+M * 40+X+Y * 88+R
2020 RETURN
```

Introduction to call

The ways in which we have just been using peek and poke are simple and obvious to explain because the effects of what we are doing are immediately obvious on the screen. However, very often the memory locations into which numbers are poked have nothing to do with the screen, and so this is not so easy to demonstrate. Indeed, once you have poked numbers into such memory locations, it is necessary to make the machine actually go to the first of these memory locations and perform the activities which the numbers placed in them are codes for. To do this we use the word *call.*

MUSIC

Call and music

This program will demonstrate how poke and call are used together to put a machine-code program into Apple's memory and then to make Apple go to that part of memory and actually run the program.

Any program written in machine-code looks like a set of numbers. The program we now list in data statements is used to make Apple play a note of music. Don't worry about how it actually works since we are using it simply to demonstrate the process. Later we will show how to decide what the pitch of the note is to be and what its duration is to be, but for the moment here is the set of numbers making up the program. We store them in data statements in two lines of BASIC. We could have used one line, but it would be a bit long.

```
 10 HOME
100 DATA 173, 48, 192, 136, 208, 5, 206, 1, 3, 240, 9
110 DATA 202, 208, 245, 174, 0, 3, 76, 2, 3, 96, 0, 0
```

We must now use poke to put these numbers into successive memory units. To do this we must choose a part of Apple's memory that is not, or is not likely to be, used for something else. How this is done is too complicated to describe here, but it is perhaps enough to know that on most Apples the memory units numbered 768 up to 1023 are normally available. (Note that the next set of memory units, starting at 1024, are the screen memory locations discussed earlier.) We will leave 768 and 769 for another purpose and begin at 770. Notice that there are 23 numbers in the program in lines 100 and 110, so the next part of the program pokes these 23 numbers into the memory units 770 to 792.

```
120 FOR N=770 TO 792
140 READ Y
160 POKE N, Y
180 NEXT N
```

Type this in and run it. The program is now entered into Apple's memory ready to be used. To do this we need to do two things:

(a) Put the pitch of the note in memory unit 768, and its duration or length in memory unit 769. We do this using poke in line 240 and 260 below, after inviting the user to choose the values in lines 200 and 220.

```
200 PRINT : INPUT "WHAT PITCH (0-255)   " ; P
220 PRINT : INPUT "WHAT DURATION (0-255)   " ; D
240 POKE 768, P
260 POKE 769, D
```

(b) Tell Apple to go to the memory unit numbered 770 and use or run the program. We do this in line 300 with the word CALL.

```
300 CALL 770
```

The whole program so far looks like this:

```
10 HOME
100 DATA 173, 48, 192, 136, 208, 5, 206, 1, 3, 240, 9
110 DATA 202, 208, 245, 174, 0, 3, 76, 2, 3, 96, 0, 0
120 FOR N=770 TO 792
140 READ Y
160 POKE N, Y
180 NEXT N
200 PRINT : INPUT "WHAT PITCH (0-255)   " ; P
```

(*continued overleaf*)

```
220 PRINT : INPUT "WHAT DURATION (0-255)   " ; D
240 POKE 768, P
260 POKE 769, D
300 CALL 770
```

Now type in RUN and press **RETURN** . The screen will look like this:

```
WHAT PITCH (0-255)
```

You respond with any number between 0 and 255 and press **RETURN**. The screen then asks "WHAT DURATION (0-255)". You again respond and when you press **RETURN** the note should sound. Run this a few times and try a variety of different numbers between 0 and 255.

Playing a tune

We can now use this as a basis for the creation of a program to play a tune. In addition to the information already available we must first decide which numbers correspond to the musical notes on a piano. Below is our attempt to do this. The first note is the A below middle C.

	First Octave	*Second Octave*
A	228	114
B	204	102
C	192	96
D	171	85
E	152	76
F	144	72
G	128	64

We can now use these to put in the pitches of the various notes of our tune. We also need fixed numbers for the duration of notes, and for this we allow the following values: Crotchet, 240; Quaver, 120; Semiquaver, 60, and so on.

The tune we have chosen is an old Irish air called *The Cliffs of Doneen*. It is shown at the top of page 107.

We first make a list of the number pairs for the notes of this tune and store them in data lines. First remove the lines numbered from 200 to 300 in the above program, and keep the lines numbered 10 to 180. Then type in lines 200 to 206 which contain the set of data for the pitches of the notes of the tune. There are 54 notes, so there are 54 numbers.

```
200 DATA 171, 152, 128, 114, 102, 85, 102, 114, 128, 152, 171, 171, 171
202 DATA 102, 96, 85, 76, 85, 102, 171, 152, 128, 114, 128, 114, 102
204 DATA 102, 96, 85, 76, 85, 102, 171, 152, 128, 114, 102, 114, 128
206 DATA 114, 102, 102, 114, 128, 114, 102, 85, 102, 114, 128, 152, 171, 171, 171
```

Then type in lines 220 to 226 which contain the set of 54 data for the lengths of these same notes.

```
220 DATA 40, 40, 40, 240, 60, 60, 240, 60, 60, 120, 180, 60, 240
222 DATA 60, 60, 240, 60, 60, 120, 120, 60, 60, 240, 60, 60, 240
224 DATA 60, 60, 240, 60, 60, 120, 120, 120, 120, 120, 40, 40, 40
226 DATA 120, 240, 60, 60, 180, 60, 60, 60, 240, 60, 60, 120, 180, 60, 240
```

Now we will store these numbers in arrays so that we can easily call them up later on.

First the pitches, in an array called P.

```
240 FOR C=1 TO 54
260 READ P(C)
280 NEXT C
```

Then the durations, in an array called D.

```
300 FOR C=1 TO 54
320 READ D(C)
340 NEXT C
```

We must now remember to declare these arrays with a DIM statement at the start of the program.

```
20 DIM P(60), D(60)
```

Then finally a loop which pokes the first pitch and duration into memory locations 768 and 769 and immediately afterwards calls the program in machine-code to play the first note. Then it cycles round to do the same for the second note; and so on for all 54 notes.

```
360 FOR C=1 TO 54
380 POKE 768, P(C)
400 POKE 769, D(C)
420 CALL 770
440 NEXT C
```

The whole program looks something like this, with the addition of some explanatory REM statements.

```
 10 HOME
 20 DIM P(60), D(60)
 99 REM MACHINE CODE PROGRAM
100 DATA 173, 48, 192, 136, 208, 5, 206, 1, 3, 240, 9
110 DATA 202, 208, 245, 174, 0, 3, 76, 2, 3, 96, 0, 0
120 FOR N=770 TO 792
140 READ Y
160 POKE N, Y
180 NEXT N
199 REM DATA FOR PITCHES OF NOTES
200 DATA 171, 152, 128, 114, 102, 85, 102, 114, 128, 152, 171, 171, 171
202 DATA 102, 96, 85, 76, 85, 102, 171, 152, 128, 114, 128, 114, 102
204 DATA 102, 96, 85, 76, 85, 102, 171, 152, 128, 114, 102, 114, 128
206 DATA 114, 102, 102, 114, 128, 114, 102, 85, 102, 114, 128, 152, 171, 171, 171
219 REM DATA FOR DURATIONS OF NOTES
220 DATA 40, 40, 40, 240, 60, 60, 240, 60, 60, 120, 180, 60, 240
222 DATA 60, 60, 240, 60, 60, 120, 120, 60, 60, 240, 60, 60, 240
224 DATA 60, 60, 240, 60, 60, 120, 120, 120, 120, 120, 40, 40, 40
226 DATA 120, 240, 60, 60, 180, 60, 60, 60, 240, 60, 60, 120, 180, 60, 240
240 FOR C=1 TO 54
260 READ P(C) : REM PITCHES
280 NEXT C
```

```
300 FOR C=1 TO 54
320 READ D(C) : REM DURATIONS
340 NEXT C
359 REM ROUTINE TO PLAY TUNE
360 FOR C=1 TO 54
380 POKE 768, P(C)
400 POKE 769, D(C)
420 CALL 770
440 NEXT C
```

The program will now allow you to play any tune, but it might be a good idea to write in two routines to save on disk and recover from disk the long lists of data in lines like 200 to 226 since these will change for each new tune.

A MACHINE-CODE PROGRAM

Translating machine-code

Very often, in books and magazines, it is possible to find a short program for the Apple written in machine-code which it would be nice to be able to use. Unfortunately, unless you know how to interpret it, the way such programs are presented is often difficult to understand. Here is an example. It doesn't do anything very dramatic, but we have deliberately chosen one which is short and has a clear and recognizable output. In fact it prints the words PRENTICE HALL in the middle of the screen.

Memory Unit Addresses	*Hex-Codes*	*Mnemonic Codes*
0300	20 58 FC	JSR FC58
0303	A2 00	LDX 00
0305	BD 11 03	LDAX 0311
0308	9D B4 04	STAX 04B4
030B	E8	INX
030C	E0 0E	CPX 0E
030E	D0 F5	BNE B
0310	60	RTS
0311	D0 D2 C5	DATA
0314	CE D4 C9	DATA
0317	C3 C5 A0	DATA
031A	A0 C8 C1	DATA
031D	CC CC	DATA

This program is perhaps slightly better presented than usual in that there are headings to the columns. This listing is in three parts. The column on the left is a list of what appears to be numbers starting at 0300 and ending at 031D. The presence of letters is perhaps a bit puzzling. These are numbers written in base sixteen and they represent the addresses of units of memory. (If you would like to know more about base sixteen see Appendix F.) When 300 is translated from base sixteen to the usual base ten it becomes 768, which is the number of the unit of memory where we usually begin to put machine-code programs. This was described on page 105.

The second column, headed hex-codes, is the machine-code program written in base sixteen. The first row is 20 58 *FC*. We must first translate these into base ten. When we do they become 32 88 252. We must then put these three numbers into the three memory units starting at 0300, that is into 0300, 0301 and 0302. In base ten these would be 768, 769 and 770. So we can set out the first few lines of the program again, like this:

Memory Unit Addresses		*Hex-Codes*		*Mnemonic Codes*
Hex	*Dec*	*Hex*	*Dec*	
0300	768	20	32	JSR FC58
0301	769	58	88	
0302	770	FC	252	
0303	771	A2	162	LDX 00
0304	772	00	0	
..	..	..	..	
..	..	..	..	
..	..	..	..	

We will discuss the third column, mnemonic codes, later. It is now a simple matter to rewrite the rest of the program in this manner, although it is also necessary to change all the hex-codes into numbers in base ten. This can be done using the table in Appendix F, but in this case the complete listing is shown below.

We are translating both the memory addresses in column 1, and the hex-codes in column 2, into base ten because that is the form in which we will need them when we use POKE and CALL in our BASIC program later on to run this machine-code program. This is because BASIC always uses base ten. But for those experienced and knowledge-able about machine-code programs, there are other simpler ways of placing the numbers in memory and running the program, for example using the monitor. This is done by inputting the numbers in base sixteen, and, since this is the most common way of doing it, programs are usually given with the numbers in base sixteen, as they were at the beginning of this section. For beginners, however, it is wiser to use BASIC programs with numbers in base ten.

An analysis of the program

We now present the whole program again in a more detailed and analysed form. This part tries to make sense of exactly what the code does at each stage, but if you do not understand this next part, or if you find it difficult, you can still go on with the rest of the activity of learning how to use machine-code programs. That is to say, you can use them without knowing exactly how they work. There are now six columns. The first two columns on the left are the memory addresses in both base sixteen and base ten. These are often described as HEX and DEC. In the next two columns the codes are given in both forms. The column headed mnemonic codes follows, and finally there is the comments column, which tries to explain what these mnemonic codes mean.

We have also divided the program up into nine sections, which we will now explain one at a time.

	Memory Unit Addresses		*Hex-Codes*		*Mnemonic Codes*	*Comments*
	Hex	*Dec*	*Hex*	*Dec*		
A	0300	768	20	32	JSR FC58	Jump to a Built-in Subroutine at FC58
	0301	769	58	88		
	0302	770	FC	252		
B	0303	771	A2	162	LDX 00	Loads Zero into X-register
	0304	772	00	0		
C	0305	773	BD	189	LDAX 0311	Puts in ACC Data From 0311
	0306	774	11	17		
	0307	775	03	3		
D	0308	776	9D	157	STAX 04B4	Store ACC in Screen Memory 04B4
	0309	777	B4	180		
	030A	778	04	4		
E	030B	779	E8	232	INX	Add One to Register X
F	030C	780	E0	224	CPX 0E	Compare Contents of X with 0E that is 14
	030D	781	0E	14		

(continued overleaf)

(continued from previous page)

G	030E	782	D0	208	BNE B	Branch Back 11 Steps if X Not Equal to 14
	030F	783	F5	245		
H	0310	784	60	96	RTS	Return From Subroutine to BASIC
I	0311	785	D0	208		
	0312	786	D2	210		
	0313	787	C5	197		
	0314	788	CE	206		
	0315	789	D4	212		
	0316	790	C9	201		
	0317	791	C3	195		
	0318	792	C5	197		
	0319	793	A0	160		
	031A	794	A0	160		
	031B	795	C8	200		
	031C	796	C1	193		
	031D	797	CC	204		
	031E	798	CC	204		

Section A has the comment, "jump to a built-in subroutine at FC58". The mnemonic code is JSR FC58. The mnemonic code means exactly the same thing, but is a shorthand version which most programmers can usually recognize. Apple does not understand this (unless an assembler is being used), so it is there for the benefit of the programmer. It tells him, or reminds him, what the hex command 20 stands for. Look again at the program and note that the first three hexes are marked 20 58 FC and then look at the MNEMONIC JSR FC58. From this you can see that 20 stands for JSR (Jump to Sub Routine): and the address of the memory location where the subroutine begins is FC58. Note that we write this back-to-front in the actual program, that is we put it 58 FC not FC58. In fact FC58 is the address of the first line of a built-in Apple subroutine which clears the screen. It works in the same way as HOME in BASIC.

The next section, B, is, "loads zero into X-register". This is the equivalent of *LET X*=0 in BASIC. The mnemonic code is LDX 00, and the hex-codes are A2 and 00.

Section C says, "puts in accumulator data from 0311". It means, "go to memory unit 0311 and take the number stored there, and put it into the accumulator". Now look down the program to line 0311 in section I. The number stored is D0, and this is put in the accumulator. In base ten it is 208 and it represents the letter P. The rest of the lines after 0311 in section I are all similar in that each contains a number representing a letter. These stand for PRENTICE HALL, with two spaces between the two words. This can be shown in a table like this:

P	R	E	N	T	I	C	E			H	A	L	L
208	210	197	206	212	201	195	197	160	160	200	193	204	204

The program will call for each of these in turn, but to begin with it has taken P. In fact the command in section C, LDAX, adds the value contained in X (0 at this stage) to the memory address given, i.e. 0311.

Section D stores the contents of the accumulator (the hex-code for this is 9D) in the screen-memory unit 04B4 (which is 1204 in base ten. You can see from Table D3 on page 196 that this is near the middle of the screen). Again the command STAX adds the number in X (still 0) to the memory address 04B4.

The next section, section E, adds one to X. This is described as INX, and the hex-code is E8.

The next section, F, compares the contents of X (which is now 1) with 0E in base sixteen or 14 in base ten. The codes are CPX and E0.

Section G is BNE B. This means, "*B*ranch back if contents of X *N*ot *E*qual to *B*" (in base ten, B is equal to 11). The hex-codes are D0 for BNE and F5 for B. (To make sense of this, you subtract F5 from FF and add 1). Since the contents of X is just one, we branch back 11 steps to line 305 again. The circuit is repeated 11 times altogether and the result is that the numbers shown above representing PRENTICE HALL are now in the 11 memory units starting at 04B4 or 1204.

So that, after 11 circuits we go on to the section H at address number 0310. This is the equivalent of "return" in BASIC.

The program in BASIC

All that now remains is to write a short program to poke the numbers making up this program into the designated memory units. Here is our version:

```
10 DATA 32, 88, 252, 162, 0, 189, 17, 3, 157, 180
11 DATA 4, 232, 224, 14, 208, 245, 96, 208, 210, 197, 206, 212
12 DATA 201, 195, 197, 160, 160, 200, 193, 204, 204
100 HOME
120 PRINT "MACHINE CODE DEMO"
140 FOR N=768 TO 798
160 READ A
180 POKE N, A
200 NEXT N
220 PRINT "CODE LOADED PRESS SPACE BAR" : GET Z$
240 CALL 768
260 PRINT "PROGRAM RUN"
```

Lines 10 to 12 contain the numbers for the program shown on page 111 under HEX-CODES, DEC. Check that they are the same. Lines 140 to 200 poke these numbers into the memory units shown beside the hex-codes. Line 240 uses CALL to run the program. The result will be that the words PRENTICE HALL appear on the screen. Try it and see.

Notice that the actual translation from the original presentation of the program on page 109 has involved nothing more than changing the addresses into base ten and the hex-codes into base ten, poking these and then calling the routine.

This technique can be used with any machine-code routine written for the 6502 microprocessor which is the one used in the Apple and in many other machines. However there are two small points to remember:

(a) The memory addresses used in other programs may not always be those most suitable for Apple so you may have to translate these into the numbers beginning with 0300, as in the example above. It may also be the case that memory addresses are referred to within the program as in sections C and D. These will then also have to be changed.

(b) Apple has a number of built-in subroutines which other machines may not have and vice-versa, so this should also be borne in mind when copying programs which were not written for Apple.

POKE AS A SWITCH

As well as being used in the ways already described, poke, peek and call have a number of other functions usually relating to specific memory locations or built-in subroutines. For example, poke can be used as a switch to change the Apple, or some aspect of its functioning, from one mode to another. There are some examples of this described in the *Applesoft-BASIC Programming Manual* (see Appendix H, page 251). The following is a useful example of this sort of routine.

Screen borders

As we know the screen is 40 spaces wide by 24 spaces high. We can, however, change these dimensions using poke. We begin with an example of how to use this facility to help to edit a program. First type this in:

```
100 HOME
120 PRINT "THE APPLE PERSONAL COMPATER FOR BEGINNERS"
```

The mis-spelling of COMPUTER in line 120 is deliberate. Now suppose you wish to correct this without having to retype the whole line. On page 78, earlier, we described a number of ways of doing this, but the simplest method is as follows.

First, to remind us of the problem, type in LIST 120, and use the **ESC** key and the I and J keys to move the cursor on top of the one in 120. Then press the space bar and use the arrow-right key to move the cursor along the line to the mis-spelling. Correct this, and continue to move the cursor out to the end of the line. Then press **RETURN** . Now list line 120 again. As a result of this editing a large space now appears between the O and the M of the word COMPUTER. Run the program and it is even more obvious.

This happens because when you list a program Apple presents it on the screen as though the screen was only 33 spaces wide, starting from the left. So, when editing, the gap on the right made up of 7 spaces becomes incorporated into the line. We need a technique for changing the width of the screen to 33 spaces. First, retype the line 120 as it was originally, then type in HOME and press **RETURN** to clear the screen. Type in POKE 33, 33 and press **RETURN**, then list line 120 again, then repeat the editing process, using **ESC** , I, J and the arrow-right key. This time, when the cursor reaches the end of the written line, at the letter O of *computer*, it moves immediately down to the beginning of the next line, and so leaves out the seven-space gap on the right.

The command POKE 33, 33 is a sort of switch. The first 33 is a memory address and the second 33 is the screen width. To return to the normal screen width, type in POKE 33, 40. (You could also press the **RESET** key or type in TEXT and press **RETURN**). Experiment with this. Try typing in POKE 33, 12 and then list the program.

In a similar way we can use poke and memory address 32 to set the position of the left border of the screen. Here is a program which combines these two:

```
100 HOME
120 VTAB 10 : PRINT "THIS IS OUTSIDE"
140 VTAB 11 : PRINT "THE WINDOW."
160 POKE 32, 20 : REM SETS LEFT BORDER
180 POKE 33, 16 : REM SETS WIDTH
200 HOME
220 PRINT "THIS IS A WINDOW"
240 PRINT "IT IS 16 SPACES WIDE"
260 FOR N=1 TO 500 : NEXT N
280 GOTO 220
```

Type it in and try it. Finally it is also possible to set a top and a bottom to the window on the screen. Add these two lines to the program above:

```
185 POKE 34, 8 : REM SETS TOP OF WINDOW
190 POKE 35, 16 : REM SETS BOTTOM
```

and change lines 220 and 240 as follows:

```
220 PRINT "TOP IS 16 WIDE"
240 PRINT "SIDE IS 8"
```

Now run the program again.
These poke numbers are summarized as shown below:

Poke Number	*Range of X*	*Normal X Value*	*Function*
Poke 32, X	0 to 39	0	Left Border
Poke 33, X	1 to 40	40	Screen Width
Poke 34, X	0 to 23	0	Screen Top
Poke 35, X	0 to 24	24	Screen Bottom

PROBLEMS

1. Use the program written in this chapter for playing a tune as a basis for the development of a full *Melody Maker* program. It should allow you to input a tune, save it on disk, play the tune, and so on.
2. Write a program so that two players can play the game *Counters*. A set of 40 counters are placed on the screen using a poke. Each player in turn "removes" one, two or three of them. The player to take the last counter loses. This means that when a player presses the keys 1, 2, or 3, an appropriate number of counters disappears from the screen. This should be done using poke.

8

Strings

INTRODUCTION

We have met strings at various times in this book (see page 12), and this chapter is about ways of manipulating and displaying them. In order to do this effectively, Apple has a set of eight quite powerful string functions. Each function either separates out a part of the string or changes numbers into strings or strings into numbers. We will consider each of them in turn.

DEFINITION OF STRINGS

More often than not strings are made up entirely of letters of the alphabet and are simply English words. However, it is not necessary for this to be so. A string can be made up of any collection of symbols or graphics or numerals, and the important point is that quotation marks must be put around strings when they are used or declared in programs.

A string can be made up entirely of numerals so that it looks exactly like a number, except for the quotation marks.

A=47	A is a number
A$="47"	A$ is a string

This may not seem to be a very important distinction, but it is vital and the importance rests in the different sort of manipulations that can be performed with numbers as opposed to strings. For example, numbers can be added together in the conventional sense. Type this in and run it:

```
100 A=20
120 B=30
140 C=A+B
160 PRINT C
```

The result of this addition of 20 and 30 is, not unexpectedly, 50! But suppose these were in the form of strings. Type in the program below and run it. (Remember to type in NEW first):

```
100 A$="20"
120 B$="30"
140 C$=A$+B$
160 PRINT C$
```

The result is 2030. That is, addition of strings results in what is called concatenation rather than normal arithmetic addition. To think of this in another way, if these two strings had contained alphabet letters or other non-numeric characters, then placing them side by side would seem less strange. This is done on page 13.

THE VAL FUNCTION

The first string function that we consider is the VAL function. It can be used to "translate" strings into numbers, according to the following rules.

Firstly, if the string in question is made up of, or begins with, letters, graphics, or any non-numeric characters, then use of the VAL function produces 0. Some examples:

```
A$="JOE"        VAL(A$)=0
B$="SD007"      VAL(B$)=0
C$="A99"        VAL(C$)=0
```

This process can be tested within a program.

```
100 PRINT VAL("JOE")
120 A$="PC49"
140 PRINT VAL(A$)
```

Type this in and run it. The result should be two zeros.

Secondly, if the string is made up entirely of numerals the VAL function translates this string into the corresponding number.

```
A$="99"         VAL(A$)=99
B$="1234"       VAL(B$)=1234
C$="4.7"        VAL(C$)=4.7
```

Again, you can test this within a program as follows. Type this in and run it:

```
100 PRINT VAL("99")
120 A$="4312"
140 PRINT VAL(A$)
```

Thirdly, if the string begins with numerals, but also contains letters or symbols, the VAL function translates this string into the initial number value, disregards the letters etc., and disregards any numbers which follow them.

```
G$="12AB"        VAL (G$)=12
H$="4X5Y"        VAL(H$)=4
I$="987Q"        VAL(I$)=987
J$="9PQ2"        VAL(J$)=9
```

This function can be useful in programs when checking whether or not an input is appropriate. Here is an input program, where the second line simply prints the input.

```
100 INPUT "WRITE YOUR NAME" ; A$
140 PRINT A$
```

Run this program and respond to the question mark with JOE – or something similar. Apple accepts this quite happily and then prints it on the screen. Now run the program again, but this time respond to the question mark with a number; say 87. Again, Apple accepts this quite happily because A$ in line 100 is a string, and both JOE and 87 are acceptable strings. Therefore, when the input variable (A$) is a string variable then Apple cannot distinguish numbers from words.

Add line 120 to the program so that it now looks like this:

```
100 INPUT "WRITE YOUR NAME" ; A$
120 IF VAL(A$) <> 0 THEN 100
140 PRINT A$
```

Then run it again and try responding with a number, say 43. This time Apple will not accept it and returns to line 100. This is because in line 120 if VAL (A$) *is not equal* to zero then the program returns to line 100. Obviously VAL(A$) is only equal to zero when A$ is not a number, that is, when A$ is a letter or symbol combination.

Many programmers would argue that all input statements should use string variables and that number variables should not be used at all. The argument is that if a number input is needed, it is possible to use the VAL function to turn it into a number once it has been input as a string. But, more importantly, when input as a string it is possible to use all the string functions to manipulate it and format it in a way that is difficult, if not impossible, with numbers.

This kind of manipulation and formatting can be demonstrated as follows. Suppose, at the start of a program, the user is invited to input the data and suppose further that this is done according to a fixed format. That is June 14th 1902 would be entered as 061402. Similarly February 5th 1912 would be 020512. The first two digits represent the month, and if it is one digit, a zero is written in front of it. The third and fourth digits represent the day, and the fifth and sixth digits represent the year.

```
100 HOME
120 INPUT "WHAT IS THE DATE" ; A$
```

We now wish to break this six-character string into three parts in order to make the date easier to read. We must first remember that, since we used A$ in line 120, this six-figure digit is a string and not a number; so we first use the VAL function as follows:

```
140 T=VAL(A$)
```

T is now a six-digit number which can be subjected to normal arithmetic manipulation, and so the rest of the program, shown below, applies simple arithmetic to this to separate the month (called M), the day (D) and the year (Y).

```
                        T=020512
160 A=INT(T/100)        A=0205
                        100*A=020500

180 Y=T-100*A           Y=12 (THE YEAR)

200 M=INT(A/100)        M=02 (THE MONTH)
                        100*M=0200

220 D=A-100*M           D=05 (THE DAY)

240 PRINT "MONTH", "DAY", "YEAR"
260 PRINT M, D, Y
```

There are also three functions which allow us to isolate particular bits of individual strings. They are **LEFT$**, **RIGHT$**, and **MID$**. We will consider each in turn, as well as the LEN function.

THE LEFT$ FUNCTION

This is best explained using examples. Type in the program below and run it. The resulting printouts are shown on the right.

Program	*Printout*
100 PRINT LEFT$("BASIC", 1)	B
120 PRINT LEFT$("BASIC", 2)	BA
140 A$="EDUCATIONAL"	
160 PRINT LEFT$(A$, 9)	EDUCATION

So the **LEFT$** function prints the specified number of characters starting on the left of the string. This function is often very useful in programs because it allows us to test input by examining its first letter only.

```
100 PRINT "DO YOU WISH TO:-"
120 PRINT : PRINT "   BEGIN AGAIN"
140 PRINT : PRINT "   READ LIST"
160 PRINT : PRINT "   SAVE ON DISK"
180 INPUT A$
200 IF LEFT$(A$, 1)="B" THEN 1000
220 IF LEFT$(A$, 1)="R" THEN 2000
240 IF LEFT$(A$, 1)="S" THEN 3000
```

In this incomplete program the first letter of the response is examined and compared with the first letter of each possible response. This technique is found most often in this next short routine, which is also incomplete. The two lines 1000 and 2000, referred to in lines 120 and 140, have not been included.

```
100 INPUT "DO YOU WISH TO PLAY AGAIN   "; A$
120 IF LEFT$(A$, 1)="Y" THEN 1000
140 IF LEFT$(A$, 1)="N" THEN 2000
160 PRINT "TRY AGAIN" : GOTO 100
```

This routine shows how to isolate the first letter of strings.

We now look at a routine which prints the first letter; then the first two letters; then the first three letters, and so on. First type in NEW and press **RETURN** . Then type in this program:

```
100 HOME
120 INPUT A$
140 FOR N=1 TO 7
160 PRINT LEFT$(A$, N)
180 NEXT N
```

Now type in RUN and, when the question mark appears, type in a word like STRETCH. The figure 7 in line 140 can be changed to whatever number you wish. Do not remove this program for a moment as it will be used again with the next string function.

THE LEN FUNCTION

This function simply counts the number of characters in a string. The word LEN is short for *length.* One immediate use of this can be found in the last program. Type in the new line 130 below and also change line 140 as shown.

```
130 L=LEN(A$)
140 FOR N=1 TO L
```

Now type in RUN and press **RETURN** . Respond to the question mark by typing in any word. Line 130 finds the number of characters in this word, and calls it L. Line 140 sets up the loop to run for L times.

We can now use this LEN function to demonstrate how long a string Apple can handle. First remove the old program by typing in NEW. Then type in the following, noting that in line 120 A$ is to contain exactly 63 As. Line 130 actually prints out the number so you can first run the program and check that it is exactly 63.

```
100 HOME
120 A$="AAAA ..."
130 PRINT LEN(A$)
```

When you are sure that the A$ in line 120 is a string made up of 63 As then remove line 130 by typing in 130 and pressing **RETURN** . Now add this line:

```
140 B$=A$+A$+A$+A$
```

B$ is, therefore, a string made up of four times 63 or 252 As. Again use a temporary line to see how this looks. Type in this line and then run the program.

```
150 PRINT B$
```

The result of this should be that over six full rows of As appear on the screen. Now remove line 150 and type in these three lines.

```
160 INPUT C$
180 B$=B$+C$
200 PRINT B$, LEN(B$)
```

Line 160 invites you to input another string. Line 180 joins this new string to the end of the 252 As already in **B$**. Line 200 prints this extended string **B$**, and its length.

When the question mark appears on the screen as a result of line 160, input a string of five As. Then press **RETURN** . Apple responds like this:

```
?STRING TOO LONG ERROR IN 180

]□
```

Therefore, the existing 252 As joined to this new input of five As (making a total of 257 As) produces a string that Apple considers to be too long. Run the program again and put in four As. Again, an error message appears. Run it again with three As and the new enlarged string, **B$**, is printed out by line 200. At the end it also prints 255, which is the length of the string, or the number of characters it contains. So the longest possible string that Apple will accept has 255 characters.

Finally, add the lines below, changing lines 160 and 200 as shown.

```
160 C$="AAA"
200 FOR N=1 TO LEN(B$)
220 PRINT LEFT$(B$, N)
240 NEXT N
```

Now run this program.

One last demonstration of the use of the LEN function concerns situations where there is a need to place a program heading, or something similar, in the center of the screen. First, remember that the screen is 40 spaces wide, and suppose the heading is a string, A$. Then find the length of that string using LEN (A$). Then, subtract this from 40 to find the total number of spaces left. Divide this number by two to find how many of these extra spaces to put on each side of A$.

In Chapter 9 we will use the TAB function with this to move the cursor to the right spot. In the meantime, you can use the direct mode to find the necessary number of spaces. Type this in directly:

```
A$="HEADING" : ?(40-LEN(A$))/2
```

The result will be 16.5. So you can choose between 16 and 17 spaces. Now type in this heading with 16 spaces:

```
110 PRINT "                HEADING"
```

THE RIGHT$ FUNCTION

This is very similar to the LEFT$ function. The difference is obvious and implicit in the word. With LEFT$ we are able to select a part of the string, starting on the left: so, with RIGHT$ we can select part of the string, starting on the right.

Some examples with the resulting printout are now shown.

Program	*Printout*
100 PRINT RIGHT$("APPLE", 1)	E
120 PRINT RIGHT$("RETURN", 4)	TURN
140 A$="ABCD" 160 FOR N=1 TO 4 180 PRINT RIGHT$(A$, N) 200 NEXT N	D CD BCD ABCD

A short example now follows which illustrates the essential difference between the LEFT$ and RIGHT$ functions. It makes use of the beginning of a famous sentence that reads the same from left to right as it does from right to left. The sentence is ABLE WAS I ERE I SAW ELBA. Type in the program below.

```
100 HOME
120 A$="ABLE WAS I"
140 FOR N=I TO LEN(A$)
160 PRINT LEFT$(A$, N), RIGHT$(A$, N)
180 NEXT N
```

Now type in RUN.

THE MID$ FUNCTION

This is probably the most useful of the string formatting functions and is in some ways the most sophisticated. First, some examples. (Remember to type in NEW to remove the old program.)

Program	*Printout*
100 PRINT MID$("DRONES", 3, 2)	ON
120 PRINT MID$("DRONES", 3, 4)	ONES
140 PRINT MID$("DRONES", 4)	NES
160 B$="ZYXWV" 180 FOR P=1 TO 4 200 PRINT MID$(B$, 2, P) 220 NEXT P	Y YX YXW UXWV

So a statement like this:

```
MID$(A$, 4, 6)
```

means, "make a substring six characters long by beginning at the fourth character of A$".

A slightly more complex use of this function is now described, line by line. The program accepts an input of a number from 1 to 7 where these numbers represent days of the week. Therefore Sunday is 1, Monday is

2, and so on. The program then translates the number you have input into the first three letters of the appropriate day.

```
100 HOME : INPUT "INPUT DAY AS A NUMBER   "; D
```

This line clears the screen and invites the input.

```
120 D$="..SUNMONTUEWEDTHUFRISAT"
```

This sets up a string made up of two dots, followed by a long word made up of the first three letters of each day. It is placed in **D$**.

```
140 A$=MID$(D$, 3*D, 3)
```

In line 140 the **MID$** function is used to select the appropriate three letters from the long string **D$**. This is done in two stages, first by using the 3, which is by itself, in the brackets, to specify a string three characters long. Then the middle part of the material inside the brackets, 3*D, will select the appropriate starting point for the three-letter string to be printed.

When D=1, we expect the outcome to be SUN. In this case 3*D becomes 3, and the **MID$** function becomes **MID$(D$**, 3, 3). This means begin at the third character and take three characters. The first two characters are dots, which are there as spacefillers, and the third character is the first letter, S, of SUN. So SUN is selected and called **A$**.

Finally, put in a print line.

```
160 PRINT A$
```

So the whole routine looks like this:

```
100 HOME : INPUT "INPUT DAY AS A NUMBER   ": D
120 D$="..SUNMONTUEWEDTHUFRISAT"
140 A$=MID$(D$, 3*D, 3)
160 PRINT A$
```

You ought to be able to write a similar routine for the 12 months. The two routines can then be put together, and the program converted to translate as follows:

Day 3, 14th day of month 7, 1850, into
Tuesday, July 14th, 1850

THE CHR$ FUNCTION

In the chapter on peek and poke we discovered that each character on the Apple keyboard has four numbers associated with it: two for normal mode, and one each for the reverse-field and flash modes. These numbers and the corresponding characters can be seen in Tables D1 and D2 on pages 194 and 195. The CHR$ function (CHR is short for *character*) is used to translate some of these numbers directly into the corresponding characters, so that you do not need to look up the table. It uses only normal mode, however, so reverse-field and flash mode characters are translated into their normal mode equivalents. Unfortunately, the numbers used for the characters in association with CHR$ do not match exactly the numbers used in association with peek and poke, although there are certain broad similarities. The CHR$ numbers are shown in Table D4, page 197. They are known generally as ASCII codes (American Standard Code for Information Interchange).

You will notice also that there are some numbers in Table D4 which have no character-equivalents and some characters which have two or more numbers. Some of the numbers with no character-equivalents are used for special control functions. For an example, type in PRINT CHR$(7) and press **RETURN** . This causes the bell to ring. Now type in the short program that follows:

```
100 HOME
120 FOR N=1 TO 10
140 INPUT A
160 A$=CHR$(A)
180 B$=B$+A$
200 PRINT B$
220 NEXT N
```

Line 100 clears the screen. Lines 120 and 220 combine to produce a loop which Apple cycles through 10 times. Inside this loop, line 140 is an input line, and the A means that this input is to be a number. Line 160 uses the CHR$ function to translate that input number into a string character as shown in Table D4, and it is called A$. Line 180 accumulates these characters into another string, B$, and line 200 prints the total B$ to date, each time.

Suppose we wished to turn B$ into N. IRELAND. Look up Table D4 and find the numbers corresponding to these characters. They are as follows:

78	46	32	73	82	69	76	65	78	68
N	.		I	R	E	L	A	N	D

Now run the program and respond to the question mark by typing in the number for N, i.e. 78, and then pressing **RETURN** . Then type in the next number, that is 46, and press **RETURN** . Continue in this way.

This CHR$ function is used most often in association with the peek statement. One example of this association has already appeared in Chapter 7 (page 103). We use the peek command to find out what number is stored in a unit of memory. For example, if we poke the character M in reverse field into a unit of memory, it is not the reverse-field M but an associated number (in this case 13, see Table D2) that is placed in the unit of memory. If we then peek at that unit of memory, what is produced is that number, i.e. 13, not the reverse-field letter M. If we want to translate the 13 into its corresponding letter, reverse-field M, we have to use the CHR$ function.

Unfortunately, as we have already said, the CHR$ numbers and the peek and poke numbers do not correspond exactly and some adjustments are necessary. For example, in Table D2, the peek and poke number associated with reverse-field M is 13. In Table D4, there is no number for the reverse-field M, so we have to use the number for M, i.e. 77. So in order to adjust the peek and poke number for reverse-field M to the corresponding CHR$ number we must add 64 to the number found by peeking. This turns it into the number to be used with CHR$. This may seem very confusing but, in practice, it works quite easily. We will now look carefully at one part of each of Tables D2 and D4 together, as shown, in order to illustrate this.

Character	*Peek number*	*CHR$ number*
@	0	64
A	1	65
B	2	66
C	3	67
.	.	.
.	.	.
.	.	.
M	13	77
.	.	.
.	.	.
∧	30	94
—	31	95

Remember that from the peek numbers these characters are in reverse-field. Now, a short program using this table.

```
100 HOME
120 POKE 1724, 13
140 A=PEEK(1724)
160 A$=CHR$(A+64)
180 PRINT A$
```

First type this in and run it. It is a little contrived since it is just designed to illustrate the point. Line 120 pokes the number 13 (standing for reverse-field M), into the screen location 1724. (Only because we wish to peek at it.) Line 140 peeks at this location and calls what it finds there A. Of course, we know it finds 13. Line 160 adds 64 to A before using the CHR$ function to translate this number, i.e. 77, into the letter M. However, we will not normally know what the peek number is in advance, so we need to carry out tests to discover what changes may need to be made. We know, for example, that if A is less than 32, it must be changed to A + 64. So we put in this test line:

```
150 IF A <32 THEN A=A+64
```

This means that if A is less than 32, then 64 will be added to it. If A is not less than 32, then the program just goes on to the next line. We now need to change line 160 to:

```
160 A$=CHR$(A)
```

This translation is also necessary for the set of numbers between 128 and 191 inclusive. To cover this we need the line:

```
155 IF A >127 AND A <192 THEN A=A+64
```

We have noticed that the reverse-field characters can not be recovered using CHR$. When the original poked symbol was in reverse-field, this table translated it into the same symbol, but in direct-field. The same is true for flashing characters. Type in this line 155 as shown, and then remove line 120 and change line 140 to:

```
140 INPUT A
```

Now run the program and when the question mark appears, use Table D2 to feed in a peek number. The rest of the program should then translate this into the appropriate character via the CHR$ function. The whole program now looks like this. Line 200 has been added to allow you to test as many numbers as you wish.

```
100 HOME
140 INPUT A
150 IF A < 32 THEN A=A+64
155 IF A > 127 AND A< 192 THEN A=A+64
160 A$=CHR$ (A)
180 PRINT A$
200 GOTO 140
```

CHR$ AND QUOTATION MARKS

A particularly useful **CHR$** number is 34. That is the one that produces a quotation mark on the screen. This makes it possible to get Apple to print quotation marks during the run of a program, thus getting round the problem that quotation marks are normally used to specify material to be printed, but are not printed themselves when the material appears on the screen.

```
100 PRINT "MY NAME IS" ; CHR$(34) ; "PRENTICE HALL" ; CHR$(34)
```

The output from this is:

```
MY NAME IS "PRENTICE HALL"
```

THE ASC FUNCTION

This is the inverse or opposite of the **CHR$** function. It translates the first letter of a string into its corresponding **CHR$** number. As an example, remember that **CHR$(65)=A** (see Table D4). Now type in this program.

```
100 A=ASC("A")
120 B=ASC("AT")
140 A$="ATE"
160 C=ASC(A$)
180 PRINT A, B, C
```

Now run this. The result should be

```
65        65        65
```

This means that the ASC function returned, in each case, the CHR$ number 65 associated with A. If we wished to have a record of the numbers associated with each letter of a string, and not just the first letter, we can use the MID$ function, as follows.

```
100 A$="APPLE"
120 FOR N=1 TO LEN(A$)
140 B$=MID$(A$, N, 1)
160 A=ASC(B$)
180 PRINT B$, A
200 NEXT N
```

This produces the CHR$ numbers for the letters of Apple as shown.

```
A  65
P  80
P  80
L  76
E  69
```

THE STR$ FUNCTION

This function acts as the opposite of the VAL function. That is, it takes a number and translates it into a string. This will not change how the set of characters making up the number looks on the screen, but it allows you to manipulate it by means of the various string formatting functions described earlier in the chapter. Some examples of this will be shown in Chapter 9 where the whole problem of formatting is discussed. To illustrate how STR$ works, type in this program:

```
100 A=44.25
120 B$=STR$(A)
140 FOR N=1 TO LEN(B$)
160 C$=MID$(B$, N, 1)
180 C=VAL(C$)
200 PRINT C
220 NEXT N
```

In line 100, the variable A represents a number. Line 120 converts it into a string. The next five lines apply string formatting techniques to this string, which results in each separate character being isolated, translated back into a number, and printed. Run it and see if it works.

ORDERING STRINGS

It is often useful to be able to put strings in alphabetical order. This is very simple using Apple because strings can be compared in exactly the same way as numbers using the signs >, = and <. When we find that A$ < B$, it means that, according to alphabetical order, A$ comes before B$. Type in this program and try it.

```
100 A$="AABC"
120 B$="ABCD"
140 IF A$< B$ THEN 200
160 PRINT B$, A$
180 GOTO 220
200 PRINT A$, B$
220 END
```

Run this program and it should put the two strings A$ and B$ in correct alphabetical order. Now change lines 100 and 120 as shown:

```
100 INPUT "FIRST WORD    "; A$
120 INPUT "SECOND WORD    "; B$
```

Now run the program, and type in whichever two words you choose. The program will put them in alphabetical order and print them.

A routine to sort a longer list of words into alphabetical order is shown in Chapter 10.

PROBLEMS

1. Use random numbers to select, from a deck of 52 cards, two poker hands each with five cards. The two hands should be presented on the screen each time. Remember to write a routine to check that any particular card has not been "dealt" already.
2. Write a program for crossword puzzlers to help them find the answer to clues where all but one or two of the letters are known. The program should print on the screen every possible word that

can be made by putting all the letters of the alphabet in the appropriate spaces. It should also allow users to decide whether they wish to use all 26 letters of the alphabet or just the five vowels.

3. Write a program which allows you to put in a passage of prose and then counts the number of occurrences of each letter of the alphabet within the passage. Use GET A$ as the input device and provide responses which allow you to:
   (a) Indicate when you have completed a passage;
   (b) Abort a piece of work and begin again;
   (c) Delete mistakes.

   Use CHR$ and ASC to allow you to edit out spaces and punctuation marks.

9

Formatting

TAB

We have already shown (Chapter 2, page 22) how the use of commas and semicolons can be used to place numbers and strings in particular columns – or at least to separate them into distinct columns. There are some disadvantages and limitations with this method of formatting information. For example, we cannot use it to choose which column we would like to use. We can solve this problem using the TAB function. This is short for *tabulation* and it allows you to specify precisely on which column to begin writing numbers or strings. Here is a simple example:

```
100 HOME
120 PRINT "NAME" TAB (25) "SCORE" TAB (32) "RANK"
140 PRINT "DOMINIC MURRAY" TAB (25) 50 TAB (32) 3
```

First line 100 clears the screen. Then line 120 prints the word NAME on the left of the screen. It then uses TAB (25) to move the cursor out 24 columns from the left edge of the screen to column 25, and prints the word SCORE on columns 25 to 29. Finally it uses TAB (32) to move the cursor to column 32 and prints the word RANK in columns 32 to 35. The use of TAB (25) and TAB (32) again on line 140 makes sure that DOMINIC MURRAY, the score 50, and the rank 3, are all printed starting on exactly the same columns, as the headings on the line above. Now add these lines to the program:

```
160 PRINT "BARRY MURPHY" TAB (25) 28 TAB (32) 15
180 PRINT "DAN BRADSHAW" TAB (25) 73 TAB (32) 1
```

and run it again. You will notice that the names are aligned on the left.

That is, the first letter of each name is lined up with the one above. It would be interesting on some occasions to have a technique to align them to the right, with the last letters in the same column.

To do this we must find the length of each name, but because the lines get a bit cluttered we will first put each word and name in a variable, as follows (first type in NEW, and then these lines):

```
100 HOME
120 A$="NAME" : B$="SCORE" : C$="RANK"
140 N1$="DOMINIC MURRAY"
160 N2$="BARRY MURPHY"
180 N3$="DAN BRADSHAW"
```

We will now find the lengths of the names as follows:

```
200 A  =LEN (A$)
220 N1=LEN (N1$)
240 N2=LEN (N2$)
260 N3=LEN (N3$)
```

We then use the TAB function to move the cursor out a fixed number of spaces, say 20, less the length of the string in question, here called either A, N1, N2 or N3. This will make each name start on such a column so that they all end on column 20. So the print part of the program now looks like this:

```
300 PRINT TAB (20–A) A$ TAB (25) "SCORE" TAB (30) "RANK"
320 PRINT TAB (20–N1) N1$ TAB (25) 50 TAB (32) 3
340 PRINT TAB (20–N2) N2$ TAB (25) TAB (32) 15
360 PRINT TAB (20–N3) N3$ TAB (25) 73 TAB (32) 1
```

We can also use TAB to center a program heading, that is to place it in the center of the top of the screen. This was discussed on page 124. Remember that there are 40 spaces across the Apple screen. First we use the LEN function to find the length of the heading. Then subtract this length from 40, and divide by two. Here is an example (first type in NEW):

```
100 HOME
120 A$="***MILK BILL***"
140 PRINT TAB ((40–LEN (A$))/2)A$
```

We can use the TAB function to draw a sine curve as follows. The main axis lies down the middle of the screen, so if you wished to see this curve in the normal way, you would have to turn Apple onto its side. First we will type in the program and then discuss it line by line:

```
100 HOME
110 PI=3.141593
120 FOR X=0 TO 4* PI STEP.2
140 Y=SIN(X)
160 Y=20*Y+20
180 IF Y < 1 THEN Y=1
200 PRINT TAB(Y) "*"
220 NEXT X
```

Line 100 clears the screen. Lines 120 and 200 together make a loop which takes *x* in small steps of 0.2 from 0 to 4*PI. Line 140 puts *y* equal to SIN(*x*) each time. However, you will remember that SIN(*x*) always lies between − 1 and + 1. That is, the range looks like this:

− 1   − 0.5   0   + 0.5   + 1

If we now multiply each number in the range by 20 it looks like this:

− 20   − 10   0   + 10   + 20

Now add 20 to each of the numbers above, and it looks like this:

0   10   20   30   40

which is exactly the range across the screen. So line 160 scales up each value according to this pattern: that is, each value of *y* is multiplied by 20 and then 20 is added to it. Line 180 takes account of a peculiarity of the TAB function, which is that if in TAB (A) the number A is less than 1, the TAB function treats A as though it were 15. This line makes sure that it is always at least A. Line 200 then moves the cursor out *y* spaces, using TAB (*y*) and prints a star on the next space.

Now run this program a few times to see what happens. Remember that the range from 0 to 4*PI in line 120 represents two full cycles of the curve. You can experiment with this by changing the range and by changing the step used. To do this, change line 120 as shown and type in lines 50 and 60.

```
 50 INPUT "NUMBER OF PI" ; A
 60 INPUT "STEP TO BE USED" ; B
120 FOR X=0 TO A* PI STEP B
```

Now run the program, and when "NUMBER OF PI" appears on the screen, type in 2. Then when STEP TO BE USED appears, type in 0.1. Run it a number of times, and each time try different numbers.

HTAB AND VTAB

HTAB behaves very much like TAB in that it moved the cursor horizontally across the screen. A simple example will demonstrate exactly how it works.

```
100 HOME
120 PRINT "1 2 3 4 5 6 7"
140 HTAB 3 : PRINT "NEXT"
```

When you run this the screen will look like this:

```
1234567
  NEXT

]▯
```

Line 120 is there only to number the columns so that we can see exactly where the first letter of the word NEXT is printed. As you can see, HTAB 3 means that the first symbol printed will be on column 3.

Now change line 140 as follows:

```
140 PRINT "A" ; : HTAB 4 : PRINT "B" ; : HTAB 7 : PRINT "C"
```

Now run this again and the screen should look like this:

```
1234567
A  B  C

]▯
```

Note the semicolons in line 140. These are there to ensure that the letters A, B and C are all printed on the same line. Try running the program with these semicolons left out.

Here is another example of the use of HTAB.

```
100 HOME
120 FOR N=1 TO 4
140 PRINT HTAB N : PRINT "LINE NUMBER" N
160 NEXT N
```

Type this in and run it.

VTAB is perhaps more interesting than HTAB in that it has no other equivalent in Applesoft BASIC. The screen has a total of 24 rows and VTAB sends the cursor to whichever row is indicated by the number following it. First, type in new, and then this program:

```
100 HOME
120 VTAB 1 : PRINT "TOP"
140 VTAB 12 : PRINT "MIDDLE"
160 VTAB 22 : PRINT "BOTTOM"
```

Now type in RUN and press **RETURN** . Notice that in line 160 we used VTAB 22 and not VTAB 24. This is because the ending of the program uses up the bottom two lines. Now type in NEW again and then this program:

```
100 HOME
120 PRINT "FIRST LINE"
160 VTAB 1 : PRINT "BURST PIPE"
```

Now type in RUN and press **RETURN** . The words BURST PIPE will appear on the top line, but the words "FIRST LINE" will seem not to appear at all. To demonstrate what is happening, put in an extra line:

```
140 GET A$
```

Now run the program again. First the screen will clear, then the words FIRST LINE will appear, from line 120. Now press the space bar (line 140) and watch the screen carefully. The words BURST PIPE (line 160) will replace FIRST LINE. Run this a few times until you are clear about what is happening.

The next short program makes use of the top line of the screen. This allows you to use the bottom part of the screen for a permanent message or a picture drawn with the poke commands (as in Chapter 7).

First type in NEW and then this program:

```
100 HOME
120 VTAB 1 : INPUT "FIRST PLAYER'S TURN–INPUT 1 OR 2   "; B
140 VTAB 1 : INPUT "SECOND PLAYER'S TURN–INPUT 1 OR 2   "; B
160 GOTO 120
```

Of course the logic of this program is not followed through since the inputs are, for the moment, ignored. But this routine could easily be adapted for use in a program which needed to keep putting instructions at the top of the screen.

SPC FUNCTION

This function is to help in formatting by allowing us to make a specified space between any two columns. It is most useful when you have a set of numbers arranged in a set of fixed columns with all the numbers in each column containing the same numbers of digits. Here is an example:

```
100 HOME
120 FOR N=10 TO 24
140 PRINT N SPC(5) N+100 SPC(5) N+1000
160 NEXT N
```

Type this in and try it.

This technique can be very useful if we are dealing with numbers that are of a specified width. For example, if we are dealing with examination results, expressed as percentages, we might assume that they would all lie between 10 and 99. Then, if we want to list the results with the marks on the left and the names on the right, the SPC function is a useful way of formatting these results. However, it has to be typed in along with each line, so it can be a bit cumbersome. Type in the example below, first remembering to clear out the old program:

```
100 HOME
120 PRINT "SCORES" SPC(4) "NAMES"
140 PRINT : PRINT
160 PRINT 34 SPC(8) "SULLIVAN P."
180 PRINT 35 SPC(8) "MARRIOTT S."
```

Now run this.

DECIMAL PLACES

When calculations are performed on numbers involving division or the square root function, the results often have eight or nine decimal places. For example, type in this program and run it:

```
100 HOME
120 FOR N=4 TO 9
```

(*continued overleaf*)

```
140 A=SQR(N)
160 PRINT N, A
180 NEXT N
```

The result is as follows:

```
4        2
5        2.23606798
6        2.44948974
7        2.64575131
8        2.82842713
9        3
```

The numbers on the right are found by taking the square root of those on the left, and this is done in line 140 using the built-in Apple function SQR.

If we wish to express these answers with only three figures after the decimal point, then we can use the following technique, which is demonstrated first of all with a single number.

A=32.1459265

To reduce this to a number with only three decimal places we do three things:

(a) Multiply by 10 three times. Remember that, in Applesoft-BASIC, this will look like this 10 ∧ 3.
(b) Take the integral part, or whole-number part, of this using the INT function.
(c) Divide by 10 three times.

This set of processes is now shown with the number chosen.

A	32.1459265
10 ∧ 3*A	32145.9265
INT (10 ∧ 3*A)	32145
INT (10 ∧ 3*A)/10 ∧ 3	32.145

As you can see, this process reduces the number of figures after the decimal point to three. This technique can be put into the original program used at the beginning of this section as follows. Type in this line and then run the program:

```
150 A=INT (10∧ 3*A)/10∧3
```

The result is as follows:

```
4    2
5    2.236
6    2.449
7    2.645
8    2.829
9    3
```

There is still a problem however in that the INT function always takes the whole number part of a decimal even when the number is much closer to the next whole number up. So the method used above may sometimes introduce an unacceptable level of inaccuracy.
Look at these examples:

INT (3.2) = 3
INT (3.9) = 3

It would clearly be more logical to consider 3.9 to be closer to 4 than to 3. Fortunately we can make this happen very easily by adding .5 to the decimal before applying the INT function, so that 3.2 would become 3.7 and its integer remains 3, whereas 3.9 becomes 4.4 and is printed out as 4.

Type in the following program which demonstrates this process.

```
100 HOME
120 FOR A=3 TO 4 STEP .1
140 B=INT (A+.5)
160 PRINT A, B
180 NEXT A
```

The result looks like this:

```
3      3
3.1    3
3.2    3
3.3    3
3.4    3
3.5    3
3.6    4
3.7    4
3.8    4
4      4
```

In other words, all numbers up to but not including 3.6 are rounded down to 3, while all numbers from 3.6 to 4 are rounded up to 4. (Surprisingly, Apple treats the integral part of 3.5 + .5 as 3). We can now combine these two facilities and, at the same time, show how to generate as many decimal figures as we wish. Remember that, when we wished to have three decimal figures in A, we used this routine:

```
A=INT(10∧3*A)/10∧3
```

So, obviously, if we wished to have four decimal figures we could use 10∧4 and, more generally, for P decimal places, we would use 10∧P. Therefore this routine becomes:

```
A=INT(10∧P*A)/10∧P
```

then, in order to ensure that correct rounding up or down takes place, we change this to:

```
A=INT(10∧P*A+.5)/10∧P
```

Now type in the program below, remembering to type in NEW to remove the old program.

```
100 NEW
120 A=SQR(2)
140 FOR P=1 TO 8
160 B=INT (10∧P*A+.5)/10∧P
180 PRINT P, B
200 NEXT P
```

Now run this program. It will print out the square root of 2 to 1, 2, 3, 4, 5, 6, 7 and finally 8 decimal places as follows:

```
1        1.4
2        1.41
3        1.414
4        1.4142
5        1.41421
6        1.414214
7        1.4142136
8        1.41421356
```

Sometimes it is necessary to apply this technique on a great variety of occasions and with a number of variables. In order to make this happen, without having to type in the whole process each time, it is useful to use a predefined function as follows:

```
DEF FNA(X)=INT (100*X+.5)/100
```

(If you have not met this facility in BASIC for creating a predefined function using DEF and FN, look it up in any introductory book.)

Here is an example of this process. First type in this program:

```
100 HOME
140 INPUT "WRITE TOTAL PROFIT   "; P
160 T=P/2 : D=P/3 : H=P/6
200 PRINT : PRINT "TOM'S SHARE IS   " T
220 PRINT : PRINT "DICK'S SHARE IS   " D
240 PRINT : PRINT "HARRY'S SHARE IS   " H
```

This program takes the annual profit (which you choose in line 140) in a company and divides it among the three owners, Tom, Dick and Harry in the proportions shown. Run the program and put in 1000 for the profit. The results given for Dick and Harry all have too many decimal figures, so add these two lines.

```
120 DEF FNA(X)=INT (100*X+.5)/100
180 T=FNA(T) : D=FNA(D) : H=FNA(H)
```

And run it again. This time the results will have two decimal figures only.

ALIGNING THE DECIMAL POINT

First type in this program:

```
100 HOME
120 PRINT "PUT IN FOUR NUMBERS"
140 FOR N=1 TO 4 : INPUT A(N) : NEXT N
160 FOR N=1 TO 4 : PRINT A(N) : NEXT N
```

Run this program. Line 100 clears the screen, and line 120 instructs you to put in four numbers. Line 140 uses a loop to allow you to put in four numbers, and these are stored in the arrays A(1), A(2), A(3) and A(4). A question mark will appear on the screen. When it does, put in 1234, and press **RETURN** . Another question mark appears, inviting the input of a second number. This time, put in 123.4 and press **RETURN** : then 12.34 and finally 1.234. Line 160 prints these four numbers as shown.

```
1234
123.4
12.34
1.234
```

Obviously it would be much more sensible if the decimal points in these numbers were always below each other. The following routine makes this possible. It involves a slightly complex mathematical technique using logarithms. This will be explained, briefly, after the program has been typed in, but even if you do not understand it fully, you will probably still be able to use it successfully in programs.

First, add these lines to the above program:

```
160 FOR N=1 TO 4
180 IF ABS(A(N)) < 1 THEN 300
200 A=ABS(A(N))
220 B=LOG(A)/LOG(10)
240 C=INT(B)
260 PRINT TAB(10-C) A(N)
280 GOTO 320
300 PRINT TAB(11) A(N)
320 NEXT N
```

Lines 160 and 320 make the loop for printing the four numbers. Line 180 checks if each number A(N) is smaller than 1. If it is, it begins with the decimal point and so can be printed directly. Apple then goes to line 300 and prints the decimal point in the 11th column, using TAB(10).

If A(N) is not less than 1, it goes on to line 200, which makes sure that A(N) is positive. Then line 220 finds the logarithm of A(N) to the base 10 and line 240 makes C the whole number part of this logarithm. This mathematics ensures that C is always one less than the number of digits to the left of the decimal point. Line 260 then uses the TAB function, with C, to align the numbers so that the decimal point lies in the 13th column again.

EXTENDING DECIMAL PLACES

We have already shown (in Chapter 6, page 89) how Apple writes decimals to at most nine significant figures. It is sometimes necessary, especially in some mathematical investigations, to know a great many more figures than this. The following program divides a number x by a number y, and gives as many decimal figures as you wish. First type it in and then read the explanation below.

```
100 HOME
110 INPUT "INPUT FIRST NUMBER"; X
120 PRINT : INPUT "INPUT SECOND NUMBER"; Y
140 : INPUT "HOW MANY DEC. PLACES" ; C
160 Z=INT(X/Y)
180 PRINT Z".";
200 X=10*(X-Z*Y)
220 IF X=0 THEN 320
240 Z=INT(X/Y)
260 PRINT Z;
280 C=C-1
300 IF C>0 THEN 200
320 END
```

Lines 100 to 140 clear the screen, input x and y for the fraction x/y, and input for c the number of decimal figures required. Lines 160 and 180 produce the number to be written in front of the decimal point and write it down with the decimal point. Line 200 computes the new x, that is the new top line of the fraction. If the division has been exact then this x will be zero, and this is checked in line 200. If not, line 240 produces the first decimal figure, and line 260 prints it. (The semicolons make sure that these numbers are all printed across the screen.) Line 280 reduces the number of decimal figures still needed by 1, and line 300 checks if the process has been completed. If it has not, the program returns to line 200 and computes the new x, and so it continues.

Now run the program and input the fraction 15/13. That is, input 15 for x and 13 for y. Then input 20 for c. It would be interesting to adapt this program to check whan a full cycle has been completed and the true decimal representation of the fraction has been achieved.

USING STR$

As mentioned in Chapter 8 (page 131), it is possible to use the **STR$** function to translate a number into a string and then use the string functions to format it. We will consider one such program now, and we will take it line by line.

```
100 HOME
120 INPUT Z
```

This clears the screen and invites the input of a number, which in this case is meant to represent a sum of money. The rest of the program will use some of the techniques developed elsewhere in this book, to arrange things so that this sum of money, Z, is always printed and aligned in this format:

```
  $14.00
 $325.10
   $6.24
```

That is, there are always two figures after the decimal point, the dollar (or pound) sign appears first, and the decimal points are aligned.

(a) 14
(b) 243.7
(c) 4.01
(d) 74.347
(e) 9

We must, therefore, take account of each of these possibilities. The next line fixes the fourth posibility, that is where there are more than two figures after the decimal point.

```
140 Z=INT(100*Z+.5)/100
```

Then use the **STR$** function to change Z into the string **Z$**. (Remember that the dollar sign is used to represent a string as well as money.)

```
160 Z$=STR$(Z)
```

Now use the LEN function to find the length of this string and subtract 1 from it.

```
180 L=LEN(Z$)-1
```

There are now four possibilities:

(a) If L=0 then the number must have taken the form of a single-digit input like (e) above, where the input is 9. Remember that the length of this would be 1. Any other form of input would make L greater than 0. In this case we wish to change the 9 into 9.00. To cover this situation we need two new lines.

```
200 IF L=0 THEN 280
280 Z$=Z$+".00"
```

In line 280 Z$ is 9, so it is changed to 9.00 by the addition of the string ".00".

(b) The second possibility is where there are two figures given after the decimal point, like (c) above, where the input is 4.01. We now use this line:

```
240 IF MID$(Z$, L-1, 1)="." THEN 300
```

Since we have taken away from the length of the string altogether, the condition in this line will be satisfied: that is the character isolated by the MID$ function will be the decimal point, so it then moves to line 300, which begins the print routine and is discussed below.

(c) The third possibility is where there is only one figure given after the decimal point, like (b) above where the input is 243.7. If this is so then the condition in line 240 above will not be satisfied, since the subtraction of 2 from the length of the string will remove this one figure, and the decimal point. So the L−1 in the MID$ function must become L. This is given in line 260 below.

```
260 IF MID$(Z$, L, 1)="." THEN 320
320 Z$=Z$+"0"
```

Changing L−1 back to L makes sure that the decimal point is included and so the condition in line 260 is fulfilled and, in line 320, the necessary extra zero is added to the end of the string **Z$**.

(d) The fourth possibility is where the number is simply a two-digit number with no decimal point, like 14. In this case, subtracting 1 from L in line 180 and another 1 in line 240 will make L equal to zero and an error will occur. This is solved by line 220.

```
220 IF L=1 THEN 260
```

The program so far looks like this (with the addition of line 300):

```
100 HOME
120 INPUT Z
140 Z=INT(100*Z+.5)/100
160 Z$=STR$(Z)
180 L=LEN(Z$)-1
200 IF L=0 THEN 280
220 IF L=1 THEN 260
240 IF MID$(Z$, L-1, 1)="." THEN 300
260 IF MID$(Z$, L, 1)="." THEN 320
280 Z$=Z$+".00"
300 GOTO 340
320 Z$=Z$+"0"
```

The four possibilities have now been taken account of and the printout routine follows:

```
340 Z$="$"+Z$
360 A=LEN(Z$)
380 PRINT TAB(20-A)Z$
```

Now run this several times and try putting in the numbers in 1 to 5 above. If you wish to put in a lot of numbers one after another to test the routine thoroughly, put in the extra line:

```
400 GOTO 120
```

PROBLEMS

1. Using some of these formatting techniques, write a program to allow you to input successive items from a shopping list or bill. For each item, there should be three other inputs: that is, price of each; percentage discount; number of each. The program should calculate a totals column and a final overall total. The complete set of information should be presented in formatted tabulated columns on the screen.

2. Write a stock-keeping program which allows you to create a list of items in stock, the number of each in stock, and the number at which reordering is necessary. This information should be presented on the screen after entry in a suitably tabulated form. There should be a further routine to allow you to update the number of each item and this should include a message about the extent to which each item is above or below the reorder number. Finally, it should be possible to save and recover the list with a disk.

10

A Structured Program

INTRODUCTION

This chapter will show you how to develop a program longer and more complex than any we have tried up to now. Its main purpose is to show how such long and apparently complex programs can be constructed out of a set of small, more-or-less compact, units. Each of these is simple, has a single function, and can be fitted easily into the overall structure.

As well as this, such a program allows us to use, in a real context, many of the techniques and facilities which earlier chapters have described. These have often been presented in isolation and this may have disguised the fact that they are routine components of the great majority of programs.

There is, further, the intention to demonstrate a general procedure for structuring BASIC programs so that not only are they easier to write, but also so that they can be read and understood easily. This structuring has two main characteristics. Firstly, it is circular, in the sense that the set of subroutines involved is thought of as being placed around a central organizing routine. The second characteristic, which has already been briefly referred to, is that each subroutine is thought of as a single unit performing a single task. The central organizing routine places the use of these subroutines in the correct order for any specified task. Therefore, if you know what each subroutine does, you can easily follow the logic of the program, by reading the chained sequence of subroutines.

It must be added that such a structuring does not allow you to avoid the kind of interactive trial-and-error programming that we have demonstrated all the way through this book. Within each subroutine it will be necessary to engage in the normal heuristic process of test-running, debugging and so on, but the organization of these separate routines into a structured whole will be relatively simple.

THE PROBLEM TO BE PROGRAMMED

The directors of a small business want to be able to keep a record of the names of all their customers and their customers' current accounts. They want to be able to update this record at any time by adding new names, deleting lapsed names, changing the current accounts of all customers, changing the current account of a specific customer, making a list of all the current accounts that are in the red, and so on. They also want to be able to send a number of standard letters to specific kinds of customers: for example, a letter to those in the red, or a letter stopping credit. Finally, they want to be able to record this information on disk and recover it at will.

It is possible to extend this list of desirable routines, according to the requirements of a particular business. However, we will demonstrate below a solution to this problem which incorporates most of the routines suggested. The final program needs just over 6K of memory. It is always possible, of course, to remove some of the routines.

THE STRUCTURE

The program structure has four major blocks, shown in the diagram below. Each block will be described in general terms to begin with, and then the routines necessary to bring it to life will be described in detail.

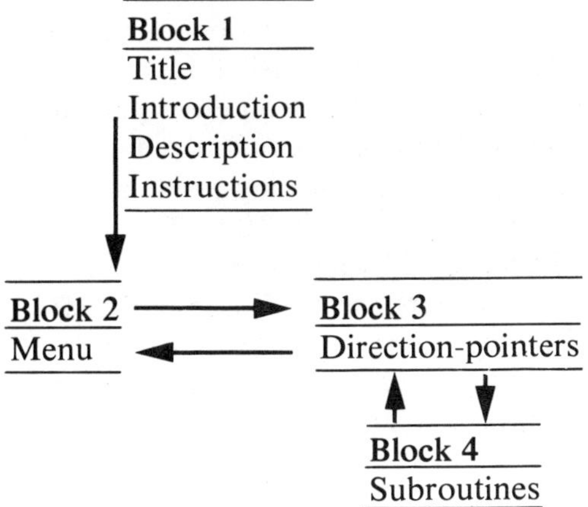

Block 1 is to do with titling the program, introducing it to the user, and presenting it in a readable manner. This is often left out, but should not be, because, although its absence does not detract from the logical flow of the program, the program is more difficult to use, to follow, and to understand without it. There are four possible components for this block suggested in the diagram, although all four will not be necessary in every program.

Block 2 is a list of the subroutines available in the program, often called a menu. The user reads this and chooses the routine that he or she wishes to use. This is the heart of the program. All roads lead out of it, but they will eventually come back to it (with one exception). Therefore, if you choose an item from the menu, the program will take you to it, but when you are finished it will return to the menu. The one exception is, of course, when you have finished using the program for a while and wish to stop the machine.

Block 3 uses a series of GOSUB statements to organize the ordering of the actual subroutines which do the work. When you choose an item from the menu it is often the case that, in order to successfully complete it, the program must go to a number of subroutines in succession. Block 3 organizes this process separately for each menu option. Of course, the last statement in any such organization returns the program to the menu.

Block 4 is simply the set of subroutines, each of which is self-contained, each of which performs a single task, and each of which, on completion, redirects the program to block 3.

THE PROGRAM

We first present an enlarged version of the initial diagram with some more detail. Several of the possible menu items are given in block 2, some of the corresponding subroutine organization is shown in block 3, and 12 possible subroutines are numbered in block 4.

Block 1, in this case, needs only a title and a few lines of description. These are shown below, in lines 10 to 910. Line 10 reserves space for 25 names in A$(25), for 25 account balances in B$(25), for the correspon-ding data for those in the red in C$(25) and D$(25) and for the reference numbers of these debtors in Z(25). Of course, this is only an example program and the capacities of the variables can be increased up to the limit of your Apple's memory.

```
10 DIM A$(25), B$(25), C$(25), D$(25), Z(25)
100 Z$="ACCOUNTS" : L=LEN (Z$)
110 HOME : PRINT TAB((40-L)/2) ; : INVERSE : PRINT Z$ : NORMAL
120 PRINT : PRINT
123 PRINT "THIS PROGRAM KEEPS A RECORD OF ALL"
125 PRINT : PRINT "CUSTOMERS AND THE STATUS OF THEIR"
```

```
130 PRINT : PRINT "CURRENT ACCOUNT. IT CAN BE UPDATED WHEN"
135 PRINT : PRINT "YOU WISH AND A SEPARATE LISTING OF ALL"
140 PRINT : PRINT "CUSTOMERS WHO ARE IN DEBT CAN BE"
145 PRINT : PRINT "GENERATED AT ANY TIME. IT IS ALWAYS"
150 PRINT : PRINT "POSSIBLE TO ADD A NEW NAME OR TAKE"
155 PRINT : PRINT "A NAME AWAY FROM THE LIST, OR TO PUT"
160 PRINT : PRINT "THE LIST INTO ALPHABETICAL ORDER."
900 PRINT : PRINT TAB(15) ; : INVERSE : PRINT "PRESS ANY KEY"
    : NORMAL
910 GET Z$
```

Block 1
Title
Introduction
Description
Instructions

Block 2
Menu
Begin again
Add a name
Delete a name
.
.
.
Finish for now

Block 3
Direction-pointers
GOSUB2500 : GOSUB3000 :
GOSUB7000 : GOTO1000
GOSUB4500 : GOSUB3000 :
GOSUB7000 : GOTO1000
.
.
.
GOTO6500

Block 4
12 Subroutines
1.Begin file creation
2. Alphabetical order
3. Updating current accounts
4. Listing customers in debt
5. Add name to list
6. Delete name from list
7. Save data on disk
8. Recover data from disk
9. End of program
10. Prints data on screen
11. Letter to debtors
12. Letter stopping credit

It is worth pointing out that, at the end of this chapter, there is a listing of the variables used in the program.

Block 2, the menu, is shown below. It includes 12 possible options and a corresponding letter code for each. The line numbers run from 1000 to 1170, and the last of these uses Z$ as the variable for holding whichever letter code is chosen. Lines 1010 and 1020 give simple instructions, and lines 1030 and 1040 give the user valuable information about how much memory is available and about the number of customers currently entered.

```
1000 HOME
1005 PRINT : PRINT TAB(18) ; : INVERSE : PRINT "MENU" : NORMAL
1010 PRINT : PRINT "CHOOSE ONE OF THE ITEMS BELOW"
1020 PRINT "AND PRESS THE APPROPRIATE KEY."
1030 PRINT : PRINT "NO. OF FREE BYTES IS   " 65536+FRE(0)
1040 PRINT : PRINT "NO. OF CUSTOMERS ENTERED   " N
1050 PRINT : PRINT : PRINT "TO BEGIN AGAIN......................B"
1060 PRINT "TO ADD A NAME TO THE LIST ..........................A"
1070 PRINT "TO DELETE A NAME FROM THE LIST ................D"
1080 PRINT "TO PUT IN A/BETICAL ORDER ........................ O"
1090 PRINT "TO UPDATE CURRENT ACCOUNT.....................U"
1100 PRINT "TO EXAMINE LIST OF DEBTORS.......................E"
1110 PRINT "TO SEND LETTER RE DEBT ...............................L"
1120 PRINT "TO SEND STOP-CREDIT LETTER .......................C"
1130 PRINT "TO PRINT LIST ON SCREEN..............................P"
1140 PRINT "TO SAVE ON DISK.............................................S"
1150 PRINT "TO RECOVER FROM DISK.................................R"
1160 PRINT "TO FINISH FOR NOW .......................................F"
1170 GET Z$
```

Block 3 runs from line 1500 to line 2220. It is shown below and has two parts. In lines 1500 to 1600 Apple examines the letter you have chosen from the menu and directs Apple to begin following an appropriate sequence of GOSUBS. Notice that line 1600 deals with the problem which arises if you input a letter which does not appear on the menu at all.

```
1500 IF Z$="B" THEN 2000
1510 IF Z$="A" THEN 2020
1520 IF Z$="D" THEN 2040
1530 IF Z$="O" THEN 2060
1540 IF Z$="U" THEN 2080
1560 IF Z$="E" THEN 2100
```

```
1580 IF Z$="L" THEN 2120
1585 IF Z$="C" THEN 2140
1590 IF Z$="P" THEN 2160
1595 IF Z$="S" THEN 2180
1597 IF Z$="R" THEN 2200
1599 IF Z$="F" THEN 2210
1600 PRINT : PRINT "TRY AGAIN" : GOTO 1000
2000 GOSUB 2500 : GOSUB 3000 : GOSUB 7000 : GOTO 1000
2020 GOSUB 4500 : GOSUB 3000 : GOSUB 7000 : GOTO 1000
2040 GOSUB 5000 : GOSUB 7000 : GOTO 1000
2060 GOSUB 3000 : GOSUB 7000 : GOTO 1000
2080 GOSUB 3500 : GOSUB 7000 : GOTO 1000
2100 GOSUB 4000 : GOTO 1000
2120 GOSUB 7500 : GOTO 1000
2140 GOSUB 8000 : GOTO 1000
2160 GOSUB 7000 : GOTO 1000
2180 GOSUB 5500 : GOTO 1000
2200 GOSUB 6000 : GOTO 1000
2210 GOTO 6500
2220 GOTO 1000
```

So, if you choose code letter B on the menu, for begin, Apple picks this up on line 1500 and directs you to line 2000. Line 2000 means that you go in turn to three different subroutines and then back to line 1000 which is, of course, the menu.

A similar structure works for each of the 12 menu options, except for "FINISH FOR NOW" which goes to line 2210, which is simple: GOTO 6500. This is a short finishing and switching off routine.

Block 4 is a set of 12 subroutines to carry out the actual tasks involved in manipulating the customers' accounts. Each of these is now shown separately, with a short comment.

Subroutine 1 is the input or the begin routine. It allows you to input names and sums of money in order to create the initial file of names and balances. It is quite a short routine running from lines 2500 to 2580.

```
2500 HOME
2505 INPUT "HOW MANY CUSTOMERS  "; N
2510 FOR C=1 TO N
2520 PRINT : PRINT "CUSTOMER NUMBER  " C
2530 PRINT : INPUT "INPUT NAME      "; A$(C)
2540 PRINT : INPUT "THE CURRENT BALANCE   "; B$(C)
2550 NEXT C
```

```
2560 PRINT : PRINT : PRINT "THAT WAS THE LAST ONE"
2565 PRINT : PRINT "   PRESS ANY KEY"
2570 GET Z$
2580 RETURN
```

Subroutine 2 is the routine for putting the names into alphabetical order. It runs from line 3000 to line 3085. The technique involved is a variation of a well-known ordering routine called a Sort, which is discussed in most introductory books. There are a number of different forms of Sort: this particular form is called a Bubblesort.

```
3000 HOME
3005 PRINT "   ALPHABETICAL ORDER"
3010 PRINT : PRINT "THIS PROCESS MAY TAKE SOME TIME."
3020 PRINT "TRY TO BE PATIENT."
3025 J=0
3030 FOR C=1 TO N-1
3035 IF A$(C) < A$(C+1) THEN 3060
3040 X$=A$(C+1) : Y$=B$(C+1)
3045 A$(C+1)=A$(C) : B$(C+1)=B$(C)
3050 A$(C)=X$ : B$(C)=Y$
3055 J=J+1
3060 NEXT C
3065 IF J > 0 THEN 3025
3070 PRINT : PRINT : PRINT "NOW IN ALPHABETICAL ORDER"
3075 PRINT : PRINT "   PRESS ANY KEY"
3080 GET Z$
3085 RETURN
```

Subroutine 3 is concerned with updating the current accounts of customers. It allows you to do this in two ways (which means that most of the internal routines have to be used twice). Either you simply look at the whole list of names, one at a time; or you choose a specific account by putting in the customer's name At every stage the routine, as written here, gives the user the fullest possible options. Because of this, the routine is a bit long and cumbersome. It might be a useful idea to change it into two separate routines, one for dealing with the whole list, the other for dealing with individual cases, or to omit one of the options if memory space is likely to be a problem. It runs from line 3500 to 3980.

```
3500 HOME
3505 Z$="FILE UPDATE" : L=LEN (Z$)
3510 PRINT TAB ((40–L)/2)Z$
```

```
3520 PRINT : PRINT "DO YOU WISH TO PICK A SPECIFIC CUSTOMER"
3530 PRINT : PRINT "OR GO THROUGH THE WHOLE LIST:-"
3540 PRINT : INPUT "INPUT W OR S   " ; Z$
3550 IF LEFT$ (Z$, 1)="S" THEN 3830
3555 IF LEFT$ (Z$, 1)="W" THEN 3570
3560 PRINT : PRINT "TRY AGAIN" : GOTO 3520
3570 FOR C=1 TO N
3580 PRINT : PRINT : PRINT "   CUSTOMER   "C"   IS   "A$(C)
3590 PRINT : PRINT : PRINT "   CURRENT BALANCE IS   " B$(C)
3600 PRINT : INPUT "DO YOU WISH TO CHANGE THIS ACCOUNT   " ; Z$
3610 IF LEFT$ (Z$, 1)="Y" THEN 3640
3620 IF LEFT$ (Z$, 1)="N" THEN 3780
3630 PRINT : PRINT "   TRY AGAIN" : GOTO 3600
3640 PRINT : PRINT "DO YOU WISH TO ADD ON OR TAKE AWAY   "
3650 PRINT : INPUT "INPUT A OR T   " ; Z$
3660 IF LEFT$ (Z$, 1)="T" THEN P=-1 : GOTO 3690
3670 IF LEFT$ (Z$, 1)="A" THEN P=1 : GOTO 3690
3680 PRINT : PRINT "TRY AGAIN" : GOTO 3640
3690 PRINT : INPUT "   HOW MUCH   " ; E
3710 Y$=STR$ (VAL (B$(C))+E*P)
3720 PRINT : PRINT "OLD BAL     CHANGE     NEW BAL"
3730 PRINT : PRINT B$(C), E*P, Y$
3740 PRINT : INPUT "IS THIS CORRECT (Y/N)   " ; Z$
3750 IF LEFT$ (Z$, 1)="Y" THEN 3775
3760 IF LEFT$ (Z$, 1)="N" THEN 3690
3770 PRINT : PRINT "TRY AGAIN" : GOTO 3740
3775 B$(C)=Y$
3780 NEXT C
3790 PRINT : PRINT "   PRESS ANY KEY"
3800 GET Z$
3810 RETURN
3830 PRINT : INPUT "NAME OF CUSTOMER   " ; Z$
3840 FOR C=1 TO N
3850 IF A$(C)=Z$ THEN 3880
3860 NEXT C
3870 PRINT : INPUT "NOT ON LIST. TRY AGAIN (Y/N)   " ; Z$
3872 IF LEFT$ (Z$, 1)="Y" THEN 3830
3874 IF LEFT$ (Z$, 1)="N" THEN 3980
3876 GOTO 3870
3880 PRINT : PRINT "   CUSTOMER   "C"   IS   "A$(C)
3890 PRINT : PRINT "   CURRENT BALANCE IS   "B$(C)
3895 PRINT : INPUT "DO YOU WISH TO CHANGE THIS ACCOUNT   " ; Z$
```

```
3900 IF LEFT$ (Z$, 1)="Y" THEN 3915
3905 IF LEFT$ (Z$, 1)="N" THEN 3810
3910 PRINT : PRINT "TRY AGAIN" : GOTO 3895
3915 PRINT : PRINT "   DO YOU WISH TO ADD ON OR TAKE AWAY"
3920 PRINT : INPUT "   INPUT A OR T   " ; Z$
3925 IF Z$="T" THEN P=-1 : GOTO 3940
3930 IF Z$="A" THEN P=+1 : GOTO 3940
3935 PRINT : PRINT "TRY AGAIN" : GOTO 3915
3940 PRINT : INPUT "   HOW MUCH   " ; E
3950 Y$=STR$ (VAL (B$(C))+E*P)
3955 PRINT : PRINT "OLD BAL    CHANGE    NEW BAL"
3960 PRINT : PRINT B$(C), E*P, Y$
3962 PRINT : INPUT "IS THIS CORRECT (Y/N)   " ; Z$
3964 IF Z$="Y" THEN 3980
3966 IF Z$="N" THEN 3940
3968 PRINT : PRINT "TRY AGAIN" : GOTO 3962
3970 NEXT C
3972 PRINT : PRINT "   PRESS ANY KEY"
3974 GET Z$
3980 B$(C)=Y$ : RETURN
```

Subroutine 4 is a technique for selecting those customers whose current balance is negative, i.e. in the red. These are counted by Z(N) and are stored in C$(N) and D$(N). (Line 4095 uses a quite complex notion which you may have to think about for a little while.) The routine runs from line 4000 to 4140.

```
4000 HOME
4005 PRINT "   CHECK  DEBT"
4010 D=1
4020 FOR C=1 TO N
4030 IF VAL (B$(C)) < 0 THEN 4050
4040 GOTO 4070
4050 Z(D)=C
4060 D=D+1
4070 NEXT C
4080 PRINT : PRINT "CUSTOMERS IN DEBT ARE:-"
4085 PRINT : PRINT
4090 FOR C=1 TO D
4095 C$(C)=A$(Z(C)) : D$(C)=B$(Z(C))
4100 PRINT C$(C), D$(C)
4110 NEXT C
```

```
4120 PRINT : PRINT "   PRESS ANY KEY"
4130 GET Z$
4140 RETURN
```

Subroutine 5 allows the user to add a name to the list of customers. It is a very simple process and needs only a short routine. It runs from line 4500 to 4530.

```
4500 HOME
4502 PRINT "   ADD NAME ROUTINE"
4505 N=N+1
4510 INPUT "   NEW NAME    "; A$(N)
4515 PRINT : INPUT "   BALANCE    "; B$(N)
4520 PRINT : PRINT "   PRESS ANY KEY"
4525 GET Z$
4530 RETURN
```

Subroutine 6 is the opposite of subroutine 5, in that it allows the user to delete a customer's name from the list. It also takes account of the situation where the name to be deleted is not typed in exactly as stored in Apple. It runs from line 5000 to line 5100.

```
5000 HOME
5002 PRINT "   DELETE A NAME"
5005 PRINT : INPUT "NAME TO BE REMOVED    "; T$
5010 FOR C=1 TO N
5015 IF A$(C)=T$ THEN 5060
5020 NEXT C
5025 PRINT : PRINT "NAME NOT ON LIST. REMEMBER TO PUT IT"
5030 PRINT : PRINT "IN EXACTLY AS ORIGINALLY."
5035 PRINT : PRINT "DO YOU WISH TO TRY AGAIN (Y/N)"
5040 PRINT : INPUT "            "; Z$
5045 IF Z$="Y" THEN 5005
5050 IF Z$="N" THEN 5100
5055 PRINT : PRINT "   TRY AGAIN" : GOTO 5035
5060 FOR D=C TO N-1
5065 A$(D)=A$(D+1) : B$(D)=B$(D+1)
5070 NEXT D
5075 A$(N)=""
5080 N=N-1
5085 PRINT : PRINT "NAME AND RECORD NOW REMOVED"
5090 PRINT : PRINT "   PRESS ANY KEY"
5095 GET Z$
5100 RETURN
```

Subroutine 7 is used to save the records on disk. It is almost identical to the one which has already been discussed at some length in Chapter 4. It runs from line 5500 to line 5580.

```
5500 HOME
5502 D$=CHR$ (4)
5503 PRINT "NAMES AND DATA BEING STORED"
5505 PRINT D$ ; "OPEN NAMES"
5510 PRINT D$ ; "WRITE NAMES"
5520 FOR C=1 TO N
5525 PRINT A$(C) : PRINT B$(C)
5530 NEXT C
5540 PRINT D$ ; "CLOSE NAMES"
5550 PRINT : PRINT "NAMES AND DATA NOW STORED"
5560 PRINT : PRINT "PRESS ANY KEY"
5570 GET Z$
5580 RETURN
```

Subroutine 8 is used to recover the records from disk and is again very similar to the one described in Chapter 4. It runs from line 6000 to line 6120. Notice that you must remember how many records you have stored, so it is always a good idea to make a note of how many records have been stored on it.

```
6000 HOME
6010 PRINT : INPUT "HOW MANY NAMES WERE STORED   ";N
6020 D$=CHR$ (4)
6025 PRINT "NAMES AND DATA BEING RECOVERED"
6030 PRINT D$; "OPEN NAMES"
6040 PRINT D$; "READ NAMES"
6050 FOR C = 1 TO N
6060 INPUT A$(C) : INPUT B$(C)
6070 NEXT C
6080 PRINT D$; "CLOSE NAMES"
6090 PRINT "   RESULTS NOW RECOVERED"
6100 PRINT : PRINT : PRINT "   PRESS ANY KEY"
6110 GET Z$
6120 RETURN
```

Routine 9 is the "finish" routine and is not a subroutine in the normal sense. It runs from line 6500 to line 6540 and ends with the word END rather than the word RETURN. In this it is different from all others.

```
6500 PRINT : PRINT : PRINT
6510 PRINT "THANK YOU FOR NOW. IF YOU WISH TO"
6520 PRINT : PRINT "BEGIN AGAIN, TYPE IN 'RUN' AND"
6530 PRINT : PRINT "PRESS RETURN."
6540 END
```

Subroutine 10 runs from line 7000 to line 7050. It prints the data on the screen for examination. Line 7015 breaks the data up into "screenfuls" of at most 15 records, so that they don't run off the top of the screen before you can read them.

```
7000 HOME
7005 PRINT "NAMES" TAB(18) "BALANCES"
7007 FOR C = 1 TO N
7012 PRINT LEFT$ (A$(C), 12) TAB(20) VAL (B$(C) )
7015 IF INT (C / 15) = (C / 15) THEN 7025
7020 GOTO 7035
7025 PRINT : PRINT "   PRESS ANY KEY"
7030 GET Z$
7035 NEXT C
7040 PRINT : PRINT "   PRESS ANY KEY"
7045 GET Z$
7050 RETURN
```

Subroutines 11 and 12, starting at lines 7500 and 8000, are not included, since they require the use of a printer, which is not discussed in this book, but space has been reserved for them by putting in a short message as shown.

```
7500 HOME
7510 PRINT "THIS ROUTINE IS NOT YET INCLUDED."
7520 PRINT : PRINT "WHEN YOU GET A PRINTER IT WILL"
7530 PRINT : PRINT "BE EASY TO PUT IT IN."
7540 PRINT : PRINT "   PRESS ANY KEY"
7550 GET Z$
7560 RETURN

8000 REM PRINTER ROUTINE
8005 HOME
8010 GOTO 7510
```

The twelve routines in block 4 are now shown together below, with a shorthand for each, and the first line number of each.

No.	Letter on menu		Shorthand	First Line
1	B	INPUT or BEGIN. File Creation	Begin	2500
2	O	Alphabetical order	Alpha	3000
3	U	Updating current accounts	Update	3500
4	E	Selecting customers in debt	Debt	4000
5	A	Add a name to list	Add	4500
6	D	Delete a name from list	Delete	5000
7	S	Save data on disk	Save	5500
8	R	Recover data from disk	Load	6000
9	F	End of program	End	6500
10	P	Print data on screen	Read	7000
11	L	Send letter to debtors	Letter	7500
12	C	Send letter stopping credit	Credit	8000

It would clearly be possible to remove any one of these subroutines or to attach any number of new subroutines by changing the appropriate parts in blocks 2 and 3, and simply deleting or inserting these routines in block 4. The program is, in a sense, modularized.

The variables used in this program are now listed.

(a) **Array Variables**
- **A$** ( ) Names of Customers
- **B$** ( ) Current account balance figures
- **C$** ( ) Names of customers in debt
- **D$** ( ) Current account balances of customers in debt
- Z(25) List of numbers of customers in debt

(b) **String Variables**
- **Z$** A casual variable used for pause routines etc.
- **X$** An auxiliary variable used in the alphabetical order routine
- **Y$** Same as **X$**
- **T$** Used in delete routine to hold temporarily the name to be removed

(c) **Other Variables**
- L Length of strings
- N Number of customers
- C Counts from 1 to N in loops
- D Counts the number of debtors
- J Conditional variable used in alphabetical order routine
- E Amount to be added to or taken from current account
- P Used to hold sign of E (i.e. plus or minus)

It is a good policy to keep a list of variable names like this in all programs, for two reasons. First, if there is a breakdown the variable involved can be more easily located. Second, it avoids the danger of using a single variable name for two different things.

It is not suggested that every single program can be modularized in exactly this way, but it ought to be possible to develop some kind of comparable structure whatever the form of the problem.

PROBLEMS

1. Write a bibliography program which allows you to input a list of books. Each entry should include the author's name, the title of the book, the publisher and the year of publication. The menu should allow the following options:

BEGIN	a new list
READ	a current list
ADD	a name to a list
DELETE	a name from a list
CHANGE	any specified entry
SAVE	the list on disk
RECOVER	the list from disk
FINISH	for now

   As well as the subroutines necessary for these, it should also include a routine for putting the list into alphabetical order and a routine for holding the screen.

2. Write a test standardization program. This should allow the input of names and scores of a class, and should then calculate the mean and standard deviation of these scores. The user should then be invited to choose a new mean and a new standard deviation and the program should then calculate a new score for each name. The data should be displayed on screen in three columns, i.e. names, scores, standardized scores. There should be routines for saving on disk, recovering from disk, putting in alphabetical order, adding and taking away names, changing all the scores, and so on.

11

Apple in the Classroom

INTRODUCTION

This section tries to describe a set of activities which a teacher might use in introducing Apple into his or her classroom. Although these activities are presented in a particular order, this does not mean that we think that this order is very important. In certain circumstances changes in the ordering would be sensible and even necessary. As well as this it has been assumed that, for some of these activities, suitable software is available or can be constructed. In some cases this is probably over-optimistic, but the quality and quantity of good Apple software is improving all the time and we hope that this book will help teachers and others to become more expert at both writing software and improving or revising bought software.

The ideas that follow are meant as a very general guide and no special kind of school or range of school ages is specified. Many of the suggestions would work very well in a primary school for example, but are generally not intended exclusively for that age.

We are very clear, however, that all school subjects can benefit from using the machine. That is to say, we would not support at all the notion that mathematics and the sciences have a better case than the other disciplines. In particular, the sophisticated string-handling and word-processing capacity of Apple makes it as capable of dealing with words as with numbers.

We also believe that the potential of machines like Apple is very great and that as time goes on the range and complexity of the tasks that they can accomplish successfully will be greatly extended.

In practical terms, therefore, we believe that all users should join an Apple User's Club either locally or nationally so as to keep in touch with developments in software and add-on hardware (see Appendix H).

APPLE AS A GAMES-PLAYER

To begin with, it is necessary to overcome any inhibitions and anxieties that children may have about playing with Apple. They must become adept at setting the machine up, loading programs from disk, pressing keys, using the **RETURN** , **CTRL** and **ESC** keys, avoiding the **RESET** key, and so on.

Games, probably bought from a software house to begin with, are the ideal introduction. Not only do they act as an immediate stimulus but they build up a degree of motivation and interest that is hard to acquire in any other way. It is even likely, after some experience, that children will take on the onerous task of typing in long game programs from books and magazines, even before they have had any experience of programming.

Although many of the most popular games are arcade-type games, like *Starwars*, not all games that can be played on Apple are trivial or unintellectual. Many of these, such as *Mastermind* or *Noughts and Crosses* (or *Tic-Tac-Toe*) have a logical or mathematical dimension that is important educationally. This is not to mention complex games like *Draughts, Chess* and *Go.*

APPLE AS A CALCULATOR

The first chapter of this book shows how to begin to use Apple as a simple calculator. This usually involves the use of the word PRINT (or its shorthand, ?). At a very elementary level children can go to Apple to check answers to arithmetical calculations. One effect of this is to put some emphasis on the importance of the "ordering" of calculations and on the ambiguity of statements like:

```
20-10-4
```

For example, we can compare the answer to:

```
?20-10-4
```

with the answer to:

```
?20-(10-4)
```

and discuss why these are different.

It is also an interesting and important mathematical notion to be able to store numbers in variables. This can be done on Apple and, at the same time, a simulation of the process can be developed in the classroom. For example, we can input the following lines, remembering to press the **RETURN** key after each.

```
A=4
B=5
C=A+B
D=A*B
?A, B, C, D
```

Alongside this we can have a set of small cardboard boxes labelled A, B, C and D. The first line A=4 can be represented visually by putting four counters in the A box. This process is then continued for each of the other boxes.

This sort of exercise allows children to develop some kind of mental imagery about the internal processes of the machine.

A similar activity is possible with strings. Suppose the school is called "St. John's Academy". Then:

```
A$="ST."
B$=" JOHN'S"
C$=" ACADEMY"
D$=A$+B$+C$
?D$
```

(Note: there is a space between the quotation marks and the J and the A in lines 2 and 3 above.) Boxes can be used again to represent the memory units and this time will be labelled A$, B$, and so on.

APPLE AS A TEACHER

At a very elementary level it is possible to write a little program to allow children to practice addition. Suppose, for example, we wish to add two two-digit numbers each time. First, we can create the numbers with these two lines:

```
100 A=INT(100*RND(4))
120 B=INT(100*RND(7))
```

We then find the answer with:

```
140 C=A+B
```

We then display the problem and invite an answer (D) from the child:

```
160 PRINT " "A
180 PRINT "+"B
200 PRINT "______"
220 INPUT D
```

Then check if the answer is correct.

```
240 IF C=D THEN ? "CORRECT" : GOTO 280
260 PRINT "SORRY. THIS IS NOT CORRECT"
280 PRINT "DO YOU WANT TO TRY ANOTHER?"
```

and so on.

This is just the bones of a program and a great deal can be done to dress it up and present it in an interesting and fascinating way. What about using graphics to make the screen "explode" when a correct answer is given!

Of course, this program can easily be adapted for subtraction, multiplication, division and so on. It can also, with very little extra thought, become a word-completion or sentence-completion program.

These are simple examples of Computer Assisted Learning (shortened to CAL). It is possible to develop these into quite a complex suite of such programs and, as time goes on, most teachers will do this. But the alternative is to buy commercial versions of such programs and adapt these to your own needs.

For older primary children more complex problems become possible, such as completing sequences, plotting points, visual representations of fractions, completing symmetrical shapes, rotations, solving simple equations, and many more. For secondary children the possibilities are even greater and are limited only by the imagination of the teacher or programmer.

The program that follows is an example which is more complex both in its content and in the amount of programming necessary to make it work. It uses two random numbers, generated in lines 120 and 140, to produce linear sequences of numbers. A set of six numbers in a linear sequence is then written on the screen with a bar, equal in length to each number, drawn beside each number. The user is then invited to put in the next two numbers in the sequence.

```
100 HOME
120 A=INT (5*RND(7)+1) : REM FIRST TERM
140 B=INT (6*RND(8)+1) : REM TERM DIFFERENCE
160 FOR C=1 TO A : PRINT "*" ; : NEXT C
180 PRINT TAB(35)A
200 PRINT
220 FOR N=1 TO 5
240 D=A+N * B
260 FOR C=1 TO D : PRINT "*" ; : NEXT C
280 PRINT TAB(35)A+N * B
300 PRINT
320 NEXT N
340 PRINT "——" TAB (36) "?"
400 PRINT : PRINT
410 INPUT "PUT IN THE NEXT NUMBER    " ; A1
420 B1=A+6 * B
440 IF A1=B1 THEN 480
460 PRINT : PRINT "TRY IT AGAIN" : GOTO 400
480 PRINT : PRINT
490 INPUT "NOW THE NEXT ONE    " ; A2
500 B2=A+7 * B
520 IF A2=B2 THEN 560
540 PRINT : PRINT "TRY IT AGAIN" : GOTO 480
560 PRINT : PRINT "WELL DONE"
```

APPLE AS A MANAGER

There are a number of ways in which Apple can be used to store and generate records of class activities. An example of this is the "Test Standardization" program in the problems attached to Chapter 10. This allows a teacher to store and, perhaps more importantly, to standardize any set of scores generated by a class.

Let us take another example. Suppose a teacher has created a set of mathematics workcards (called C1, C2, etc.) which has a complex organizational structure. A very small subset of this structure is shown below:

Stage 1. Choose one of: C1 C2 C3
Stage 2. Do C4 — which includes short test.
Stage 3. If score 50, or less, do C5.
If score greater than 50, do C6.

Stage 4. After C5, do C7 and C8.
After C6 do C9
Stage 5. Do card 10.

It would be a relatively simple task to write a program which would "advise" each pupil about which card to use next.

The first few steps in such a program are shown below. To begin with, the child is asked to indicate whether or not he/she is a beginner. If he/she is a beginner then the problem is immediately solved: do C1, C2 or C3. If the child is not a beginner then further information is necessary:

```
100 HOME : PRINT "ARE YOU A BEGINNER?"
120 INPUT A$ : IF A$="YES" THEN 180
140 IF A$="NO" THEN 240
160 GOTO 100
180 PRINT : PRINT "CHOOSE ONE OF THE CARDS NUMBERED:-"
200 PRINT "C1, C2, C3"
220 END
240 PRINT : PRINT "WHAT CARD HAVE YOU JUST COMPLETED?"
260 INPUT A$
280 IF A$="C1" OR A$="C2" OR A$="C3" THEN 1000
```

Again, commercial programs for purposes of this sort will often be available, and will certainly become available as time goes on.

In more general terms the machine can be used to manage or advise about, or to control any complex set of educational decisions or structures. In this sort of system the machine acts simply as a record-keeper and patternkeeper and so is able, very quickly, to compare individual performances or courses or patterns with a more general established or expected set.

APPLE AS AN AID IN SIMULATIONS

The programs on "tossing a coin" and "tossing a dice" in Chapter 6 are elementary examples of simulation programs. Instead of actually throwing a dice or a coin 200 times, it is possible to get Apple to simulate this process and produce a set of likely outcomes. Clearly the random number function will allow Apple to be used to produce figures of this sort for any such problem.

There are many situations in subjects like biology and geography where such random number techniques are useful in that they allow a complex set of natural phenomena linked by probabilistic relationships to be observed and studied in the classroom. Usually the real complexity of the situation and the interrelationships have to be severely oversimplified but, nonetheless, their structure and the processes through which they operate can be partially retained even in an oversimplified simulation model. An example now follows.

A factory is about to employ a new workforce of 1,000 people. Some of these will be junior managers and some will be shopfloor workers. No exact figures are decided upon, but it is expected that the probability of becoming a junior manager is 1/4 or 0.25, so that the probability of working on the shopfloor is therefore 3/4 or 0.75.

After three years there will be a promotions exercise. Of the junior managers some will become senior managers, and the probability of this is about 1/10 or 0.1. The others will remain junior managers, and the probability of this is therefore 9/10 or 0.9. Of those working on the shopfloor, some will be promoted to foremen. The probability of this is reckoned to be 1/3 or 0.33. The others will remain on the shopfloor and so the probability of this is 2/3 or 0.67.

Use a simulation exercise based on random numbers to see how many of the 1,000 workers might end up in each of the four employment categories, that is,

(a) Senior management
(b) Junior management
(c) Foremen
(d) Shopfloor workers

Admittedly, this problem is fairly easily solved using simple arithmetic and the rules of probability. But that would leave out to some extent the random element and the "real-life" notion that the probabilities quoted are not precise.

Here is a program which can be used. As always, it is fairly unadorned and a great deal more can be done with it, but at the end it produces figures of those actually in each of the four categories, and compares these with the numbers "expected" if precise arithmetic were used.

```
100 HOME
120 INPUT "INPUT TOTAL NO. OF WORKERS   "; W
140 C1=0 : C2=0 : C3=0 : C4=0
160 FOR N=1 TO W
180 A=INT (4 * RND(3) + 1) : REM WORKERS OR MANAGEMENT
200 B=INT (5 * RND(5) + 1) : REM MANAGEMENT PROMOTION
```

```
220 C=INT (3 * RND(3)+1) : REM WORKERS PROMOTION
240 IF A=1 THEN 280 : REM MANAGEMENT
260 GOTO 360 : REM WORKERS
280 REM C1 IS NEW SENIOR MANAGEMENT
300 IF B < 3 THEN C1=C1+1 : GOTO 440
320 REM C3 IS JUNIOR MANAGEMENT
340 C2=C2+1 : GOTO 440
360 REM C3 IS NEW FOREMEN
380 IF C=1 THEN C3=C3+1 : GOTO 440
400 REM C4 IS THE NUMBER NOT PROMOTED
420 C4=C4+1 : GOTO 440
440 NEXT N
450 PRINT : PRINT : PRINT : PRINT
460 PRINT "SENIOR" TAB(8) "JUNIOR" TAB(16) "FORE" TAB(24) "SHOP"
480 PRINT "MANAG" TAB(8) "MANAG" TAB(16) "MEN" TAB(24)
    "FLOOR"
500 PRINT : PRINT
520 PRINT C1 TAB(8) C2 TAB(16) C3 TAB(24) C4 TAB(28) "ACTUAL  NOS"
540 PRINT W / 10 TAB(8)3*W / 20 TAB(16)W / 4 TAB(24)W / 2
    TAB(28) "EXPECTED NOS"
```

APPLE FOR LEARNING PROGRAMMING

This aspect of Apple's potential use in schools can easily be forgotten in all the other more obviously functional and applied uses which we have described. But for those children who wish to learn how to program and who may take examinations in computer science, or similar subjects, then a machine like Apple is most valuable.

In the past, learning to program was often a theoretical exercise with long delays between writing the program and testing it. With Apple there is an immediate feedback and any attempt at programming can be tested on the spot. A great deal can be done with a very limited set of BASIC statements and commands and, once these have been taken in, there is tremendous scope for experiment and practical work.

There are also many side-effects from this kind of exercise. These range from the development of physical skills, like typing, to the logical skills necessary to predict the consequences of a series of simple statements and commands.

Appendix A Apple Variations and Hardware

INTRODUCTION

The Apple which you are using will be either an Apple II or an Apple II Plus. This will be written on the front, just above the keyboard. There are two main differences between these two versions of Apple, as follows.

When it is switched on normally, without a disk-drive attached, Apple II comes up with Integer BASIC and this is indicated by a prompt on the screen like this, >. This means that Integer BASIC is built into the machine and is available as soon as Apple is switched on. You cannot harm or destroy the language because it is stored in Read-Only-Memory chips called ROM chips. As the name suggests, these can be read from but cannot be written to. However, Apple II Plus has Applesoft BASIC in ROM instead, and when you switch it on this is what becomes available and this is indicated by the prompt,], on the screen.

The other main difference is that Apple II Plus has an autostart ROM which, as the name suggests, automatically switches on a disk-drive (if attached) and loads the operating system from a diskette in drive 1. This is not true of Apple II and the method for using disks with this is described below.

CARDS AND SLOTS

Now switch your Apple off and remove the cover by pulling up at the rear edge until it comes apart from the box. Now slide this cover off carefully and look into the Apple. At the very back, furthest away from the keyboard, there is a row of eight slots numbered 0 to 7. These are used to plug or slot in a variety of additional boards or cards to the Apple so that it is possible to attach numerous peripherals like disk-drives, printers, graphics boards and so on. It is also possible to plug in cards which add new facilities to Apple. For example, if you have an Apple II Plus and wish to have Integer BASIC as well as the resident Applesoft BASIC, then it is possible to buy an Integer BASIC card and instal it in slot 0.

DISK DRIVES

We have assumed in this book that your Apple will have at least one floppy disk-drive attached. If this is so you will find that a card for this has been installed, and it is most likely to be in slot 6, although it could be in any slot from 1 to 7. This card should have marked on it very clearly the words Drive 1 and Drive 2 with arrows pointing to the appropriate connectors. So this single card can be used to operate either a single disk-drive or two disk-drives.

It is possible to have up to three of these disk-drive cards and so to have up to six disk-drives, and ways of addressing these are given in the Apple DOS manuals (see Appendix H). These cards again can be installed in any of the slots except number 0, but normally they appear in slots 4, 5 and 6.

BOOTING DOS

In order to be able to use the disks it is necesary to add some new commands to the BASIC language. These commands take the form of words like OPEN, CATALOG, RENAME and so on. If no disk-drive is attached these words are not required, and so normally BASIC does not contain them. The process of adding these commands is called *booting DOS,* where DOS stands for Disk Operating System.

There are currently two established versions of DOS being used by Apples. These are called DOS 3.2 and DOS 3.3. A further complication is the possibility that your Apple may have what is called a *language card* (sometimes mistakenly called a Pascal card and sometimes a RAM card) installed in slot 0. We will discuss all of these variations below.

The procedure for booting the DOS depends on which version of Apple you are using, so there are essentially two possibilities, and we will consider each in turn.

(a) If you have the Apple II system with DOS 3.2 this means that you will not have the automatic ROM, so proceed as follows:

(i) Check which slot contains the disk-drive card. It is normally slot 6.
(ii) Turn the Apple on at the back, and turn the monitor on as usual.
(iii) Put the disk called *Sytem Master* into disk-drive 1.
(iv) Type in PR#6, and press **RETURN**. The red light on the front of the disk-drive will come on, there will be a whirring sound and the screen will print something like this:

```
DISK II    MASTER DISKETTE      VERSION 3.2
                                DATE
□
```

The result is that DOS has been booted and the new operating commands have been added to BASIC although the Apple will not appear to do anything very different.

There are two further points to be made.
(i) You could have typed in IN#6 instead of PR#6.
(ii) The 6 refers to the slot number, so if your disk-drive card has been placed in some other slot then this number must be changed accordingly.

(b) If you have Apple II Plus with the automatic ROM and DOS 3.3 then proceed as follows:
(i) As always check which slot contains the disk-drive card. It is normally slot 6.
(ii) Put the disk called *System Master* into disk-drive number 1.
(iii) Switch Apple on at the back. The red light will come on, there will be a whirring sound and the screen will print a message like that shown above, but referring to DOS 3.3. The essential difference in this case is that you do not have to type in PR 6.

VERSIONS OF DOS

The essential difference between the two versions of DOS being used is in the way they format the diskettes. In the earlier version of DOS the diskette was divided into 13 sectors, but DOS 3.3 divides the diskette into 16 sectors. This is done mainly to accommodate the language card which is discussed below. The main consequences of the change is an increase in the amount of storage space available on each diskette (from approximately 103,000 bytes to 127,000 usable bytes).

For someone who has diskettes formatted in both ways (i.e. with 13 sectors and with 16 sectors), DOS 3.3 allows the use of both sets, but DOS 3.2 only allows the use of those with 13 sectors.

In DOS 3.3 then there are two systems depending on the format of the diskette to be used. With a 16 sector diskette the normal booting system as described above is used. However, if you have a developed system written or saved on a 13-sector diskette there are two possibilities open to you. One is to transfer all the programs and data from the 13-sector diskette to a new 16-sector diskette using a program called *Muffin*. This is available on the DOS 3.3 systems disk. The other alternative involves using a conversion disk called BASICS, which allows DOS 3.3 systems to deal directly with 13-sector diskettes. The procedure is to insert this BASICS disk into disk-drive 1 and turn Apple on at the back. In response to this Apple will print on the screen the words, "INSERT YOUR 13 SECTOR DISKETTE AND PRESS RETURN". You should then insert your 13-sector diskette into Disk-Drive 1 as instructed.

The final variation occurs if you have what is called the *Language Card* installed in slot 0. The main reason for installing the language card is that it is then possible to use other languages like *Pascal* and *FORTRAN*. These languages use 16-sector diskettes and so it is necessary to have DOS 3.3 installed. The parts necessary to do this are normally included when you buy the language card.

You will also be given a BASICS diskette and a DOS 3.3 diskette so that it is possible for you to use both 13-sector and 16-sector diskettes, as described above. If you are also going to use Pascal (or another language), the appropriate disks will be included and there is some discussion of these in Appendix E.

ITT 2020

A version of the Apple is produced in Europe and is called the ITT 2020. It is almost identical to Apple and much Apple software will run on it, and vice versa. The most immediately obvious difference is the color of the plastic case, although it looks like the Apple shape. As well as this, underneath the lid the design of the main inside board is a bit different.

The important difference is in the software and in particular in the way the two machines treat high resolution graphics. The main BASIC is called Palsoft rather than Applesoft and they differ with respect to their treatment of graphics.

As we have described in Chapter 5 the Apple high resolution screen is divided into 280 points across the screen and 160 down the screen. The ITT has 360 points across the screen and 160 down. One consequence of this is that, on the ITT 2020, horizontal and vertical lines are differently scaled. For example, a program which will draw a square on Apple will produce a rectangle on the ITT 2020.

As well as this, the HPLOT command differs on the two systems. On Apple you can write:

```
HPLOT 0,0 TO 0,100 TO 100,100.
```

On the ITT 2020 this must be changed into two statements, i.e.:

```
HPLOT 0,0 TO 0,100
HPLOT 0,100 TO 100,100.
```

The result of these differences is that some Apple programs will not run on the ITT 2020 either because of the BASIC or because the video system is different.

BELL AND HOWELL

A similar Apple-based look-alike machine is sold in the USA by Bell and Howell. This is in fact an Apple in another case, and there are no incompatibility problems.

LOWER-CASE LETTERS

Although Apple does not have the facility for producing lower-case letters there are a number of devices on the market which can be added to the machine to make this possible. This can be in the form of a ROM chip which is simply plugged in, or a slot-in card which is put into one of the eight slots at the back of the Apple board.

Appendix B Tape Management

INTRODUCTION

Although most Apple systems are likely to have disk-drives, not all owners will be able to afford them, so this is a short introduction to the use of cassette tapes and a tape recorder for the purposes of saving and recovering programs.

The process of connecting a tape recorder to Apple and of making sure that it can "listen" properly and "talk" properly to Apple is described in the Applesoft tutorial and will not be repeated here. The essential point is that the volume control on the recorder must be set properly and this proper position is found by trial and error in the first instance. When it has been found it should be marked clearly so that it can be properly aligned each time the recorder is used. It is worth pointing out that saving and loading text or data files is not dealt with here as the processes are either impossible or too complex to describe.

SAVING A PROGRAM

The procedure for doing this is now outlined in detail. The steps to be followed are given in the correct order, so you should proceed exactly as described.

(a) If you have not already done so, type in the program that you wish to keep.

(b) Put a cassette into the tape recorder and make sure it is rewound.

(c) Type the word SAVE but do not as yet press the **RETURN** key.

(d) Hold the *record* key and press the *play* key so that both stay down. The cassette tape will begin to move as it begins to record.

(e) Press the RETURN key. The cursor will then disappear, and after ten to fifteen seconds Apple will give a "beep" sound. This indicates that recording has begun. When the recording has been completed this "beep" will sound again and the cursor will reappear.

(f) When the cursor reappears, press the stop key on the tape recorder. Your program has now been saved.

(g) Remove the cassette, and label it carefully so that you know what program has been saved on it.

LOADING A PROGRAM FROM TAPE

This is the opposite process and it echoes the "save" process fairly faithfully. Again the steps should be carefully followed.

(a) Insert the tape and make sure it is rewound.

(b) Type the word LOAD but do not as yet press the RETURN key.

(c) Press the *play* key and make sure that it stays down so that the tape is running.

(d) Press the RETURN key. The cursor will then disappear. After some seconds (less than twenty usually) Apple will give a "beep" sound to indicate that the program is being loaded into Apple. When this loading has been completed this "beep" will sound again and the cursor will reappear.

(e) When the cursor reappears, press the *stop* key on the tape recorder. Your program has now been loaded.

(f) Now type in RUN and press RETURN .

For the benefit of the disk users it is as well to point out that using LOAD or SAVE without a file name implies that cassette tape is being used, so that if a system with disks is being used, the cursor disappears, and nothing happens. In other words, disk users must always include a file name.

Appendix C Apple Vocabulary

INTRODUCTION

Apple recognizes certain words, symbols and letters as having a special meaning. For example, the question mark means "print" and the dollar sign indicates a string. A complete list of these reserved words now follows, as well as a list of all Apple symbols, such as the comma. Included in this list are all the words used in DOS commands and a small number of words associated with machine-code commands.

The expressions are listed in alphabetical order, and beside each expression there are three pieces of information.

(a) A short description of the meaning or purpose of the words. However, it is emphasized that these are by their nature sketchy descriptions and the reader should check the syntax carefully in the *Applesoft BASIC Programming Reference Manual,* details on page 251).

(b) A reference to the appropriate page number in this book, where it occurs.

(c) An indication of the categories into which the word fits according to these divisions:

DIR — Can be typed in directly outside a program.
PRG — Used mainly within a program.
FN — Is a function.
STRFN — Is a string function.
DOS — Is used by the Disk Operating System.

(This is not adhered to with complete strictness because although many words can in theory be used directly, they rarely are and are not so classified).

WORDS

Expression	*Description*	*Page*
ABS	Used with numbers, and always produces the number as positive even when used with a negative number. (PRG, FN)	—
AND	This is the logical AND to combine two conditionals. (PRG)	—
APPEND	A DOS command used within a program with PRINT CHR$(4) to add data to the end of a sequential file. (PRG, DOS)	—
ASC	Produces a number corresponding to the first character of the string in brackets. (PRG, STRFN)	130
ATN	A mathematical function, the inverse TAN function. The result will be in radians. (PRG, FN)	—
BLOAD	A DOS command which loads a machine-code file. (DIR, DOS)	—
BRUN	A DOS command which executes a machine-code file. (DIR, DOS)	—
BSAVE	A DOS command which saves a machine-code file. (DIR, DOS)	—
CALL	Used to call or execute a machine-code routine. It is followed by a number which is the address of the memory location of the beginning of the routine. (DIR, PRG)	94
CATALOG	A DOS command used to list on the screen the contents of a diskette inserted in one of the disk drives. Can be used with a drive number as in CATALOG, D2. (DIR, DOS)	43

Expression	*Description*	*Page*
CHR$	Produces a character corresponding to the number in brackets. (PRG, STRFN)	48
CLEAR	Used to set all variables to zero or equivalent. Can also be used as a statement within a program. (DIR, PRG)	—
CLOSE	A DOS command used, both within a program and directly, with PRINT CHR$(4) to close a data file. (DIR, PRG, DOS)	48
COLOR	Used in low-resolution graphics to choose a color, using an appropriate number as in COLOR = 4. (See HCOLOR.) (DIR, PRG, GRAPH)	56
CONT	Used to make Apple continue with a program after it has gone into direct mode as a consequence of the word STOP or the word END. (DIR)	—
COS	The mathematical cosine function. The number used with COS (in brackets) must be in radians. (PRG, FN)	70
DATA	*See* READ.	74
DEF FN	Used to define a function which can then be used again and again. (DIR, PRG, FN)	143
DEL	Removes or deletes lines from a program as in DEL 100, 160. This removes all lines from 100 to 160 inclusive. Notice that the numbers are separated by a comma. (DIR, PRG)	20
DELETE	(a) A DOS command used to remove a file from a diskette. The title of the file must be used, as in DELETE FILENAME. Again it is possible to specify the drive to be used	

Expression	*Description*	*Page*
	as in DELETE FILENAME, D2. (DIR, DOS)	46
DELETE	(b) A DOS command used with PRINT CHR$(4) to remove a data file from a diskette. (DIR, PRG, DOS)	—
DIM	Allows for booking of a set of units of memory for numbers or strings. (PRG)	108
DRAW	Draws a shape, defined by a shape-table, in high-resolution graphics. Not used in this book. (DIR, PRG, GRAPH)	182
END	Ends a program. Need not be the last line of the program. (PRG)	33
EXEC	A DOS command similar to RUN used to execute files containing BASIC statements as data. (DIR, PRG, DOS)	—
EXP	The exponential function produces a number equal to the mathematical constant e, raised to the power of the number in brackets. (PRC, FN)	—
FLASH	This causes all output to the screen to flash, that is to change quickly and repeatedly from black on white to white on black. It is turned off by NORMAL. (DIR, PRG)	10
FOR	Used with TO and NEXT (and sometimes STEP). Creates a loop. Rarely used as a direct command. Used mainly within programs as a statement. Use colons as separators. (DIR, PRG)	47

Expression	*Description*	*Page*
FP	If Apple is in Integer BASIC this puts it into Applesoft (i.e. floating point) BASIC, if it is posible. (See INT.) (DIR)	—
FRE	Used with a number in brackets, so may be thought of as either a statement or a function. Produces a number indicating the number of bytes of memory still free or available. (PRG, FN)	26
GET	Apple anticipates a single character input from the keyboard. (PRG)	38
GOSUB	Used with RETURN and, sometimes with ON. Sends Apple to a specified subroutine. RETURN acts as the end of the subroutine and sends Apple back to the line after GOSUB. (PRG)	32
GOTO	Sends Apple to appropriate line in program, as in GOTO 200. Most often used as a statement. Used with ON, IF and THEN. (DIR, PRG)	51
GR	Changes the screen for low-resolution graphics. The top 20 lines are then reserved for graphics, while the bottom four lines are used for text. This is turned off by TEXT. (See HGR and HGR 2.) (DIR, PRG, GRAPH)	55
HCOLOR	Used in high-resolution graphics to choose a color, using an appropriate number as in HCOLOR=4. (See COLOR.) (DIR, PRG, GRAPH)	67
HGR	Changes the screen for high-resolution graphics. The top 20 lines are then reserved for graphics, while the bottom	

Expression	*Description*	*Page*
	four lines are used for text. Uses page one of high resolution graphics. This is turned off by TEXT. (See HGR2 and GR). (DIR, PRG, GRAPH)	66
HGR2	Same as HGR, except that the complete screen is reserved for high-resolution graphics. Can only work if Apple has at least 24K of memory. (DIR, PRG, GRAPH)	—
HIMEM	Changes the address of the highest memory location available to programs in BASIC. (DIR, PRG)	—
HLIN	Used in low-resolution graphics to draw a horizontal line across the screen. For example HLIN 12, 30 at 20. (DIR, PRG, GRAPH)	63
HOME	Clears all text off the screen and moves the cursor to the top left-hand corner. (DIR, PRG)	10
HPLOT	Used in high-resolution graphics to plot a point, or to draw a line using the word TO. (DIR, PRG, GRAPH)	68
HTAB	This is followed by a number between 1 and 255, as in HTAB 25. This moves the cursor out to the twenty-fifth position on the current line. (DIR, PRG)	137
IF	Used with THEN and with GOTO. Sets up a condition which allows Apple to decide which of two things to do next. (PRG)	39
INIT	A DOS command used to initialize a new diskette. (DIR, DOS)	42
INPUT	Apple anticipates an input from the key-	

Expression	*Description*	*Page*
	board (or from the diskette) which may be a number or string. (PRG)	20
INT	(a) Produces the integral part of the number inside the brackets. (PRG, FN)	86
	(b) If Apple is in Applesoft BASIC this puts it into Integer BASIC (if available). See FP. (DIR)	—
INVERSE	This causes all output to the screen to be printed as black on a white background. It is turned off by NORMAL. (DIR, PRG)	10
IN#	This is followed by a number between 1 and 7 and this refers to one of the eight slots for extra cards at the back of the Apple. It tells Apple to expect INPUT from whatever device is attached to this slot. (DIR, PRG)	174
LEFT$	Produces a part of the string in brackets, starting from the left. (PRG, STRFN)	121
LEN	Produces a number equal to the number of characters in the string. (PRG, STRFN)	121
LET	An optional word used to set a variable equal to a constant. (PRG)	11
LIST	Puts a listing of the current program on the screen. (DIR)	18
LIST A—B	List that part of the program between lines A and B, including A and B. (PRG)	18
LIST—B	List all lines in a program up to a specified line, i.e. B. (PRG)	18
LIST—A	List all lines in a program from a specified line onwards, i.e. A. (PRG)	18

Expression	*Description*	*Page*
LOAD	Used with disk drive to copy a program from diskette or cassette to Apple's memory. Must be followed by the program's name, as in LOAD FILENAME, when loading from diskette, but is used without a file name when loading from cassette. (DIR)	45
LOCK	A DOS command used to ensure that a file on a diskette cannot be erased, as in LOCK FILE. This lock can be removed by the UNLOCK command. A locked file on a diskette will have a star beside it in the CATALOG. (DIR, DOS)	—
LOG	The mathematical logarithm function to the exponential base. (PRG, FN)	144
LOMEM	Changes the address of the lowest memory location available to programs in BASIC. (DIR, PRG)	—
MAXFILES	A DOS command used to specify the number of active files to be permitted When it is not used three files are assumed. It should be used with caution. (DIR, DOS)	—
MID $	Produces a part of the string in brackets, according to fixed rules. (PRG, STRFN)	121
MON	A DOS command used to monitor the information passing between Apple and disks. Useful mainly when having problems with disk files. Turned off by NOMON. (DIR, DOS)	—
NEW	Wipes any existing program from Apple's memory. Can be used within a program. (DIR, PRG)	19

Expression	*Description*	*Page*
NEXT	See FOR — used to make a loop. (DIR)	47
NOMON	A DOS command used to turn off the MON command. (DIR, DOS)	—
NORMAL	Used to turn off the INVERSE or the FLASH command, so that output to the screen is normal again. (DIR, PRG)	10
NOT	Used to present a negative conditional. (PRG)	—
NOTRACE	Used to turn off the TRACE command. (DIR, PRG)	91
ON	Used with GOTO and GOSUB to direct Apple to one of a set of lines or subroutines according to an index number. (PRG)	—
ONERR GOTO	This may be used to stop Apple from leaving a program and halting execution when an error occurs. Used with RESUME. (PRG)	—
OPEN	A DOS command used within a program with PRINT CHR$(4) to open a data file. (PRG, DOS)	48
OR	This is the normal OR to distinguish two conditionals. (PRG)	—
PDL	Used to make effective the paddles or game controls. PDL(0) or PDL(1) normally refers to first two paddles. The values of these range from 0 to 255. (DIR, PRG)	—
PEEK	Used to find the number stored in a particular unit of memory. (PRG)	94

Expression	*Description*	*Page*
PLOT	Used in low-resolution graphics to plot a point. (DIR, PRG, GRAPH)	56
POKE	Used to place a particular number in a specified (numbered) unit of memory. (PRG)	94
POP	This has the effect of RETURN without a corresponding GOSUB. (DIR, PRG)	—
POS	Used with PRINT to specify the position of the cursor with respect to the left-hand margin. Positions are numbered from 0 to 39. (DIR, PRG)	—
POSITION	A DOS command used within a program with PRINT CHR$ to extract data from a specified field in a data file. (PRG, DOS)	—
PRINT	Can be used to print characters and numbers on the screen or on other specified devices. Can often be shortened to ?. (DIR, PRG)	5
PR#	This is used in the same way as IN# except that it implies PRINTING out to a device attached to the slot number specified. (DIR, PRG)	174
READ	(a) Used with DATA and RESTORE to allow a set of numerical data (or string) to be placed within a program from the start rather than input during a program run. (PRG)	74
READ	(b) A DOS command used within a program with PRINT CHR$(4) to read from a data file. (PRG, DOS)	48
RECALL	This loads or recalls arrays of data from a cassette tape. Used with STORE. (DIR, PRG)	—

Expression	*Description*	*Page*
REM	Short for REMARK, this allows a program to be annotated. (PRG)	25
RENAME	A DOS command used to change or RENAME a file on a diskette. (DIR, DOS)	47
RESTORE	Used with READ and DATA to reinstitute a set of data already used within a program. (DIR, PRG)	—
RESUME	Used with ONERR GOTO. (PRG)	—
RETURN	Used in association with GOSUB as an indication that a subroutine has ended. (PRG)	32
RIGHT $	Produces a part of the string in brackets, starting on the right. (PRG, STRFN)	121
RND	Produces a random number of up to nine digits between 0 and 1. (PRG, FN)	84
ROT	Used with DRAW and XDRAW to establish angle of rotation for the shape. (DIR, PRG, GRAPH)	—
RUN	Causes program to be executed. Can be used with a line number, such as RUN 200. (DIR, PRG)	18
SAVE	Used with disk-drive to copy a program from memory to diskette or cassette. Normally used outside a program as a direct command, but can be used in a program. When saving a program on diskette this command must be followed by the name of the program. If it is used without a file name this implies the use of a cassette tape rather than a diskette. *See* LOAD. (DIR, PRG)	44

Expression	*Description*	*Page*
SCALE	Used to establish an enlargement factor when using DRAW and XDRAW. (DIR, PRG, GRAPH)	—
SCRN	Used to establish the color code of any point on the low-resolution graphics screen. (DIR, PRG, GRAPH)	—
SGN	Changes a negative number to − 1 and a positive number to + 1 and leaves zero as zero. (PRG, FN)	—
SHLOAD	This loads a shape table from a cassette tape. (DIR, PRG)	—
SIN	The mathematical sine function. The number in brackets must be in radians. (PRG, FN)	70
SPC	Produces the number of spaces specified in the brackets following the function. (PRG, FN)	139
SPEED	Establishes the speed at which characters are sent to the screen (or other devices). The range is 0 to 255 and the format is, SPEED = 120. (DIR, PRG)	—
SQR	Produces the square root of the number in brackets. (PRG, FN)	140
STEP	See FOR and TO. Used to indicate size of step used in a loop. (PRG)	136
STOP	Used as a temporary stop. (PRG)	31
STORE	Used to save or store arrays of data on cassette tape. Used with RECALL. (DIR, PRG)	—
STR $	Changes a number into an "identical" string. (PRG, STRFN)	131

Expression	*Description*	*Page*
TAB	Used to move the cursor out the number of spaces specified in the brackets. (PRG, FN)	86
TAN	The mathematical tangent function. The number in brackets must be in radians. (PRG, FN)	—
TEXT	This turns off the graphics screen modes established with the words GR or HGR or HGR2. (DIR, PRG, GRAPH)	56
THEN	Used with IF to indicate one of two possible results of conditional statements. (PRG)	39
TO	See FOR. Used with FOR, STEP and NEXT in loops. (PRG)	47
TRACE	Used to debug programs. It causes the line number of each executed line to appear on the screen as it is executed. It is turned off by NOTRACE. (DIR, PRG)	91
UNLOCK	A DOS command used to remove the effect of LOCK on a diskette file. This makes it possible for the file to be erased. (DIR, DOS)	—
USR	A machine-code transferral statement. (PRG)	—
VAL	Produces a number, from the left of a string, if it is numeric. (PRG, STRFN)	118
VERIFY	Used with SAVE to check that APPLE has copied program correctly on to diskette. Must specify name of program. (DIR)	44
VLIN	Used in Low Resolution Graphics to draw	

Expression	*Description*	*Page*
	a vertical line down the screen. For example VLIN 10, 30 at 20. (DIR, PRG, GRAPH)	63
VTAB	This is followed by a number between 1 and 24, as in VTAB 12. This moves the cursor to the beginning of the twelfth line across the screen starting from the top. (DIR, PRG)	137
WAIT	Used to make a program pause, this being dependent on the status of a specified memory location. (DIR, PRG)	—
WRITE	A DOS command used within a program with PRINT CHR$(4) to write to a data file. (PRG, DOS)	48
XDRAW	Used with DRAW to erase shapes drawn on the screen. (DIR, PRG, GRAPH)	—

SYMBOLS

Expression	*Description*	*Page*
=	There are two meanings of this: the normal equality meaning and the notion of a variable Ax becoming a specified value.	11
^	This means "to the power of".	89
/	The symbol for division.	6
*	The symbol for multiplication. It must not be left out, as it sometimes is in algebra.	6
+	The symbol for addition.	6
−	The symbol for subtraction.	6

Expression	*Description*	*Page*
<	This means "is less than".	62
>	This means "is greater than".	62
< >	This means "is not equal to".	119
< =	This means "is less than or equal to".	—
> =	This means "is greater than or equal to".	—
:	Used to separate two or more statements used in a single line of BASIC.	12
;	Used in PRINT statements to place numbers side by side or to concatenate strings.	23
,	Used in PRINT statements to space out the numbers and strings being printed.	22
?	Used as shorthand for PRINT.	7
$	Used with variable names to indicate string variables.	13
%	Used with variable names to indicate integer variables.	87
RETURN key	This key is pressed when the user wishes to indicate that he has completed an input of some sort.	4
" "	Used around strings to indicate beginning and end.	8

Appendix D Tables of Peek, Poke and CHR$ Numbers

Table D1 Keyboard Peek and Poke Numbers

The bottom number represents the symbol in reverse mode; the second number represents the symbol in flash mode; the top two numbers represent the symbol in normal mode.

225	226	227	228	229	230	231	232	233		234	253
161	162	163	164	165	166	167	168	169		170	189
97	98	99	100	101	102	103	104	105		106	125
33	34	35	36	37	38	39	40	41		42	61
!	"	#	$	%	&	'	(	)		*	=
241	242	243	244	245	246	247	248	249	240	250	237
177	178	179	180	181	182	183	184	185	176	186	173
113	114	115	116	117	118	119	120	121	112	122	109
49	50	51	52	53	54	55	56	57	48	58	45
1	2	3	4	5	6	7	8	9	0	:	—

209	218	197	210	212	217	213	201	207	208	192
145	151	133	146	148	153	149	137	143	144	128
81	87	69	82	84	89	85	73	79	80	64
17	23	5	18	20	25	21	9	15	16	0
Q	W	E	R	T	Y	U	I	O	P	@

193	211	196	198	199	200	202	203	204	251	235
129	147	132	134	135	136	138	139	140	187	171
65	83	68	70	71	72	74	75	76	123	107
1	19	4	6	7	8	10	11	12	59	43
A	S	D	F	G	H	J	K	L	;	+

218	216	195	214	194	206	205	236	238	239	222	252	254	255
154	152	131	150	130	142	141	172	174	175	158	188	190	191
90	88	67	86	66	78	77	108	110	111	94	124	126	127
26	24	3	22	2	14	13	44	46	47	30	60	62	63
Z	X	C	V	B	N	M	,	.	/	^	<	>	?

	224
	160
	96
SPACE BAR	32

Table D2 Peek and Poke Numbers

Symbols	*Rev. Mode*	*Flash Mode*	*Normal Mode*		*Symbols*	*Rev. Mode*	*Flash Mode*	*Normal Mode*	
@	0	64	128	192		32	96	160	224
A	1	65	129	193	!	33	97	161	225
B	2	66	130	194	"	34	98	162	226
C	3	67	131	195	#	35	99	163	227
D	4	68	132	196	$	36	100	164	228
E	5	69	133	197	%	37	101	165	229
F	6	70	134	198	&	38	102	166	230
G	7	71	135	199	'	39	103	167	231
H	8	72	136	200	(	40	104	168	232
I	9	73	137	201	)	41	105	169	233
J	10	74	138	202	*	42	106	170	234
K	11	75	139	203	+	43	107	171	235
L	12	76	140	204	,	44	108	172	236
M	13	77	141	205	—	45	109	173	237
N	14	78	142	206	.	46	110	174	238
O	15	79	143	207	/	47	111	175	239
P	16	80	144	208	0	48	112	176	240
Q	17	81	145	209	1	49	113	177	241
R	18	82	146	210	2	50	114	178	242
S	19	83	147	211	3	51	115	179	243
T	20	84	148	212	4	52	116	180	244
U	21	85	149	213	5	53	117	181	245
V	22	86	150	214	6	54	118	182	246
W	23	87	151	215	7	55	119	183	247
X	24	88	152	216	8	56	120	184	248
Y	25	89	153	217	9	57	121	185	249
Z	26	90	154	218	:	58	122	186	250
[	27	91	155	219	;	59	123	187	251
\	28	92	156	220	<	60	124	188	252
]	29	93	157	221	=	61	125	189	253
∧	30	94	158	222	>	62	126	190	254
—	31	95	159	223	?	63	127	191	255

Table D3 Peek and Poke Screen Numbers

Columns 1 2 3 4 5 6 7 8 9 0 1 2 3 4 5 6 7 8 9 0 1 2 3 4 5 6 7 8 9 0 1 2 3 4 5 6 7 8 9 0

First no. on row	*Rows*	Numbers marked in the grid	Row	Last no. on row
1024	1		1	1063
1152	2		2	1191
1280	3		3	1319
1408	4		4	1447
1536	5	1546, 1566	5	1575
1664	6		6	1703
1792	7		7	1831
1920	8		8	1959
1064	9		9	1103
1192	10	1197, 1212	10	1231
1320	11		11	1359
1448	12		12	1487
1576	13		13	1615
1704	14		14	1743
1832	15	1862	15	1871
1960	16		16	1999
1104	17		17	1143
1232	18		18	1271
1360	19		19	1399
1488	20	1503	20	1527
1616	21		21	1655
1744	22		22	1783
1872	23		23	1911
2000	24		24	2039

Missing numbers 1144 – 1151, 1272 – 1279, 1400 – 1407, 1528 – 1535, 1656 – 1663, 1784 – 1791, 1912 – 1919, 2040 – 2047

Table D4 CHR$ Numbers

No symbols	*As shown*	*No symbols*	*As shown*	*As shown*			
0	64 @	128	192 @	32	96	160	224
1	65 A	129	193 A	33 !	97 !	161 !	225 !
2	66 B	130	194 B	34 ”	98 ”	162 ”	226 ”
3	67 C	131	195 C	35 #	99 #	163 #	227 #
4	68 D	132	196 D	36 $	100 $	164 $	228 $
5	69 E	133	197 E	37 %	101 %	165 %	229 %
6	70 F	134	198 F	38 &	102 &	166 &	230 &
7	71 G	135	199 G	39 ′	103 ′	167 ′	231 ′
8	72 H	136	200 H	40 (	104 (	168 (	232 (
9	73 I	137	201 I	41)	105)	169)	233)
10	74 J	138	202 J	42 *	106 *	170 *	234 *
11	75 K	139	203 K	43 +	107 +	171 +	235 +
12	76 L	140	204 L	44 ,	108 ,	172 ,	236 ,
13	77 M	141	205 M	45 —	109 —	173 —	237 —
14	78 N	142	206 N	46 .	110 .	174 .	238 .
15	79 O	143	207 O	47 /	111 /	175 /	239 /
16	80 P	144	208 P	48 0	112 0	176 0	240 0
17	81 Q	145	209 Q	49 1	113 1	177 1	241 1
18	82 R	146	210 R	50 2	114 2	178 2	242 2
19	83 S	147	211 S	51 3	115 3	179 3	243 3
20	84 T	148	212 T	52 4	116 4	180 4	244 4
21	85 U	149	213 U	53 5	117 5	181 5	245 5
22	86 V	150	214 V	54 6	118 6	182 6	246 6
23	87 W	151	215 W	55 7	119 7	183 7	247 7
24	88 X	152	216 X	56 8	120 8	184 8	248 8
25	89 Y	153	217 Y	57 9	121 9	185 9	249 9
26	90 Z	154	218 Z	58 :	122 :	186 :	250 :
27	91 [	155	219 [	59 ;	123 ;	187 ;	251 ;
28	92 \	156	220 \	60 <	124 <	188 <	252 <
29	93]	157	221]	61 =	125 =	189 =	253 =
30	94 ∧	158	222 ∧	62 >	126 >	190 >	254 >
31	95 _	159	223 _	63 ?	127 ?	191 ?	255 ?

(These are ASCII codes. ASCII is short for American Standard Code for Information Interchange. Although the numbers 96 to 255 produce codes which are the same as those produced by the smaller numbers, there are occasions when Applesoft BASIC does not recognize them as being the same. This is true, for example, with logic operations on strings and when using a printer.)

Appendix E Other Languages and Software

INTRODUCTION

Applesoft Extended Floating Point BASIC is the language used in the descriptions, explanations and examples throughout this book. It is probably the language most often used on Apple, but other languages are available, and a few notes about some of these will now be given.

INTEGER BASIC

On most Apples, Integer BASIC is available as well as Applesoft (see Appendix A). You can tell when you are in Integer BASIC by the form of the prompt sign which appears with the flashing cursor. In Applesoft BASIC this is a closing square bracket,], but in Integer BASIC it is >, that is a right-facing arrowhead. The main difference between the two BASICs is, as suggested by their names, that Applesoft Floating Point BASIC can work directly with numbers involving decimal fractions, whilst Integer BASIC can only operate directly with whole numbers or integers. There are, also, a number of important differences between the commands used in the two languages and between the ways in which they execute commands.

A considerable range of commands which can be included in an Applesoft program will not work in Integer BASIC. This means either that the facility in question is not available at all or that it has to be achieved through some other programming technique.

Commands which are available in Applesoft, but not in Integer BASIC, are shown in the list at the end of this Appendix. The most important differences from our point of view restrict both the graphics facilities and the string-handling facilities of Integer BASIC as compared with Applesoft BASIC.

SPECIAL INTEGER BASIC COMMANDS

There are, however, a few commands in Integer BASIC which have no equivalent in Applesoft.

AUTO. This is a command which tells Apple to number the lines in a program automatically, starting at a specified initial number and increasing in tens. For example this command:

AUTO 100

will make Apple begin numbering the program lines at line 100, followed by 110, 120, and so on. You will not have to put in any line numbers, as they will appear automatically on the screen when you press RETURN at the end of a line. If you want a gap other than 10 between successive line numbers you can specify this. For example, AUTO 500, 100 will make Apple begin numbering lines at 500 and it will then go up in hundreds as follows: 500, 600, 700.

Indeed, Apple will number anything you type in whilst the AUTO command is in operation, including a RUN command. This means that when you type in RUN and press RETURN to test your program, RUN will become part of the program. To get out of this problem, hold the CTRL key and press X. Then you can type in RUN without it being numbered as a line. CTRL and X can also be used to insert lines with numbers out of the automatic sequence. So if you suddenly realize you have forgotten a line or need some extra operation you can hold CTRL and press X and then type in a line with a number of your own choice.

MAN. The CTRL and X command will allow you to insert one line or type in the RUN command, but if you want to stop the AUTO function altogether you need to use CTRL and X, and follow this by typing in MAN. This returns you to a situation where you must number each line yourself.

DSP. This is short for DISPLAY and is a facility which allows you to look at the current value of any particular variable. If you type DSP A this will cause Apple to print out the current value of the variable A. If you want the DSP function to operate during the run of a program, that is to show you the current value of one or more variable at some point or points during the operation of the program, you must use DSP as part of the program, that is with a line number: for example, 140 DSP A.

MOD. This function is related to Integer BASIC's inability to handle decimals. When a calculation involving division is carried out a problem arises in Integer BASIC if the answer is not a whole number. Thus while

```
PRINT 25/5
```

will produce the expected answer, that is 5

```
PRINT 28/5
```

will also produce the answer 5 because Integer BASIC cannot use decimal fractions, but will only give you the number of times 5 can be divided into 28. It does this and then ignores the remainder. To get information about the remainder it is necessary to use MOD, which is short for MODULO. So in a division calculation where we need to know whether there is a remainder and, if so, what it is, we have to use a two-stage operation. Here is an example:

```
10 PRINT 28/5
20 PRINT 28 MOD 5
```

If we run this Apple will respond

```
5
3
```

that is, 5 goes into 28 five times and their is a remainder or 3.

COMMON FACILITIES

There are a number of cases where the same facility is available in both Applesoft and Integer BASIC, but the command used to activate it differs. These are now listed with comments.

Applesoft command	*Integer command*
CLEAR	CLR
HOME	CALL—936
INVERSE	POKE 50, 127
NORMAL	POKE 50, 255
X%	X
< >	#

These differences are almost self-explanatory. The alternative form of HOME, that is CALL–936, can also be used as a substitute for HOME in Applesoft. The X% means that the variable in question in Applesoft is an integer, and, of course, it is unnecessary to give it a special symbol in Integer BASIC so X by itself will do. The signs < > and #, of course, mean "is not equal to".

There are a few other differences that need mention.

(a) Applesoft has two words which do more or less the same job, that is TAB and HTAB, whereas Integer BASIC just has TAB.

(b) In Applesoft we can use the word ON as follows:

```
ON X GOTO 100, 120, 140, 160
ON X GOSUB 100, 120, 140, 160,
```

In Integer BASIC this is replaced by a function version of the same notion:

```
GOTO    100 + 20*X
GOSUB   100 + 20*X
```

(c) In Applesoft BASIC a program line is checked for syntax errors by the machine when the program is run, so that error messages usually appear only when the program is tested by running it (except in obvious cases, such as where you have omitted the line number). With Integer BASIC, however, each line is checked when you press RETURN after typing it in. This means that some types of errors are more immediately signalled.

(d) Only the first two characters of a variable name are significant in Applesoft BASIC, whilst in Integer BASIC all the characters in a variable name are significant. So whilst variables called DULL and DUCK would be regarded as the same in Applesoft, Integer BASIC would be able to distinguish them.

(e) The END command is optional in Applesoft BASIC programs.

(f) In Applesoft BASIC, NEXT may be used alone in a loop.

```
10 FOR N=1 TO 10
20 NEXT
```

In Integer BASIC the NEXT must always be followed by a variable name, so line 20 above would have to be NEXT N.

APPLESOFT WORDS NOT IN INTEGER BASIC

ATN
CHR$
COS
DATA
DEF FN
DRAW
EXP
FLASH
FN
FRE
GET
H COLOR
HGR
HGR2
H PLOT
INT
INVERSE
LEFT$
LOG
LOMEM
MID$
NORMAL
ON——GOSUB
ON——GOTO
ONERR——GO TO
POS
READ
RECALL
RESTORE
RESUME
RIGHTS
ROT
SCALE
SH LOAD
SIN
SPC
SPEED
SQR
STOP
STORE
STR$
TAN
USR
VAL
WAIT
X DRAW

PASCAL

This language is also now available on Apple. However, you must first instal a language card (see Appendix A) and, if necessary, update from DOS 3.2 to DOS 3.3. There is a considerable amount of literature available about Pascal and Apple Computers produce a manual about how to use their particular version of it (see also Appendix H). Here we will refer only to the ways in which it differs from BASIC and to some aspects of its use that are of some interest.

WHY PASCAL

Pascal is the best known example of what is called a *structured* language, or rather a language that allows and encourages structured programming. In detail this is a complex notion but its general meaning is obvious. A structured program is one where each routine is isolated and self-dependent and where the complete set of routines are put together in a coherent and logical way. As well as this the programming techniques to be used, especially in programming loops, discourage the undisciplined movement from one section of the program to another. This is usually done, for example in BASIC, by writing GOTO with a line number. To do this is to go against the modular spirit of structured programming.

USING PASCAL

First of all Pascal is not an interactive language on Apple. This means that you do not get quick and repeated feedback at regular intervals while generating and debugging a program. You must write the whole program, or at least a full routine from the program, then ask Apple to compile it, that is (essentially) to translate it into machine-code, and then, if it is bug-free, to run it. If it has mistakes in it these may be found during the compiling stage and they will be reported on the screen; alternatively they may not become obvious until you try to run the program. This last normally means that, although the program is technically acceptable in that it does compile, it does not do the job that you want it to do.

PASCAL AND BASIC

Perhaps the best way to illustrate the way Pascal differs from BASIC is to show a short program in each language doing precisely the same thing. That is, it asks for a set of data and draws a bar-graph to illustrate this data.

First the BASIC program. This accepts the data input, checks each input against a number of criteria – is it greater than zero? Is it an integer? Is it greater than forty? And so on – and uses a subroutine (lines 170 to 200) to actually draw the bars of the graph on the screen. It is not a very elegant program, full of GOTO and GOSUB statements, and it is quite difficult to be sure about what is going on. (We may have cheated a bit by making it more awkward than it needed to be.)

```
  5 HOME
 10 INPUT "INPUT THE NUMBER OF DATA POINTS    "; N
 25 PRINT "NOW INPUT EACH DATA POINT"
 27 PRINT
 29 FOR I = 1 TO N
 30 INPUT "   "; NUMBER
 40 LTH = INT (NUMBER)
 50 IF NUMBER > (LTH + 0.5) THEN LTH = LTH + 1
 60 IF LTH > 0 GOTO 100
 70 LTH = 0
 80 GOSUB 170
 90 GOTO 150
100 IF LTH < 40 GOTO 140
```

```
110 LTH = 40
120 GOSUB 170
130 GOTO 150
140 GOSUB 170
150 NEXT I
160 END
170 FOR J = 1 TO LTH
180 PRINT "*";
190 NEXT J
193 IF LTH = 40 GOTO 200
195 PRINT
200 RETURN
```

Now the Pascal program to do the same job:

```
PROGRAM EXPASCAL ;

VAR X, Y, N : INTEGER ;
    NUMBER : REAL ;

PROCEDURE DRAW (LENGTH : INTEGER) ;
VAR I : INTEGER ;
BEGIN
    FOR I : = 1 TO LENGTH DO
    WRITE ('*') ;
    WRITELIN ;
END ;

BEGIN
    PAGE (OUTPUT) ;
    WRITE ('INPUT THE NUMBER OF DATA POINTS    ') ;
    READLN(N) ;
    WRITELN ('NOW INPUT EACH DATA POINT') ;
    WRITELN ;
    FOR X : = 1 TO N DO
    BEGIN
    READLN(NUMBER) ;
    Y : = ROUND(NUMBER) ;
    IF Y < 0 THEN DRAW (0)
    ELSE IF Y > 40 THEN DRAW (40)
    ELSE DRAW (Y)
    END
END.
```

The first line names the program and the next two lines declare the variables to be used. This is done in every Pascal program, but it only happens at the beginning, no matter how long the program. Then a procedure called DRAW is defined. The procedure will be called on later to draw the bars, and is seven lines long. The rest of the program accepts input, rounds off the input to integers using the ROUND statement, and in the last three lines before the two END lines checks the data against the same criteria as before, using IF and ELSE. In each case it calls on the DRAW procedure already defined to make the bar lines.

The advantages of this should already be obvious to some extent, but in larger programs this method, that is declaring procedures and then calling on them, lends to better program legibility and the probability of fewer bugs. Notice also that we can use full-length words like LENGTH and NUMBER for variables.

OTHER LANGUAGES

A great many other languages are now available on Apple and the existence of the language card adds greatly to the variety of possibilities. As well as this, other language implementations are being produced regularly. For example, the well-known educational language LOGO is now available and part of its graphics system is also available in Apple Pascal using the name *Turtle Graphics*.

Apple Pilot is a version of another educational language specially designed for Apple. It allows inexperienced programmers to produce programs in a fairly straightforward Computer-Assisted Learning mode using a very small number of simple commands.

There is now an Apple FORTRAN, which allows those who have become used to this language over the years to use it on the Apple, and there is also an Apple COBOL system. Finally, the artificial intelligence language LISP is now also available.

SOFTWARE

It would be impossible to do more than skim the surface of the range of software that can now be purchased to be used with Apple. Some of this like VISICALC can, with a range of business problems, actually function as a sort of language in itself. In fact VISICALC is now just one of a range of programs for businessmen which appear under this label and which cover a variety of techniques.

Data base management systems are also now available with considerable levels of sophistication for a great variety of uses. Programs dedicated to the needs of specific types of businesses such as Hotel Management, Estate Agencies, Investment Houses, Stock Control Agencies, and so on are also available.

Finally, there is a system of television viewdata accession available, and a number of quite sophisticated music programs allowing for composition, playing and analysis.

Appendix F Base Sixteen Numbers

INTRODUCTION

We discovered in Chapter 7 that we need sometimes to be able to translate numbers from base ten to base sixteen and vice versa. In order to describe properly the whole idea of bases in arithmetic and the particular importance of base sixteen in computing we would need much more space than we have available here. We can, however, try to make the actual translation process as simple and direct as possible. We do this now in two ways: firstly by describing briefly the process and secondly by using reference tables.

BASE SIXTEEN

Our number system is based on two important practices. Firstly, we use a limited or finite number of symbols to represent numbers. In our normal counting we need only use ten symbols, that is the set: 0, 1, 2, 3, 4, 5, 6, 7, 8, 9. We know that we can represent any number by using these ten symbols in various combinations and repetitions. This raises the second practice, which is that the meaning or value of each symbol depends on its position with respect to the other symbols. For example we know that the four in 347 means four tens because the seven must mean seven units. So in base-ten arithmetic we need ten symbols and we know what they mean by looking at where they are placed.

This means that, in base sixteen, we need sixteen symbols and to make up the full set we make use of letters of the alphabet as follows:

Base sixteen	–	0	1	2	3	4	5	6	7	8	9	A	B	C	D	E	F	10
Base ten	–	0	1	2	3	4	5	6	7	8	9	10	11	12	13	14	15	16

We have written the same numbers in base ten for comparison. Note that in base ten when we reach 9, the next number, i.e. ten, uses the symbols 0 and 1 again like this, 10, meaning one ten and zero units. So in base sixteen in parallel to this, when we reach F (or 15), then the next number, i.e. sixteen, uses the symbols 0 and 1 again in the same way. Therefore in base sixteen, 10 means one sixteen and zero units. Similarly 20 means two sixteens and zero units (that is 32 in base ten), and so on. This also means that the base ten number 99 — which means nine tens and nine units — is paralleled in base sixteen by FF — which means fifteen sixteens and fifteen units. In both cases the next number is 100 which means ten tens in base ten, and sixteen sixteens in base sixteen. The process continues in this way.

REFERENCE TABLES

We now present two tables which allow us to translate directly, from and to base sixteen, all base sixteen numbers from 00 to FF.

Table F1 translates from base sixteen to base ten. It is used as follows. Suppose we wish to change the number C7 into base ten. We start on the left, where it says First Digit, and find the row with a C. Then move along this row to the column with 7 at the top where it says Second Digit. The number you will find there is 199. So C7 in base sixteen is equivalent to 199 in base ten.

Table F2 does the translation from base ten to base sixteen. Start on the left where it says First Digits and find the row with a 12. Then move along this row to the column with a 7 at the top where it says Last Digit. The number you will find is 7F. So 124 in base ten becomes 7F in base sixteen.

Table F1. Base Sixteen to Base Ten

		Second Digit															
		0	1	2	3	4	5	6	7	8	9	A	B	C	D	E	F
	0	000	001	002	003	004	005	006	007	008	009	010	011	012	013	014	015
	1	016	017	018	019	020	021	022	023	024	025	026	027	028	029	030	031
	2	032	033	034	035	036	037	038	039	040	041	042	043	044	045	046	047
	3	048	049	050	051	052	053	054	055	056	057	058	059	060	061	062	063
	4	064	065	066	067	068	069	070	071	072	073	074	075	076	077	078	079
	5	080	081	082	083	084	085	086	087	088	089	090	091	092	093	094	095
First	6	096	097	098	099	100	101	102	103	104	105	106	107	108	109	110	111
Digit	7	112	113	114	115	116	117	118	119	120	121	122	123	124	125	126	127
	8	128	129	130	131	132	133	134	135	136	137	138	139	140	141	142	143
	9	144	145	146	147	148	149	150	151	152	153	154	155	156	157	158	159
	A	160	161	162	163	164	165	166	167	168	169	170	171	172	173	174	175
	B	176	177	178	179	180	181	182	183	184	185	186	187	188	189	190	191
	C	192	193	194	195	196	197	198	199	200	201	202	203	204	205	206	207
	D	208	209	210	211	212	213	214	215	216	217	218	219	220	221	222	223
	E	224	225	226	227	228	229	230	231	232	233	234	235	236	237	238	239
	F	240	241	242	243	244	245	246	247	248	249	250	251	252	253	254	255

Table F2. Base Ten to Base Sixteen

Last Digit

First Digits	0	1	2	3	4	5	6	7	8	9
0	00	01	02	03	04	05	06	07	08	09
1	0A	0B	0C	0D	0E	0F	10	11	12	13
2	14	15	16	17	18	19	1A	1B	1C	1D
3	1E	1F	20	21	22	23	24	25	26	27
4	28	29	2A	2B	2C	2D	2E	2F	30	31
5	32	33	34	35	36	37	38	39	3A	3B
6	3C	3D	3E	3F	40	41	42	43	44	45
7	46	47	48	49	4A	4B	4C	4D	4E	4F
8	50	51	52	53	54	55	56	57	58	59
9	5A	5B	5C	5D	5E	5F	60	61	62	63
10	64	65	66	67	68	69	6A	6B	6C	6D
11	6E	6F	70	71	72	73	74	75	76	77
12	78	79	7A	7B	7C	7D	7E	7F	80	81
13	82	83	84	85	86	87	88	89	8A	8B
14	8C	8D	8E	8F	90	91	92	93	94	95
15	96	97	98	99	9A	9B	9C	9D	9E	9F
16	A0	A1	A2	A3	A4	A5	A6	A7	A8	A9
17	AA	AB	AC	AD	AE	AF	B0	B1	B2	B3
18	B4	B5	B6	B7	B8	B9	BA	BB	BC	BD
19	BE	BF	C0	C1	C2	C3	C4	C5	C6	C7
20	C8	C9	CA	CB	CC	CD	CE	CF	D0	D1
21	D2	D3	D4	D5	D6	D7	D8	D9	DA	DB
22	DC	DD	DE	DF	E0	E1	E2	E3	E4	E5
23	E6	E7	E8	E9	EA	EB	EC	ED	EE	EF
24	F0	F1	F2	F3	F4	F5	F6	F7	F8	F9
25	FA	FB	FC	FD	FE	FF				

Appendix G Answers to Problems

CHAPTER 1

1. (a) ?4.27+31.28+173.1 **CR**

   208.65

   (b) ?13452/12 **CR**

   1121

   (c) ?(6.5/100)*73216 **CR**

   4759.04

   (d) ?12345+(11/100)*12345 **CR**

   13702.95

   (e) ?5–(1.34+1.78+0.69) **CR**

   1.19

2. A=650 : B=.02 : C=71 **CR**

   D=A+B* A–C : ?D **CR**

   592

   D=D+B*D–C : ?D **CR**

   532.84

   472.4968

   410.946736

   348.165671

3. The result is that eventually there are four complete rows made up entirely of the letter A.

   The result this time is that four rows fill up more quickly with repetitions of 12345.

CHAPTER 2

1.

```
 20 REM NAMES AND
 30 REM BANK BALANCES
 40 PRINT "INPUT 6 NAMES. IN EACH CASE PUT IN"
 50 PRINT "NAME AND THEN PUT BALANCE ON NEXT LINE"
 55 PRINT : PRINT "THE FREE MEMORY IN BYTES IS"
 60 PRINT 65535+FRE (0)
100 INPUT A$
110 INPUT A
120 INPUT B$
130 INPUT B
140 INPUT C$
150 INPUT C
160 INPUT D$
170 INPUT D
180 INPUT E$
190 INPUT E
200 INPUT F$
210 INPUT F
220 PRINT A$, A
230 PRINT B$, B
240 PRINT C$, C
250 PRINT D$, D
260 PRINT E$, E
270 PRINT F$, F
275 PRINT : PRINT "THE FREE MEMORY NOW IS"
280 PRINT 65536+FRE (0)
```

2.

```
 20 REM NAMES
 30 REM AND
 40 REM ADDRESSES
 45 PRINT "FREE MEMORY IS"
 47 PRINT 65535+FRE (0)
 50 PRINT "INPUT 4 NAMES AND ADDRESSES, IN EACH"
 60 PRINT "CASE PUT THE NAME IN AND"
 70 PRINT "THEN THE ADDRESS IN 3 LINES"
 80 PRINT "DO NOT USE ANY COMMAS OR FULL COLONS"
 90 PRINT "FIRST ONE"
100 INPUT A1$
110 INPUT B1$
```

```
120 INPUT C1$
130 INPUT D1$
135 PRINT "NEXT ONE"
140 INPUT A2$
150 INPUT B2$
160 INPUT C2$
170 INPUT D2$
175 PRINT "NEXT ONE"
180 INPUT A3$
190 INPUT B3$
200 INPUT C3$
210 INPUT D3$
215 PRINT "LAST ONE"
220 INPUT A4$
230 INPUT B4$
240 INPUT C4$
250 INPUT D4$
255 REM PRINT OUT BEGINS
260 PRINT A1$, B1$
270 PRINT, C1$
280 PRINT, D1$
290 PRINT A2$, B2$
300 PRINT, C2$
310 PRINT, D2$
320 PRINT A3$, B3$
330 PRINT, C3$
340 PRINT, D3$
350 PRINT A4$, B4$
360 PRINT, C4$
370 PRINT, D4$
380 PRINT "FREE MEMORY NOW IS"
390 PRINT 65535+FRE (0)
```

3.

```
10 REM STANDARD LETTER
15 HOME
20 PRINT "   STANDARD LETTER"
30 PRINT "WHEN RESPONDING TO QUESTIONS DO NOT
   USE ANY COMMAS"
40 PRINT "PUT IN TODAY'S DATE"
50 INPUT A$
60 PRINT "NOW INPUT LETTER RECIPIENT"
```

```
70 INPUT B$
80 PRINT "NOW INPUT REASON FOR MEETING"
90 INPUT C$
100 PRINT "NOW TYPE IN THE DATE WHEN"
105 PRINT "YOU WILL BE AVAILABLE"
110 INPUT D$
120 PRINT "NOW TYPE IN THE TIME WHEN"
125 PRINT "YOU WILL BE AVAILABLE"
130 INPUT E$
140 PRINT "FINALLY TYPE IN WHERE"
145 PRINT "YOU WILL BE AVAILABLE"
150 INPUT F$
200 PRINT "EDUCATION CENTER"
210 PRINT "NEW UNIVERSITY OF ULSTER"
220 PRINT "COLERAINE, N. IRELAND"
230 PRINT A$
240 PRINT "DEAR     "B$
250 PRINT "          I WOULD LIKE TO ARRANGE"
260 PRINT "A MEETING TO DISCUSS"
270 PRINT "              "C$
280 PRINT "I WOULD BE AVAILABLE ON "D$
290 PRINT "IN"F$"AT"E$
300 PRINT "I WOULD BE GRATEFUL IF YOU COULD"
310 PRINT "   COME AT THIS TIME"
320 PRINT "   YOURS SINCERELY"
340 PRINT "              STUART MARRIOTT"
```

CHAPTER 3

1.
```
5 HOME
10 PRINT "      **WEIGHT CONVERSION**"
15 PRINT
17 GOSUB 2000
20 PRINT "THIS PROGRAM CONVERTS POUNDS WEIGHT": PRINT
25 PRINT "INTO GRAMS. ONE POUND IS TAKEN": PRINT
30 PRINT "TO BE EQUAL TO 435.592 GRAMS" : PRINT
40 PRINT "WHEN YOU SEE THE QUESTION MARK": PRINT
50 PRINT "PUT IN THE NUMBER OF POUNDS YOU": PRINT
60 PRINT "WISH TO CONVERT"
65 GOSUB 2000
70 GOSUB 3000
```

```
75 GOSUB 2000
80 PRINT "NOW INPUT THE NUMBER AND PRESS RETURN"
85 GOSUB 2000
200 INPUT A
210 B=A * 453.592
220 GOSUB 2000
230 PRINT "THE NUMBER OF POUNDS IS:-     "A
240 PRINT "THE NUMBER OF GRAMS IS:-     "B
250 GOSUB 2000
260 PRINT "DO YOU WISH TO MAKE ANOTHER CONVERSION?": PRINT
270 PRINT "IF SO, INPUT YES, OTHERWISE NO.": PRINT
280 INPUT A$: IF A$ = "YES" THEN 5
290 GOSUB 2000
300 PRINT "THANK YOU. IF YOU WISH TO START AGAIN"
310 PRINT : PRINT "TYPE IN 'RUN' AND PRESS 'RETURN' "
320 PRINT : PRINT "GOODBYE FOR NOW."
330 END
2000 FOR N=1 TO 4: PRINT : NEXT : RETURN
3000 PRINT "          **PRESS ANY KEY**"
3010 GET A$
3020 RETURN
```

2.

```
5 HOME
10 PRINT "       ***AVERAGING***"
20 GOSUB 2000
40 PRINT "THIS PROGRAM ACCEPTS A SET OF NUMBERS": PRINT
50 PRINT "FINDS THEIR TOTAL AND CALCULATES": PRINT
60 PRINT "AN AVERAGE. PUT THEM IN ONE AT A    " : PRINT
70 PRINT "TIME. AFTER THE LAST ONE PUT IN -99."
80 GOSUB 2000
82 GOSUB 3000
85 GOSUB 2000
90 C=0 : T=0
100 INPUT A
110 IF A=-99 THEN 160
120 T=T+A
130 C=C+1
140 GOSUB 2000
150 GOTO 100
160 AV=T/C
170 GOSUB 2000
```

```
 180 PRINT "YOU PUT IN " C "NUMBERS"
 190 PRINT "   THEIR TOTAL IS:-    " T
 200 PRINT "THEIR AVERAGE IS:-        "AV
 210 END
2000 PRINT : PRINT : PRINT : RETURN
3000 PRINT "        ***PRESS ANY KEY***"
3010 GET A$
3020 RETURN
```

3.

```
  5 HOME
 10 PRINT "        ***MONEY CONVERSION***"
 20 GOSUB 2000
 40 PRINT "THIS PROGRAM ACCEPTS A SUM OF MONEY": PRINT
 50 PRINT "IN ONE CURRENCY AND CONVERTS IT": PRINT
 60 PRINT "INTO THE EQUIVALENT AMOUNT IN 4": PRINT
 70 PRINT "OTHER CURRENCIES. YOU CHOOSE THE OTHER ": PRINT
 71 PRINT "CURRENCIES AND INPUT THE ": PRINT
 72 PRINT "RATE OF EXCHANGE FOR EACH": PRINT
 80 GOSUB 2000
 82 GOSUB 3000
 85 GOSUB 2000
 90 PRINT "INPUT THE NAME OF THE FIRST OF THE FOUR": PRINT
 95 PRINT "CURRENCIES YOU WANT TO CONVERT": PRINT
 97 PRINT "YOUR OWN MONEY INTO": PRINT
100 INPUT A$
110 PRINT : PRINT "INPUT THE NAME OF THE SECOND CURRENCY":
    PRINT
120 INPUT B$
130 PRINT : PRINT "INPUT THE NAME OF THE THIRD CURRENCY": PRINT
140 INPUT C$
150 PRINT : PRINT "INPUT THE NAME OF THE FOURTH CURRENCY":
    PRINT
160 INPUT D$
170 GOSUB 2000
180 PRINT "NOW PUT IN THE CURRENT EXCHANGE RATE": PRINT
190 PRINT "FOR EACH OF THESE CURRENCIES." : PRINT
200 PRINT A$ : INPUT A : PRINT
210 PRINT B$ : INPUT B : PRINT
220 PRINT C$: INPUT C : PRINT
230 PRINT D$: INPUT D : PRINT
240 PRINT "NOW INPUT THE NUMBER OF UNITS OF": PRINT
```

```
 250 PRINT "YOUR OWN CURRENCY THAT YOU WISH ": PRINT
 260 PRINT "TO HAVE CONVERTED TO THE OTHER 4": PRINT
 270 INPUT T
 280 A1=T * A
 290 B1=T * B
 300 C1=T * C
 310 D1=T * D
 320 PRINT "THE AMOUNT GIVEN IS:-     "T: PRINT : PRINT
 330 PRINT "     ***EXCHANGE VALUES***"
 340 PRINT : PRINT A$,A1
 350 PRINT : PRINT B$,B1
 360 PRINT : PRINT C$,C1
 370 PRINT : PRINT D$,D1
 400 END
2000 PRINT : PRINT : PRINT : RETURN
3000 PRINT "        ***PRESS ANY KEY***"
3010 GET A$
3020 RETURN
```

CHAPTER 4

1.
```
100 HOME
105 PRINT "SAVING NUMBERS 1-100 ON DISK"
110 PRINT : PRINT "WHICH ROUTINE DO YOU WISH TO USE"
120 PRINT : PRINT "           DATA SAVING......S"
130 PRINT : PRINT "           DATA RECOVERY......R"
140 PRINT : PRINT "CHOOSE ONE OF THE TWO LETTERS"
150 INPUT B$
170 IF B$="S" THEN 300
180 IF B$="R" THEN 500
190 GOTO 100
300 HOME
310 D$=CHR$ (4)
320 PRINT D$; "OPEN NUMBERS"
330 PRINT D$; "WRITE NUMBERS"
340 FOR C=1 TO 100
350 PRINT C
360 NEXT C
370 PRINT D$; "CLOSE NUMBERS"
380 PRINT : PRINT : PRINT "NUMBERS 1 TO 100 NOW STORED ON DISK"
```

```
390 GOTO 110
500 HOME
510 REM RECOVER NUMBERS
520 D$=CHR$ (4)
530 PRINT D$; "OPEN NUMBERS"
540 PRINT D$; "READ NUMBERS"
550 FOR C=1 TO 100
560 INPUT C
570 NEXT C
580 PRINT D$; "CLOSE NUMBERS"
590 PRINT : PRINT "NUMBERS 1 TO 100 NOW RECOVERED FROM DISK"
600 GOTO 110
```

2.
```
 10 REM MENU
 20 C=0
 23 HOME
 30 PRINT "       ***MAILING LIST***"
 40 PRINT : PRINT "THIS PROGRAM ACCEPTS A LIST OF NAMES"
 50 PRINT : PRINT "AND ADDRESSES AND ALLOWS YOU TO"
 60 PRINT : PRINT "STORE THEM ON DISK AND RECOVER THEM"
 70 GOSUB 3000
 80 PRINT : PRINT : PRINT "DO YOU WISH TO  :-"
 90 PRINT : PRINT "       BEGIN A NEW LIST ...B"
100 PRINT : PRINT "       LOOK AT THE CURRENT LIST ...L"
110 PRINT : PRINT "       RECOVER A LIST FROM DISK ...R"
120 PRINT : PRINT "       SAVE A LIST ON DISK ...S"
130 PRINT : PRINT "CHOOSE THE APPROPRIATE LETTER"
140 INPUT Z$: IF Z$="B" THEN 200
150 IF Z$="L" THEN 700
160 IF Z$="R" THEN 900
170 IF Z$="S" THEN 500
180 GOTO 130
200 C=1
210 HOME
215 PRINT : PRINT "       BEGINNING A LIST"
220 PRINT : PRINT "PUT IN THE NAME, SURNAME FIRST"
230 PRINT : PRINT "DO NOT USE ANY COMMAS"
240 INPUT A$(C)
250 PRINT : PRINT "THE ADDRESS WILL BE LIMITED TO 3 LINES"
260 PRINT : PRINT "DO NOT USE ANY COMMAS"
```

```
270 PRINT : PRINT : PRINT "INPUT THE FIRST LINE OF THE ADDRESS"
280 INPUT B$(C)
290 PRINT : PRINT : PRINT "INPUT THE SECOND LINE OF THE ADDRESS"
300 INPUT C$(C)
310 PRINT : PRINT : PRINT "INPUT THE THIRD LINE OF THE ADDRESS"
320 INPUT D$(C)
330 PRINT : PRINT : PRINT "DO YOU WISH TO ADD ANOTHER NAME?"
340 PRINT : PRINT "IF SO INPUT 'YES', OTHERWISE 'NO' "
350 INPUT Z$: IF Z$="YES" THEN 380
360 IF Z$="NO" THEN 70
370 GOTO 330
380 C=C+1: GOTO 220
500 HOME
505 PRINT "    SAVING ON DISK"
510 D$=CHR$ (4)
520 PRINT D$; "OPEN ADDRESS"
530 PRINT D$; "WRITE ADDRESS"
540 FOR N=1 TO C
550 PRINT A$(N)
560 PRINT B$(N)
570 PRINT C$(N)
580 PRINT D$(N)
590 NEXT N
600 PRINT D$; "CLOSE ADDRESS"
610 PRINT "NOW SAVED ON DISK"
615 GOSUB 3000
620 GOTO 80
699 REM LISTING ON SCREEN
700 HOME
705 PRINT : PRINT "NAMES            ADDRESSES"
710 FOR N=1 TO C
720 PRINT : PRINT "NUMBER",N
730 PRINT : PRINT
740 PRINT A$(N),B$(N)
750 PRINT ,C$(N)
760 PRINT ,D$(N)
770 PRINT : PRINT
780 PRINT "***************************************"
790 GOSUB 3000
800 NEXT N
```

```
810 PRINT : PRINT : PRINT "THAT WAS THE LAST ONE"
820 GOSUB 3000
830 GOTO 80
900 HOME
905 PRINT "   RECOVERING FROM DISK"
910 PRINT "HOW MANY ADDRESSES WERE STORED"
920 INPUT C
930 REM RECOVER ADDRESSES FROM DISK
940 G$=CHR$ (4)
950 PRINT G$; "OPEN ADDRESS"
960 PRINT G$; "READ ADDRESS"
970 FOR N=1 TO C
980 INPUT A$(N)
990 INPUT B$(N)
1000 INPUT C$(N)
1010 INPUT D$(N)
1020 NEXT N
1030 PRINT G$; "CLOSE ADDRESS"
1040 PRINT "   NAMES NOW RECOVERED"
1050 GOSUB 3000
1060 GOTO 80
2000 PRINT : PRINT : PRINT : RETURN
3000 PRINT : PRINT : PRINT "PRESS ANY KEY"
3010 GET A$ : IF A$= "" THEN 3010
3020 RETURN
```

CHAPTER 5

1.
```
100 HOME
180 X=0 : REM FIRST X
200 HGR : REM   SETS GRAPHICS MODE
220 Y1=0 : REM FIRST Y
240 CH=4 : REM CHANGE IN Y
260 Y2=Y1+CH: REM   NEXT Y
279 REM   NEXT LINE ENSURES THAT Y IS WITHIN LIMITS
280 IF Y2 > =0 AND Y2 < 160 THEN 380
319 REM   NEXT 3 LINES EFFECT CHANGEOVER
320 HCOLOR=0 : HPLOT X, Y1
340 CH=   -CH
350 X=X+4
360 GOTO 260
```

```
379 REM    NEXT FEW LINES PLOT POINTS
380 HCOLOR=3
400 HPLOT X,Y2
420 HCOLOR=0
440 HPLOT X,Y1
460 Y1=Y2
480 GOTO 260
```

2.

```
  5 DIM X(30),Y(30)
 50 X=10 : Y=17.3 : REM COORDS OF A HEXAGON SIDE
100 HGR
110 HCOLOR=7
120 FOR M=0 TO 3 : REM M COUNTS HEXAGONS ACROSS
130 FOR N=0 TO 6 STEP 2 : REM N COUNTS HEXAGONS DOWN
139 REM    NEXT 4 LINES MAKE SIDES OF A HEXAGON
140 HPLOT (6 * M+1) * X,N *Y TO 6 * M * X, (N+1) * Y
150 HPLOT 6 * M * X, (N+1) * Y TO (6 * M+1) * X, (N+2) * Y
160 HPLOT (6 * M+3) * X,N * Y TO (6 * M+4) * X, (N+1) * Y
170 HPLOT (6 * M+4) * X, (N+1) * Y TO (6 * M+3) * X, (N+2) * Y
250 NEXT N
260 NEXT M
299 REM    NEXT LINES MAKE TOP AND BOTTOM OF HEXAGONS
300 FOR A=0 TO 180 STEP 60
302 HPLOT X+A, 0 TO X+A+20,0
304 NEXT A
310 FOR N=2 TO 8 STEP 2
320 FOR M=0 TO 3
330 HPLOT (6 * M+1) * X,N * Y TO (6 * M+3) * X,N * Y
335 IF M=3 THEN 360
340 HPLOT (6 * M+4) * X, (N-1) * Y TO (6 * M+6) * X, (N-1) * Y
360 NEXT M
370 NEXT N
375 END
```

3.

```
100 HOME
120 PRINT "THIS PROGRAM MAKES ALL THE NUMERALS"
125 PRINT "FROM 0 TO 9 ON THE HIGH RESOLUTION"
130 PRINT "SCREEN."
140 PRINT : PRINT "EACH NUMERAL IS MADE INSIDE A BOX"
145 PRINT "WHICH LOOKS LIKE THIS."
150 PRINT : PRINT "TO SEE THE BOX PRESS ANY KEY."
```

```
155 PRINT "WHEN YOU HAVE LOOKED AT IT AND WISH"
160 PRINT "TO GO ON, PRESS ANY KEY AGAIN."
170 GET Z$
180 HGR : HCOLOR=3
200 HPLOT 20,20 TO 20,120 TO 120,120 TO 120,20 TO 20,20
210 HPLOT 20,80 TO 120,80
220 HPLOT 80,20 TO 80,120
250 GET A$
260 TEXT : HOME
280 PRINT "FIRST YOU MUST CHOOSE WHERE ON THE"
290 PRINT : PRINT "SCREEN YOU WISH TO PLACE THE TOP"
300 PRINT : PRINT "LEFT-HAND CORNER OF THE BOX FOR THE"
310 PRINT : PRINT "NUMERAL. REMEMBER THAT THE TOP OF THE"
320 PRINT : PRINT "SCREEN RUNS FROM 0 TO 279 AND THE    "
330 PRINT : PRINT "SIDE RUNS FROM 0 TO 191."
340 PRINT : INPUT "    HOW FAR ACROSS THE TOP    ";X
350 PRINT : INPUT "HOW FAR DOWN THE SIDE    ";Y
360 PRINT : INPUT "NOW CHOOSE A NUMERAL    ";N
365 IF N=0 THEN N=10
370 A=X : B=X+3 : C=X+5
380 P=Y : Q=Y+3 : R=Y+5
400 HGR : HCOLOR=3
420 ON N GOSUB 2000, 2005, 2010, 2015, 2020, 2025, 2030, 2035, 2040, 2045
440 GET A$
450 TEXT : HOME
460 PRINT : INPUT "DO YOU WANT ANOTHER    ";A$
470 IF A$="YES" THEN 340
480 IF A$="NO" THEN 500
490 GOTO 460
500 END
2000 HPLOT B,P TO B,R : RETURN : REM 1
2005 HPLOT A,P TO C,P TO C,Q TO A,Q TO A,R TO C,R : RETURN : REM 2
2010 HPLOT A,P TO C,P TO C,R TO A,R : HPLOT C,Q TO A,Q : RETURN :
     REM 3
2015 HPLOT A,P TO A,Q TO C,Q : HPLOT B,P TO B,R : RETURN : REM 4
2020 HPLOT C,P TO A,P TO A,Q TO C,Q TO C,R TO A,R : RETURN : REM 5
2025 HPLOT A,P TO A,R TO C,R TO C,Q TO A,Q : RETURN : REM 6
2030 HPLOT A,P TO C,P TO C,R : RETURN : REM 7
2035 HPLOT A,P TO C,P TO C,R TO A,R TO A,P : HPLOT A,Q TO C,Q :
     RETURN : REM 8
2040 HPLOT C,R TO C,P TO A,P TO A,Q TO C,Q : RETURN : REM 9
2045 HPLOT A,P TO C,P TO C,R TO A,R TO A,P : RETURN : REM 0
```

CHAPTER 6

1.
```
 90 HOME
100 PRINT "*** TOSSING A DICE ***"
110 PRINT : PRINT : PRINT "HOW MANY TIMES DO YOU WISH TO"
120 PRINT : PRINT "TOSS THE DICE" : PRINT
130 INPUT N
140 PRINT : PRINT "THE RESULTS OF EACH TOSS ARE NOW SHOWN."
150 PRINT : PRINT "WITH A SUMMARY AT THE END": PRINT
160 FOR CO=1 TO N
170 R=INT (6 * RND (5)+1)
180 PRINT R;
190 IF R=1 THEN A=A+1
200 IF R=2 THEN B=B+1
210 IF R=3 THEN C=C+1
220 IF R=4 THEN D=D+1
230 IF R=5 THEN E=E+1
240 IF R=6 THEN F=F+1
250 NEXT CO
260 PRINT : PRINT : PRINT : PRINT : PRINT "NUMBER OF TIMES 1
    OCCURS IS  "A
270 PRINT : PRINT "NUMBER OF TIMES 2 OCCURS IS   "B
280 PRINT : PRINT "NUMBER OF TIMES 3 OCCURS IS   "C
290 PRINT : PRINT "NUMBER OF TIMES 4 OCCURS IS   "D
300 PRINT : PRINT "NUMBER OF TIMES 5 OCCURS IS   "E
310 PRINT : PRINT "NUMBER OF TIMES 6 OCCURS IS   "F
```

2.
```
 40 DIM A$(12),B$(12)
 50 FOR N=1 TO 12 : READ A$(N) : NEXT N
 60 FOR N=1 TO 12 : READ B$(N) : NEXT N
 90 REM   VERSES LOOP
100 FOR C=1 TO 12
110 HOME
120 PRINT "ON THE   "B$(C) "   DAY OF CHRISTMAS"
130 PRINT "MY TRUE LOVE SENT TO ME :        " : PRINT
132 REM   LOOP FOR A SINGLE VERSE
135 FOR K=C TO 1 STEP -1
136 IF C=1 THEN 140
137 IF K <> 1 THEN 140
138 PRINT "                    AND"
140 PRINT A$(K)
150 NEXT K
```

```
 170 REM    DELAY INCREASING FOR
 171 REM    LONGER VERSES
 180 FOR Q=1 TO 3200+1200 * C : NEXT Q
 190 NEXT C
1000 DATA   A PARTRIDGE IN A PEAR TREE, TWO TURTLE DOVES,
     THREE FRENCH HENS
1005 DATA   FOUR COLLY BIRDS, FIVE GOLD RINGS, SIX GEESE
     A-LAYING
1010 DATA   SEVEN SWANS A-SWIMMING, EIGHT MAIDS A-MILKING
1012 DATA   NINE DRUMMERS DRUMMING
1015 DATA   TEN PIPERS PIPING, ELEVEN LADIES DANCING,
     TWELVE LORDS A-LEAPING
1030 DATA   FIRST,SECOND,THIRD,FOURTH
1040 DATA   FIFTH,SIXTH,SEVENTH,EIGHTH
1050 DATA   NINTH, TENTH, ELEVENTH, TWELFTH
```

CHAPTER 7

1.
```
100 DATA   173,48,192,136,208,5,206,1,3,240,9,202,208,245,174,0,3,76,2,3,96,0,0
110 FOR X=770 TO 792
120 READ Y
130 POKE X,Y
140 NEXT X
300 DIM A(200),B(200)
400 HOME : PRINT "        WRITING MUSIC"
405 PRINT : PRINT "DO YOU WISH TO:-"
407 PRINT : PRINT
410 PRINT "        BEGIN A NEW TUNE.............................B"
415 PRINT "        FINISH FOR NOW...............................F"
420 PRINT : PRINT"        LIST NOTES ON SCREEN.....................L"
425 PRINT "        SAVE A TUNE ON DISK..........................S"
430 PRINT : PRINT "        RECOVER A TUNE FROM DISK.................R"
432 PRINT "        PLAY THE TUNE................................P"
433 PRINT : PRINT "        CHANGE A NOTE ON TUNE....................C"
434 PRINT "        ADD NEW NOTE TO TUNE.........................A"
435 INPUT Y$ : IF Y$="B" THEN 451
437 IF Y$="F" THEN 452
438 IF Y$="L" THEN 454
440 IF Y$="S" THEN 456
442 IF Y$="C" THEN 458
444 IF Y$="A" THEN 460
```

```
445 IF Y$="R" THEN 462
447 IF Y$="P" THEN 464
450 PRINT : PRINT "       TRY AGAIN" : GOTO 400
451 GOSUB 500 : GOTO 400
452 GOSUB 3000 : GOTO 400
454 GOSUB 2500 : GOTO 400
456 GOSUB 1500 : GOTO 400
458 GOSUB 1700 : GOTO 400
460 GOSUB 1800 : GOTO 400
462 GOSUB 1600 : GOTO 400
464 GOSUB 2000 : GOTO 400
500 HOME : PRINT "       WRITING MUSIC" : Z=0
501 PRINT
502 PRINT "             *************"
505 PRINT "INPUT EACH NOTE AS A 3-SYMBOL"
507 PRINT "COMBINATION AS SHOWN BELOW. N STANDS"
509 PRINT "FOR NATURAL AND S FOR SHARP."
510 PRINT : PRINT "      G       G2N OR G2S"
512 PRINT "   F---------F2N OR F2S"
515 PRINT "      E       E2N"
517 PRINT "   D---------D2N OR D2S"
520 PRINT "      C       C2N OR C2S
522 PRINT "   B---------B2N"
525 PRINT "      A       A2N OR A2S"
527 PRINT "   G---------G1N OR G1S"
530 PRINT "      F       F1N OR F2S"
532 PRINT "   E---------E1N"
535 PRINT "      D       D1N OR D1S"
537 PRINT "   C---------C1N OR C1S    MIDDLE C"
540 PRINT "      B       B1N"
545 PRINT "   A---------A1N OR A1S"
550 PRINT : PRINT "        PRESS A KEY"
560 GET Y$
565 PRINT : PRINT "NOTE THAT EACH OCTAVE RUNS FROM A TO G"
570 PRINT : PRINT "WHEN YOU SEE THE QUESTION MARK INPUT"
575 PRINT "THE 3-LETTER COMBINATION FOR THE FIRST"
580 PRINT "NOTE AND PRESS RETURN. THEN INPUT THE"
585 PRINT "NUMBER, AS REQUESTED, FOR THE DURATION OF"
590 PRINT "THE NOTE. AT THE END, TYPE IN END."
650 PRINT : PRINT : PRINT "NOW INPUT A NOTE IN THE 3-LETTER
    FORM:-"
651 PRINT : PRINT : INPUT "REMEMBER TO USE END TO STOP   " ; Z$
```

```
652 IF Z$="END" THEN 1030
653 L$=LEFT$ (Z$,1) : M$=MID$ (Z$,2,1) : R$=RIGHT$ (Z$,1) : Z=Z+1
655 IF X1 > 0 THEN Z1=Z : Z=X1
660 L=ASC (L$)-64
661 IF L > 7 THEN 680 : IF L < 1 THEN 680
665 M=VAL (M$) : IF M=2 THEN M=15 : GOTO 670
666 IF M=1 THEN 670
667 GOTO 680
670 R=ASC (R$)
672 IF R=78 THEN R=1 : GOTO 685
675 IF R=83 THEN R=8 : GOTO 685
680 PRINT : PRINT "    TRY AGAIN    " : GOTO 650
685 PRINT : PRINT : PRINT "NOW INPUT LENGTH OF NOTE :-"
687 PRINT : PRINT "240 FOR A MINIM"
690 PRINT : PRINT "120 FOR A CROTCHET"
694 PRINT : PRINT " 30 FOR A SEMI-QUAVER"
695 PRINT : PRINT : INPUT "    " ; W : B(Z)=W
696 IF INT (W / 15)=W / 15 THEN 700
698 PRINT : PRINT : PRINT "    TRY AGAIN" : GOTO 695
700 N=L+M+R-2
710 ON N GOTO 750, 760, 770, 780, 790, 800, 810, 820, 830, 840, 850, 860, 870,
    880, 890, 900, 910, 920, 930, 940, 950, 960, 970, 980, 990, 1000, 1010, 1020
750 A(Z)=228 : GOTO 650
760 A(Z)=204 : GOTO 650
770 A(Z)=192 : GOTO 650
780 A(Z)=171 : GOTO 650
790 A(Z)=152 : GOTO 650
800 A(Z)=144 : GOTO 650
810 A(Z)=128 : GOTO 650
820 A(Z)=216 : GOTO 650
830 A(Z)=192 : GOTO 650
840 A(Z)=181 : GOTO 650
850 A(Z)=161 : GOTO 650
860 A(Z)=144 : GOTO 650
870 A(Z)=136 : GOTO 650
880 A(Z)=121 : GOTO 650
890 A(Z)=114 : GOTO 650
900 A(Z)=102 : GOTO 650
910 A(Z)=  96 : GOTO 650
920 A(Z)=  85 : GOTO 650
930 A(Z)=  76 : GOTO 650
```

```
 940 A(Z)=  72 : GOTO 650
 950 A(Z)=  64 : GOTO 650
 960 A(Z)=108 : GOTO 650
 970 A(Z)=  96 : GOTO 650
 980 A(Z)=  90 : GOTO 650
 990 A(Z)=  80 : GOTO 650
1000 A(Z)=  72 : GOTO 650
1010 A(Z)=  68 : GOTO 650
1020 A(Z)=  60 : GOTO 650
1030 IF X1 > 0 THEN Z=Z1
1040 RETURN
1500 D$=CHR$ (4)
1502 PRINT : PRINT : INPUT "    WHAT FILE NAME    " ; N$
1505 PRINT D$ ; "OPEN    " ; N$
1510 PRINT D$ ; "WRITE    " ; N$
1515 FOR J=1 TO Z
1520 PRINT A(J) : PRINT B(J)
1525 NEXT J
1530 PRINT D$ ; "CLOSE    " ; N$
1535 PRINT "    NOW SAVED ON DISK. PRESS ANY KEY"
1540 GET Y$
1550 RETURN
1600 INPUT "HOW MANY NOTES WERE SAVED    " ; Z
1605 PRINT : PRINT : INPUT "    WHAT FILE NAME    " ; N$
1610 D$=CHR$ (4)
1615 PRINT D$ ; "OPEN    " ; N$
1620 PRINT D$ ; "READ    " ; N$
1625 FOR J=1 TO Z
1630 INPUT A(J) : INPUT B(J)
1635 NEXT J
1640 PRINT D$ ; "CLOSE    " ; N$
1645 PRINT "NOW RECOVERED FROM DISK. PRESS ANY KEY"
1650 GET Y$
1660 RETURN
1700 HOME : PRINT "WHAT IS THE NO. OF THE NOTE"
1705 PRINT : INPUT "THAT YOU WANT TO CHANGE    " ; X1
1710 PRINT : PRINT "REMEMBER TO INPUT END AFTER THIS"
1715 PRINT : PRINT "    PRESS ANY KEY " : GET Y$
1720 GOTO 650
1800 HOME
1810 HOME : PRINT "THE NOTES WILL BE ADDED TO THE"
```

```
1820 PRINT : PRINT "END OF THE TUNE. AS USUAL WHEN"
1830 PRINT : PRINT "YOU WISH TO STOP, TYPE IN END."
1840 GOTO 650
2000 FOR J=1 TO Z
2010 POKE 768,A(J) : POKE 769,B(J) : CALL 770
2020 NEXT J
2030 RETURN
2500 HOME : FOR J=1 TO Z
2510 PRINT A(J), B(J)
2515 IF INT (J / 20)=J / 20 THEN 2517
2516 GOTO 2520
2517 PRINT "    PRESS A KEY" : GET Y$
2520 NEXT J
2530 PRINT : PRINT "    PRESS ANY KEY" : GET Y$ : RETURN
3000 HOME : PRINT "THANK YOU FOR NOW." : END
```

2.

```
10 HOME
15 PRINT "    COUNTERS"
20 PRINT : PRINT "A GAME FOR 2 PLAYERS. EACH PLAYER"
30 PRINT : PRINT "CHOOSES ONE OF THE NUMBERS 1, 2 OR 3"
40 PRINT : PRINT "EACH TIME. THAT NUMBER OF COUNTERS"
50 PRINT : PRINT "IS THEN TAKEN AWAY"
60 PRINT : PRINT "FROM AN ARRAY OF 40 COUNTERS."
70 PRINT : PRINT "THE PLAYER WHO TAKES THE LAST "
80 PRINT : PRINT "COUNTER IS THE LOSER."
90 GOSUB 2000 : REM PRESS A KEY
100 HOME
105 INPUT "NAME OF 1ST PLAYER    " ; Z$
110 PRINT : INPUT "NAME OF 2ND PLAYER    " ; Y$
120 REM A-SYMBOL NO : B-POKE NUMBER : C-STOP NUMBER
140 HOME
150 A=32 : B=281 : C=4
160 REM FIRST ROW
170 FOR Z=B TO B+39 STEP C
180 FOR Y=0 TO 2
185 N=Z+Y : GOSUB 3000
190 POKE P, A
192 N=N+40 : GOSUB 3000 : POKE P, A
194 N=N+40 : GOSUB 3000 : POKE P, A
200 NEXT Y : NEXT Z
210 B=B+160 : REM NEXT ROW
```

```
220 IF B=921 THEN 240
230 GOTO 170
240 Z=281
250 G=G+1
260 REM CHOOSE WHOSE TURN
265 FOR W=1024 TO 1063 : POKE W, 160 : NEXT W : REM CLEARS TOP
    ROW
270 IF INT (G / 2)=G / 2 THEN 300
280 VTAB 1 : PRINT "YOUR TURN    " Z$ : PRINT
290 GOTO 310
300 VTAB 1 : PRINT "YOUR TURN    " Y$ : PRINT
310 INPUT " . . .? " ; N
320 ON N GOTO 340, 360, 380
330 GOTO 270
340 GOSUB 1000 : Z=Z+4
350 GOTO 250 : REM NEXT TURN
360 FOR V=1 TO 2 : GOSUB 1000 : Z=Z+4 : NEXT V
370 GOTO 250 : REM NEXT TURN
380 FOR V=1 TO 3 : GOSUB 1000 : Z=Z+4 : NEXT V
390 GOTO 250 : REM NEXT TURN
400 IF INT (G / 2)=G / 2 THEN 430
410 G$=Z$ : Z1=Z1+1
420 GOTO 440
430 G$=Y$ : Y2=Y2+1
440 PRINT : PRINT "HARD LUCK    " G$ "    YOU LOSE"
450 PRINT : INPUT "PLAY AGAIN -Y OR N ——" ; A$
460 IF A$="Y" THEN 500
470 IF A$="N" THEN 510
480 GOTO 440
490 GOTO 510
500 G=G+1 : HOME : GOTO 150
510 PRINT : PRINT Y$ " 'S SCORE IS    " Z1
520 PRINT : PRINT Z$ " 'S SCORE IS    " Y2
530 END
1000 A=160 : FOR Y=0 TO 2
1005 N=Z+Y : GOSUB 3000 : POKE P, A
1010 N=N+40 : GOSUB 3000 : POKE P, A
1015 N=N+40 : GOSUB 3000 : POKE P, A
1020 NEXT Y
1021 IF Z=317 THEN Z=Z+120
1022 IF Z=477 THEN Z=Z+120
```

```
1023 IF Z=637 THEN Z=Z+120
1024 IF Z=797 THEN 400
1040 RETURN
2000 PRINT : PRINT : PRINT "    PRESS ANY KEY"
2010 GET A$
2020 RETURN
3000 REM CONVERTS SCREEN NUMBERS
3010 M=INT (N / 40)+1
3020 R=N-40 * (M-1)
3030 R=R-1
3040 IF M < 9 THEN 3070
3050 IF M     17 THEN 3080
3060 X1=56 : Y1=M-24 : GOTO 3100
3070 X1=0 : Y1=M-1 : GOTO 3100
3080 X1=72 : Y1=M-13 : GOTO 3100
3090 REM P IS SCREEN NO FOR POKE
3100 P=984+M * 40+X1+Y1 * 88+R
3110 RETURN
```

CHAPTER 8

1.
```
 40 REM 5 CARD POKER
 45 HOME
 60 PRINT : PRINT : PRINT "THIS GAME DEALS 2 HANDS OF 5 CARDS"
 90 DIM Z$(13), A$(13, 4), X(13)
 95 REM READ CARD NUMBERS
100 FOR Z=1 TO 13
110 READ Z$(Z)
120 NEXT Z
125 REM READ CARD SUITS
130 FOR Y=1 TO 4
140 READ Y$(Y)
150 NEXT Y
160 X$="OF"
205 REM STORE ALL CARDS IN A$(13, 4)
210 FOR Y=1 TO 4
220 FOR Z=1 TO 13
230 A$(Z, Y)=Z$(Z)+" "+X$+" "+Y$(Y)
240 NEXT Z
```

```
250 NEXT Y
270 X=0
275 REM CHOOSE TWO HANDS
280 FOR M=1 TO 2
290 FOR N=1 TO 5
300 A=INT (52 * RND (2)+1)
310 X=X+1
315 REM CHECK IF THE CARD IS NEW
320 FOR W=1 TO 10
330 IF X(W)=A GOTO 300
340 NEXT
350 X(X)=A
360 IF A < 14 THEN Y=1 : GOTO 400
370 IF A > 13 AND A < 27 THEN Y=2 : GOTO 420
380 IF A > 26 AND A < 40 THEN Y=3 : GOTO 440
390 IF A > 39 THEN Y=4 : GOTO 460
400 PRINT A$(A, Y), N : PRINT
410 GOTO 480
420 PRINT A$(A-13, Y), N : PRINT
430 GOTO 480
440 PRINT A$(A - 26, Y), N : PRINT
450 GOTO 480
460 PRINT A$(A - 39, Y), N : PRINT
470 GOTO 480
480 NEXT N
485 PRINT "————————————————"
490 NEXT M
500 DATA "ACE", "2", "3", "4", "5", "6"
510 DATA "7", "8", "9", "10"
520 DATA "JACK", "QUEEN", "KING"
530 DATA "HEARTS", "CLUBS", "SPADES", "DIAMONDS"
```

2.

```
  5 DIM B$(26), A$(50)
 20 FOR Z=1 TO 26 : READ B$(Z) : NEXT Z
 30 FOR Z=1 TO 5 : READ C$(Z) : NEXT Z
 40 HOME
100 PRINT "        ****CROSSWORDS****"
110 PRINT: PRINT "IF YOU HAVE A WORD WITH 'ONE' OR 'TWO' " : PRINT
120 PRINT "LETTERS MISSING THIS PROGRAM WILL" : PRINT
130 PRINT "HELP YOU" : PRINT
200 PRINT : PRINT : PRINT "FIRST COUNT THE NUMBER OF LETTERS"
```

```
202 PRINT : PRINT : PRINT
205 INPUT "IN THE WORD AND INPUT THIS ———" ; N
210 GOSUB 2000
225 PRINT : PRINT : PRINT "NOW INPUT THE LETTERS OF THE WORD"
230 PRINT : PRINT "ONE AT A TIME. WHEN THE LETTER IS NOT"
235 PRINT : PRINT "KNOWN INPUT A DASH LIKE '–' "
237 PRINT : PRINT "USE THE MINUS SIGN FOR THIS" : PRINT : PRINT
238 FOR C=1 TO N
239 INPUT " : : : : : : : : " ; A$
240 IF A$="–" THEN 250
245 GOTO 255
250 B=B+1
255 A$(C)=A$
260 NEXT C
270 PRINT : PRINT : PRINT "THE WORD SO FAR IS :-"
275 PRINT : PRINT : PRINT
280 FOR C=1 TO N
290 PRINT A$(C) "   " ;
300 NEXT C
305 PRINT
310 INPUT "CHECK THIS. IS IT CORRECT?———" ; Z$
320 IF Z$="NO" THEN 200
330 IF Z$="YES" THEN 350
340 GOTO 310
350 IF B=1 THEN 400
355 IF B=2 THEN 500
400 PRINT : PRINT : PRINT : PRINT : PRINT
402 FOR Z=1 TO L
403 PRINT "        " ;
405 FOR C=1 TO N
410 IF A$(C)="–" THEN 440
420 PRINT A$(C) ;
430 GOTO 460
440 GOSUB 3000
460 NEXT C
465 PRINT : PRINT : PRINT
467 FOR G=1 TO 1000 : NEXT G
470 NEXT Z
480 END
500 FOR Z=1 TO L
505 FOR Y=1 TO L
```

```
507 PRINT : PRINT : PRINT : PRINT "        ";
510 FOR C=1 TO N
515 IF A$(C)="-" THEN 540
520 PRINT A$(C) ;
530 GOTO 560
540 IF X=1 THEN 550
541 X=1
543 GOSUB 3000
544 GOTO 560
550 GOSUB 3500
555 FOR W=1 TO 1000 : NEXT W
560 NEXT C
561 X=0
565 PRINT : PRINT : PRINT
570 NEXT Y
580 NEXT Z
585 END
1000 DATA A,B,C,D,E,F,G,H,I,J,K,L,M,N,O,P, Q,R,S,T,U,V,W,X,Y,Z
1010 DATA A,E,I,O,U
2000 PRINT : PRINT : PRINT "DO YOU WISH TO INCLUDE 'ALL'
     THE LETTERS"
2005 PRINT : PRINT "IN YOUR LIST OF POSSIBLE SOLUTIONS"
2010 PRINT : PRINT "OR CAN IT BE CONFINED TO THE VOWELS?"
2015 PRINT : PRINT
2020 INPUT "INPUT 'A' OR 'V' ————" ; P$
2030 IF P$="A" THEN 2050
2040 IF P$="V" THEN 2055
2045 GOTO 2000
2050 L=26 : RETURN
2055 L=5 : RETURN
3000 IF L=26 THEN PRINT B$(Z) ; : RETURN
3010 IF L=5 THEN PRINT C$(Z) ; : RETURN
3500 IF L=26 THEN PRINT B$(Y) ; : RETURN
3510 IF L=5 THEN PRINT C$(Y) ; : RETURN
```

3.
```
 1 HOME
 5 PRINT "      ***LETTER COUNTER***" : PRINT
10 PRINT : PRINT "THIS PROGRAM ALLOWS YOU TO TYPE IN A"
20 PRINT : PRINT "PASSAGE OF PROSE ; IT THEN COUNTS THE"
30 PRINT : PRINT "NUMBER OF TIMES EACH LETTER OCCURS"
40 PRINT : PRINT : PRINT "THE FOLLOWING CODES ARE USED :-"
```

```
 50 PRINT : PRINT "9 . . . MEANS STOP ALTOGETHER."
 60 PRINT : PRINT " < . . . MEANS DELETE THE LAST ENTRY."
 70 PRINT : PRINT "* . . . MEANS END OF INPUT."
 75 PRINT : PRINT : PRINT : PRINT "    PRESS ANY KEY"
 76 GET Z$ : IF Z$=" " THEN 76
 80 PRINT : PRINT : PRINT "AFTER ABOUT 160 LETTERS THE MACHINE"
 90 PRINT : PRINT "DOES AN INTERIM COUNT SO THERE WILL BE"
100 PRINT : PRINT "A SHORT DELAY EACH TIME YOU REACH"
110 PRINT : PRINT "THIS NUMBER OF LETTERS."
120 PRINT : PRINT : PRINT "AS SOON AS YOU SEE THE QUESTION MARK"
130 PRINT : PRINT "BEGIN TO TYPE IN YOUR PASSAGE" : PRINT : PRINT
180 DIM K(26)
190 REM B$ CUMULATES THE LETTERS
200 B$=" "
210 A=0 : REM A COUNTS THE LETTERS
220 REM A$ IS THE CURRENT LETTER
229 PRINT "?" ;
230 GET A$ : IF A$= " " THEN 230
240 IF A$="9" THEN 500 : REM ABORT
250 IF A$="< " THEN GOSUB 1000 : REM REMOVES THE LAST LETTER
260 IF A$="*" GOTO 340 : REM END OF PASSAGE
270 B$=B$+A$
280 PRINT A$ ;
290 IF A$=" " THEN 230
300 REM TESTS FOR STRING TOO LONG
310 A=A+1
320 IF A  > 160 THEN 350
330 GOTO 230
340 PRINT
350 L=LEN (B$)
360 FOR C=1 TO L
370 C$=MID$ (B$, C, 1)
380 K=ASC (C$)
390 REM TESTS FOR PUNCTUATION MARKS
400 IF K <  64 THEN 430
410 K=K-64
420 K(K)=K(K)+1
430 NEXT C
440 IF A$= "*" THEN 460
450 A=0 : GOTO 230
460 REM PRINT OUT OF RESULTS
```

```
 469 PRINT : PRINT : PRINT : PRINT : PRINT
 470 FOR C=1 TO 13
 472 P1$=CHR$ (C+64) : P2$=CHR$ (C+77)
 480 PRINT P1$ TAB ( 8)K(C) TAB ( 15)P2$ TAB ( 22)K(C+13)
 490 NEXT
 500 END
 999 REM DELETION SUBROUTINE
1000 LE=LEN (B$)
1005 PRINT
1010 B$=LEFT$ (B$, LE-1)
1020 PRINT B$ ;
1030 A$=" "
1040 RETURN
```

CHAPTER 9

1.

```
 20 DIM A$(20), A1$(20), D$(20)
 30 DIM A(20), B(20), C(20), D(20)
 40 T=0
100 A$="DETAILED ACCOUNT"
110 L=(40-LEN (A$)) / 2
115 HOME
120 PRINT TAB ( L)A$
130 PRINT : PRINT : PRINT : PRINT "YOU PUT IN THE LIST OF
    ITEMS BOUGHT,"
140 PRINT : PRINT "THE PRICE OF EACH, THE DISCOUNT ON"
150 PRINT : PRINT "EACH IN % TERMS, THE NUMBER OF EACH "
160 PRINT : PRINT "BOUGHT. AN ITEMIZED AND DETAILED"
170 PRINT : PRINT "BILL IS THEN PRODUCED."
200 REM INPUT ROUTINE
210 PRINT : PRINT : PRINT : PRINT
215 INPUT "HOW MANY 'ITEM-TYPES' WERE BOUGHT? . . ." ; N
230 FOR C=1 TO N
240 PRINT : PRINT "NUMBER    " C
245 PRINT : PRINT
250 INPUT "INPUT NAME OF ITEM . . ." ; A$(C)
260 PRINT : PRINT "INPUT PRICE OF THIS ITEM. IF IN"
263 PRINT : PRINT
265 INPUT "PENNIES PUT DECIMAL POINT IN . . . " ; A(C)
266 M=A(C) : GOSUB 1000 : A1$(C)=M$ : REM FORMATTING
```

```
268 PRINT : PRINT
270 INPUT "INPUT % DISCOUNT ON THIS ITEM . . ." ; B(C)
275 PRINT : PRINT
280 INPUT "INPUT NUMBER OF THIS ITEM BOUGHT . . ." ; C(C)
290 NEXT C
300 PRINT : PRINT : PRINT "THAT WAS THE LAST 'ITEM-TYPE' "
400 FOR C=1 TO N
410 D(C)=C(C) * (A(C)-(A(C) * B(C) / 100) ) : REM TOTAL PRICE PER
    ITEM TYPE
412 T=T+D(C)
415 M=D(C)
420 GOSUB 1000 : REM FORMATTING
425 D$(C) =M$
430 NEXT C
498 REM PRINTING ON SCREEN
499 HOME
500 PRINT : PRINT "ITEM" TAB( 10) "PRICE" TAB( 18);
505 PRINT "DIS" TAB( 24) "NO" TAB( 32) "TOTAL"
510 PRINT "NAME" TAB( 10) "EACH" TAB( 18) ;
512 PRINT "COUNT" TAB(24) "  " TAB(32) "PRICE"
515 PRINT : PRINT
520 FOR C=1 TO N
525 P=LEN (D$(C) ) : Q=38-P
526 R=LEN (A1$(C) ) : S=15-R
530 PRINT A$(C) TAB( S)A1$(C) TAB( 18)B(C) TAB( 24)C(C) TAB( Q)D$(C)
540 NEXT C
550 M=T : GOSUB 1000 : T$=M$ : REM FORMATTING
570 PRINT : PRINT : PRINT "COMPLETE TOTAL IS :-    " T$
999 END
1000 REM FORMATS AS DOLLARS
1020 M=INT (100 * M+.5) / 100
1030 M$=STR$ (M)
1040 A=LEN (M$)-2
1050 IF A=0 THEN 1090
1060 IF MID$ (M$,A,1)="." THEN 1120
1070 A=A+1
1080 IF MID$ (M$,A,1)="." THEN 1110
1090 M$=M$+".00"
1100 GOTO 1120
1110 M$=M$+"0"
```

```
1120 M$="$"+M$
1140 RETURN
```

2.

```
  5 OA$="STOCK CONTROL"
 10 DIM A$(20), A(20), B(20), C(20)
 50 A$="STOCK CONTROL"
 55 HOME
 57 PRINT TAB( (40-LEN (A$) ) / 2)A$
 60 PRINT : PRINT : PRINT "CHOOSE ONE OF THE FOLLOWING BY"
 61 PRINT : PRINT "PRESSING THE APPROPRIATE KEY"
 65 PRINT : PRINT : PRINT "   BEGIN A NEW LIST..............................B"
 67 PRINT : PRINT "   SAVE ON DISK..........................................S"
 69 PRINT : PRINT "   RECOVER FROM DISK...............................R"
 70 PRINT : PRINT "   PRINT LIST ON SCREEN...............................P"
 72 PRINT : PRINT "   UPDATE QUANTITIES ...............................U"
 74 PRINT : PRINT "   FINISH FOR NOW .....................................F"
100 GET B$ : IF B$="" THEN 100
102 IF B$="B" THEN 120
104 IF B$="S" THEN 125
106 IF B$="R" THEN 130
108 IF B$="P" THEN 135
110 IF B$="U" THEN 140
112 IF B$="F" THEN 145
118 GOTO 55
120 GOSUB 200 : GOTO 50
125 GOSUB 400 : GOTO 50
130 GOSUB 600 : GOTO 50
135 GOSUB 800 : GOTO 50
140 GOSUB 1000 : GOTO 50
145 GOTO 2500
200 REM BEGIN INPUT ROUTINE
205 HOME
210 INPUT "   HOW MANY ITEMS?" ; N
220 FOR C=1 TO N
225 PRINT : PRINT : PRINT "NUMBER   "C
230 INPUT "   NAME OF ITEM   " ; A$(C)
235 GOSUB 2000
240 PRINT : PRINT : PRINT "   NUMBER OF THIS"
250 INPUT "   ITEM IN STORE   " ; A(C)
255 A(C)=INT (A(C) )
```

```
260 PRINT : PRINT "    PRICE OF    "
270 INPUT "    THIS ITEM    "; B(C)
275 B(C)=INT (100 * B(C)+.5) / 100
280 PRINT : PRINT "MINIMUM NUMBER ALLOWABLE"
290 INPUT "BEFORE RE-ORDERING    "; C(C)
295 C(C)=INT (C(C) )
300 NEXT C
310 RETURN
400 REM    SAVE ON DISK
410 D$=CHR$ (4)
412 PRINT D$
415 PRINT D$; "OPEN STORES"
420 PRINT D$; "WRITE STORES"
425 FOR C=1 TO N
430 PRINT A$(C): PRINT A(C): PRINT B(C): PRINT C(C)
440 NEXT C
445 PRINT D$; "CLOSE STORES"
450 PRINT : PRINT "NOW SAVED ON DISK. PRESS ANY KEY"
460 GET Z$
470 RETURN
600 REM    RECOVER FROM DISK
605 PRINT : INPUT "HOW MANY ITEMS WERE SAVED    ";N
610 PRINT "NOW BEING RECOVERED FROM DISK"
615 D$=CHR$ (4)
620 PRINT D$; "OPEN STORES"
625 PRINT S$; "READ STORES"
630 FOR C=1 TO N
635 INPUT A$(C): INPUT A(C)
640 INPUT B(C) : INPUT C(C)
645 NEXT C
650 PRINT D$; "CLOSE STORES"
655 PRINT : PRINT "NOW RECOVERED FROM DISK.    PRESS ANY KEY"
660 GET Z$
665 RETURN
800 REM    PRINT LIST ON SCREEN
810 A1$="NAME OF ITEM":A2$="NUMBER"
815 A3$="PRICE":A4$="MIN"
820 HOME
825 PRINT    TAB(2)A1$ TAB( 15)A2$ TAB( 22)A3$ TAB( 32)A4$
830 PRINT : PRINT
835 FOR C=1 TO N
```

```
840 PRINT TAB ( 12- LEN (A$(C)))A$(C) TAB( 15)A(C) TAB (22)B(C)
    TAB(32)C(C)
845 IF   INT (C/15)=C/15 THEN 855
850 GOTO 880
855 PRINT : PRINT "   PRESS ANY KEY"
860 GET Z$
880 NEXT C
970 PRINT : PRINT "   PRESS ANY KEY"
975 PRINT : PRINT
980 GET Z$
990 RETURN
1000 REM   UPDATE LISTS
1020 FOR C=1 TO N
1025 HOME
1030 PRINT "HOW MANY OF   "A$(C)"   WERE SOLD"
1035 PRINT
1040 INPUT "   "; N1
1050 A(C)=A(C)-N1
1060 IF A(C)=C(C) THEN 1100
1065 IF A(C) < C(C) THEN 1130
1070 PRINT : PRINT "YOU HAVE   "A(C)-C(C) "   MORE THAN"
1080 PRINT "PREFERRED MINIMUM IN STOCK."
1085 PRINT : PRINT "REMEMBER THAT THE PREFERRED MIN   IS  ";C(C)
1090 GOTO 1170
1100 PRINT : PRINT "YOU ARE NOW AT THE DECLARED MIN   "C(C)
1110 PRINT "OF THIS ITEM. YOU SHOULD NOW REORDER"
1120 GOTO 1170
1130 PRINT : PRINT "YOU HAVE NOW GOT   "C(C)-A(C)"   LESS"
1140 PRINT "THAN THE DECLARED MINIMUM OF   "C(C)
1150 PRINT "YOU SHOULD REORDER URGENTLY."
1170 PRINT : PRINT "   PRESS ANY KEY"
1180 GET Z$
1185 NEXT C
1190 RETURN
2000 REM   REDUCE LENGTH OF NAME
2010 L=   LEN (A$(C))
2020 IF L < 13 THEN 2030
2025 A$(C)=   LEFT$ (A$(C),12)
2030 RETURN
2500 PRINT : PRINT "GOODBYE FOR NOW."
2510 END
```

CHAPTER 10

1.
```
9 DIM A$(100),A(100),B(100)
10 HOME
11 PRINT "______________________________"
12 PRINT
13 PRINT "**********CLASS TESTS***********"
14 PRINT
15 PRINT "______________________________"
20 PRINT : PRINT : PRINT "THIS PROGRAM ACCEPTS THE NAME AND
   TEST"
21 PRINT : PRINT "   MARK OF 60 OR MORE CLASS MEMBERS. IT"
22 PRINT : PRINT "WILL THEN STANDARDIZE THE SCORES TO"
23 PRINT : PRINT "ANY GIVEN MEAN AND STANDARD DEVIATION"
44 GOSUB 8000
45 GOTO 1630
100 GOSUB 2400: GOSUB 1700: GOSUB 13000
110 GOSUB 14000: GOSUB 3000: GOTO 1630
120 GOSUB 2000: GOSUB 3000: GOTO 1630
140 GOSUB 4500: GOSUB 13000: GOSUB 14000: GOSUB 3000: GOTO 1630
160 GOSUB 4000: GOTO 1630
180 GOSUB 1612: GOSUB 13000: GOSUB 14000
181 GOTO 1630
190 GOSUB 1600: GOSUB 3000: GOSUB 13000: GOSUB 14000: GOTO 1630
200 GOSUB 5000: GOTO 1630
210 GOSUB 7000 : GOSUB 2500 : GOSUB 2600 : GOTO 1630
220 GOSUB 1600: GOSUB 3000: GOSUB 13000: GOSUB 14000: GOTO 1630
240 PRINT "BYE"
245 END
1600 HOME
1601 PRINT "INPUT NEW SCORES"
1602 FOR I=1 TO N : PRINT A$(I) ; TAB (15) ; : INPUT A(I)
1604 NEXT I
1606 PRINT : PRINT "NEW MARKS ENTERED.": GOSUB 8000
1610 RETURN
1612 HOME
1613 INPUT "NAME OF STUDENT    ";N$
1615 FOR I=1 TO N: IF A$(I)=N$ THEN 1625
1616 NEXT I
1617 PRINT : PRINT "NOT ON LIST": GOSUB 8000: GOTO 181
1625 INPUT "NEW MARK";A(I)
1628 RETURN
```

```
1630 HOME
1632 PRINT FRE (0) "   FREE BYTES   "N"   PUPILS"
1633 PRINT : PRINT "DO YOU WISH TO :-"
1637 PRINT : PRINT "BEGIN AGAIN ............................................................B"
1638 PRINT : PRINT "READ LIST ..................................................................R"
1639 PRINT : PRINT "ADD NAME TO...............................................................A"
1640 PRINT : PRINT "DELETE NAME FROM LIST ...................................D"
1641 PRINT : PRINT "CHANGE ONE SCORE..............................................C"
1642 PRINT : PRINT "CHANGE ALL SCORES............................................T"
1643 PRINT : PRINT "SAVE ON DISK ............................................................S"
1644 PRINT : PRINT "INPUT FROM DISK......................................................I"
1645 PRINT : PRINT "FINISH FOR NOW.......................................................F"
1648 PRINT : INPUT "   CHOOSE A LETTER   "; A$
1649 A=VAL (A$): IF A < > 0 THEN 1648
1650 IF A$="B" THEN 100
1652 IF A$="R" THEN 120
1655 IF A$="A" THEN 140
1656 IF A$="D" THEN 160
1657 IF A$="C" THEN 180
1658 IF A$="T" THEN 190
1659 IF A$="S" THEN 200
1660 IF A$="I" THEN 210
1661 IF A$="F" THEN 240
1662 GOTO 1630
1700 HOME
1701 PRINT "DATA IS NOW PRINTED AGAIN FOR CHECKING"
1702 FOR I=1 TO N
1703 PRINT : PRINT
1704 PRINT A$(I); TAB( 22)A(I)
1706 GOSUB 8000
1708 NEXT I
1710 RETURN
2000 HOME
2010 FOR I=1 TO N
2020 IF INT (I/20)=I/20 THEN GOSUB 8000
2040 PRINT A$(I); TAB( 22);A(I), INT (10 * B(I) + .5) / 10
2050 NEXT I
2055 GOSUB 8000
2060 RETURN
2400 HOME
2405 INPUT "HOW MANY PUPILS?   ";N
2413 PRINT : PRINT : PRINT : FOR I=1 TO N
```

```
2415 IF I=1 THEN 2417
2416 PRINT "NOW NEXT PUPIL": PRINT
2417 INPUT "PUPIL'S NAME    ";A$(I)
2418 PRINT : PRINT
2419 INPUT "NOW THE SCORE    ";A(I)
2420 PRINT : PRINT
2422 NEXT I
2425 PRINT "THAT WAS THE LAST PUPIL"
2430 GOSUB 8000
2450 RETURN
2500 PRINT : PRINT : PRINT "MEAN NOW BEING COMPUTED"
2502 S1=0:S2=0
2505 FOR I=1 TO N:SI=S1+A(I):S2=S2+(A(I)) ∧ 2
2510 NEXT I
2515 M1=S1 / N : S=S2 / N-M1 ∧ 2 : P=SQR (S)
2517 M2=INT (10 * M1+.5) / 10 : P1=INT (10 * P+.5) / 10
2520 PRINT : PRINT "MEAN OF ORIGINAL SCORES "M2," STD.DEV. "P1
2525 GOSUB 8000: RETURN
2600 PRINT : PRINT : PRINT "MEAN BEING COMPUTED"
2602 S1=0:S2=0
2605 FOR I=1 TO N:S1=S1+B(I):S2=S2+(B(I)) ∧ 2
2610 NEXT I
2615 M1=S1/N:S=S2/N-M1 ∧ 2:P=SQR (S)
2618 M3=INT (10 * M1+.5)/10 : P2=INT (10 * P+.5)/10
2620 PRINT : PRINT "MEAN OF STD.SCORES        "M3"STD.DEV.        "P2
2625 GOSUB 8000: RETURN
3000 HOME
3001 INPUT "DO YOU WISH ALPHABETICAL ORDER?   " ; A$
3004 IF LEFT$ (A$, 1)="Y" THEN 3009
3005 IF LEFT$ (A$, 1)="N" THEN 3220
3006 PRINT : PRINT "TRY AGAIN": GOTO 3001
3009 PRINT : PRINT "NAMES BEING ALPHABETIZED"
3010 J=0
3011 FOR I=1 TO N-1
3020 IF A$(I) < A$(I+1) THEN 3200
3030 X$=A$(I+1):X1=A(I+1):X2=B(I+1)
3040 A$(I+1)=A$(I):A(I+1)=A(I):B(I+1)=B(I)
3050 A$(I)=X$:A(I)=X1:B(I)=X2
3060 J=J+1
3200 NEXT I
```

```
3210 IF J > 0 THEN 3010
3215 PRINT : PRINT "NOW IN ALPHABETICAL ORDER": GOSUB 8000
3220 RETURN
4000 HOME
4005 INPUT "NAME TO BE REMOVED       ";B$
4010 FOR I=1 TO N
4020 IF A$(I)=B$ THEN 4100
4030 NEXT I
4035 PRINT : PRINT "NOT ON LIST": PRINT
4037 GOTO 4125
4100 FOR J=I TO N-1
4110 A$(J)=A$(J+1):A(J)=A(J+1):B(J)=B(J+1)
4120 NEXT J
4122 A$(N)="   ":A(N)=0:B(N)=0
4123 N=N-1
4124 PRINT : PRINT "NOW REMOVED": GOSUB 8000
4125 PRINT : INPUT "ANOTHER   ";A$
4126 IF LEFT$ (A$,1)="Y" THEN 4000
4127 IF LEFT$ (A$, 1)="N" THEN 4130
4128 PRINT : PRINT "TRY AGAIN": GOTO 4125
4130 RETURN
4500 HOME
4501 INPUT "NAME OF NEW STUDENT   ";C$
4510 PRINT : INPUT "SCORE OF STUDENT   ";C
4520 N=N+1
4530 A$(N)=C$:A(N)=C
4540 PRINT : PRINT "NEW STUDENT ENTERED"
4542 PRINT : INPUT "ANOTHER   " ; A$
4543 IF LEFT$ (A$,1)="Y" THEN 4501
4544 IF LEFT$ (A$,1)="N" THEN 4550
4545 PRINT : PRINT "TRY AGAIN": GOTO 4542
4547 GOSUB 8000
4550 RETURN
5000 D$=CHR$ (4)
5005 PRINT D$; "OPEN RECORDS"
5010 PRINT D$; "WRITE RECORDS"
5015 FOR I=1 TO N
5020 PRINT A$(I)
5030 NEXT I
5040 PRINT D$; "CLOSE RECORDS"
```

```
5078 PRINT D$; "OPEN MARKS"
5079 PRINT D$; "WRITE MARKS"
5120 FOR I=1 TO N
5130 PRINT A(I)
5140 NEXT I
5170 PRINT D$; "CLOSE MARKS"
5210 PRINT D$; "OPEN STD.MARKS"
5215 PRINT D$; "WRITE STD.MARKS"
5220 FOR I=1 TO N
5225 PRINT B(I)
5230 NEXT I
5235 PRINT D$; "CLOSE STD.MARKS"
5275 PRINT : PRINT "NOW SAVED ON DISK"
5277 GOSUB 8000
5280 RETURN
7000 HOME
7001 PRINT "HOW MANY PUPILS WERE RECORDED"
7002 INPUT "ON THIS DISK    ";N
7005 D$=CHR$ (4)
7006 PRINT D$; "OPEN RECORDS"
7007 PRINT D$; "READ RECORDS"
7008 FOR I=1 TO N
7009 INPUT A$(I)
7010 NEXT I
7020 PRINT D$; "CLOSE RECORDS"
7060 PRINT D$; "OPEN MARKS"
7065 PRINT D$; "READ MARKS"
7070 FOR I=1 TO N
7075 INPUT A(I)
7080 NEXT I
7090 PRINT D$; "CLOSE MARKS"
7100 PRINT D$; "OPEN STD.MARKS"
7105 PRINT D$; "READ STD.MARKS"
7110 FOR I=1 TO N
7120 INPUT B(I)
7130 NEXT I
7150 PRINT D$; "CLOSE STD.MARKS"
7155 PRINT : PRINT "RESULTS NOW RECOVERED"
7156 GOSUB 8000
7160 RETURN
8000 PRINT : PRINT : PRINT "          PRESS ANY KEY"
```

```
8010 GET A$
8020 RETURN
13000 PRINT : PRINT "MEAN BEING COMPUTED"
13002 S1=0:S2=0
13005 FOR I=1 TO N:S1=S1+A(I):S2=S2+(A(I)) ∧ 2
13010 NEXT I
13020 M1=S1 / N : S=S2 / N-M1 ∧ 2 : P=SQR (S) : Q=INT (10 * P+.5) / 10
13030 PRINT : PRINT "MEAN IS "INT (10 * M1+.5) / 10, "STD.DEV IS"Q
13035 GOSUB 8000
13040 RETURN
14000 HOME
14010 INPUT "CHOSEN MEAN   ";M2
14020 INPUT "STD DEV IS   ";SN
14030 IF Q=0 THEN 14080
14040 FOR I=1 TO N
14050 B(I)=M2+((A(I)-M1) / SQR (S)) * SN
14060 NEXT I
14070 GOTO 14090
14080 FOR I=1 TO N:B(I)=M2: NEXT I
14090 PRINT : PRINT "SCORES NOW STANDARDIZED"
14100 GOSUB 8000
14110 RETURN
```

2.

```
 10 DIM A$(2, 35), A(35)
 20 HOME
 30 PRINT "      BIBLIOGRAPHY"
 40 PRINT : PRINT : PRINT
 50 PRINT "THIS PROGRAM ALLOWS YOU TO ENTER A"
 55 PRINT : PRINT "BIBLIOGRAPHY, SAVE IT, RECOVER AND"
 60 PRINT : PRINT "AMEND IT."
 65 GOSUB 420
 70 GOSUB 440
 75 GOSUB 462
 80 PRINT : PRINT
 85 INPUT "   READ LIST AGAIN   ";A$
 90 IF LEFT$ (A$, 1)="Y" THEN 115
 95 IF LEFT$ (A$, 1)="N" THEN 120
100 PRINT : PRINT "TRY AGAIN": GOTO 80
115 GOSUB 500
120 GOSUB 530: GOSUB 440
```

```
130 GOSUB 500: GOSUB 530: GOTO 440
140 GOSUB 560
150 PRINT : PRINT
160 INPUT "    ADD ANOTHER    ";A$
162 IF LEFT$ (A$, 1)="Y" THEN 140
163 IF LEFT$ (A$, 1)="N" THEN 170
165 PRINT : PRINT "TRY AGAIN": GOTO 150
170 GOSUB 530: GOTO 440
190 GOSUB 580
191 PRINT : INPUT "    ANOTHER    ";A$
192 IF LEFT$ (A$, 1)="Y" THEN 190
193 IF LEFT$ (A$,1)="N" THEN 200
194 PRINT : PRINT "TRY AGAIN": GOTO 191
200 GOTO 440
220 GOSUB 600
221 PRINT : INPUT "    CHANGE ANOTHER    ";A$
223 IF LEFT$ (A$, 1)="Y" THEN 220
224 IF LEFT$ (A$, 1)="N" THEN 230
225 PRINT : PRINT "TRY AGAIN": GOTO 221
230 GOTO 440
250 GOSUB 650: GOTO 440
280 GOSUB 750: GOTO 440
300 PRINT : PRINT "    BYE"
310 END
420 PRINT : PRINT : PRINT "PRESS ANY KEY"
425 GET A$: RETURN
440 HOME : PRINT 65536+FRE (0) " FREE BYTES "N" BOOKS IN"
441 PRINT : PRINT "DO YOU WISH TO : "
442 PRINT : PRINT "BEGIN A NEW LIST.......................................B"
443 PRINT : PRINT "READ A CURRENT LIST...................................R"
444 PRINT : PRINT "ADD A BOOK TO LIST ..................................A"
445 PRINT : PRINT "DELETE A BOOK FROM LIST ..........................D"
446 PRINT : PRINT "CHANGE A BOOK ON LIST ............................C"
447 PRINT : PRINT "SAVE LIST ON DISK......................................S"
448 PRINT : PRINT "INPUT LIST FROM DISK .................................I"
450 PRINT : PRINT "FINISH FOR NOW..........................................F"
451 PRINT : INPUT "CHOOSE A LETTER    "; A$
452 IF A$="B" THEN 75
453 IF A$="R" THEN 130
454 IF A$="A" THEN 140
455 IF A$="D" THEN 190
```

```
456 IF A$="C" THEN 220
457 IF A$="S" THEN 250
458 IF A$="I" THEN 280
459 IF A$="F" THEN 300
461 PRINT : PRINT "TRY AGAIN" : GOTO 451
462 HOME : INPUT "HOW MANY BOOKS   " ; N
463 PRINT : FOR I=1 TO N : PRINT "THIS IS BOOK NUMBER   " I
465 PRINT : PRINT "INPUT AUTHOR LIKE THIS   JONES M."
466 INPUT "USE NO COMMAS   " ; A$(0, I)
467 PRINT : INPUT "NAME OF BOOK   " ; A$(1, I)
470 PRINT : INPUT "PUBLISHER   " ; A$(2, I)
473 PRINT : INPUT "DATE OF PUBLICATION. 0 IF UNKNOWN " ; A(I)
475 PRINT : PRINT : NEXT I
477 PRINT : PRINT "THAT WAS THE LAST ONE" : GOSUB 420
480 RETURN
500 HOME : FOR I=1 TO N : PRINT I
501 FOR J=0 TO 2 : PRINT A$(J, I) : PRINT
505 NEXT J : PRINT A(I) : PRINT
510 GOSUB 420 : NEXT I
515 PRINT : PRINT : PRINT "THAT WAS THE LAST ONE" : GOSUB 420
520 PRINT : PRINT : RETURN
530 PRINT : INPUT "ALPHABETICAL ORDER —— YES OR NO ——" ; A$
532 IF LEFT$ (A$, 1)="Y" THEN 538
533 IF LEFT$ (A$, 1)="N" THEN 536
535 PRINT : PRINT "   TRY AGAIN" : GOTO 530
536 GOSUB 420
537 RETURN
538 J=0 : FOR I=1 TO N-1 : IF A$(0, I) < A$(0, I+1) THEN 542
539 X$=A$(0, I+1) : Y$=A$(1, I+1) : Z$=A$(2, I+1) : X=A(I+1)
540 A$(0, I+1)=A$(0, I) : A$(1, I+1)=A$(1, I) : A$(2, I+1)=A$(2, I) :
    A(I+1)=A(I)
541 A$(0, I)=X$ : A$(1, I)=Y$ : A$(2, I)=Z$ : A(I)=X : J=J+1
542 NEXT I
543 IF J > 0 THEN 538
544 PRINT : PRINT : PRINT "IN ALPHABETICAL ORDER."
545 GOSUB 420
549 RETURN
560 N=N+1 : HOME : INPUT "NAME OF AUTHOR   " ; A$(0, N)
562 PRINT : INPUT "BOOK TITLE   " ; A$(1, N)
564 PRINT : INPUT "PUBLISHER   " ; A$(2, N)
565 PRINT : INPUT "PUBL. YEAR   " ; A(N)
```

```
570 RETURN
580 HOME : INPUT "INPUT NAME    " ; T$
587 FOR I=1 TO N
589 IF A$(0, I)=T$ THEN 592
590 NEXT I
591 PRINT : PRINT "NAME NOT ON LIST" : PRINT
592 FOR J=I TO N-1
593 A$(0, J)=A$(0, J+1) : A$(1, J)=A$(1, J+1) : A$(2, J)=A$(2, J+1) :
    A(J)=A(J+1)
594 NEXT J
596 A$(0, N)=" " : A$(1, N)=" " : A$(2, N)=" "
597 N=N-1
598 PRINT : PRINT : PRINT "BOOK HAS BEEN REMOVED." : GOSUB 420
599 RETURN
600 HOME
601 INPUT "AUTHOR TO BE CHANGED?    " ; S$
604 FOR I=1 TO N
606 PRINT : IF A$(0, I)=S$ THEN 620
608 NEXT
609 PRINT : PRINT : PRINT "NOT ON LIST"
610 RETURN
620 PRINT : PRINT "NAME ENTRY    " ; A$(0, I)
621 PRINT : PRINT
622 INPUT "NEW NAME?    " ; A$(0, I)
623 PRINT : PRINT "BOOK TITLE    " A$(1, I)
624 PRINT : PRINT
625 INPUT "NEW TITLE?    " ; A$(1, I)
626 PRINT : PRINT "PUBLISHER    " ; A$(2, I)
628 PRINT : PRINT
629 INPUT "NEW NAME?    " ; A$(2, I)
630 PRINT : PRINT "YEAR    " ; A(I)
631 PRINT : PRINT
632 INPUT "YEAR? " ; A(I)
635 RETURN
650 HOME
652 PRINT : PRINT : PRINT "DATA BEING SAVED"
655 PRINT : PRINT : INPUT "WHAT FILE NAME    " ; K$
657 Z$=CHR$ (4)
659 PRINT Z$ ; "OPEN" ; K$
660 PRINT Z$ ; "WRITE" ; K$
662 FOR V=0 TO 2
```

```
664 FOR I=1 TO N
665 PRINT A$(V, I)
666 NEXT I
669 NEXT V
688 FOR I=1 TO N
690 PRINT A(I)
692 NEXT I
696 PRINT Z$ ; "CLOSE" ; K$
698 RETURN
750 HOME
751 INPUT "HOW MANY BOOKS ARE STORED ON THE DISK" ; N
752 PRINT : INPUT "WHAT IS THE FILE NAME    " ; K$
753 PRINT : PRINT : PRINT "DATA BEING RECOVERED"
755 Z$=CHR$ (4)
757 PRINT Z$ ; "OPEN" ; K$
760 PRINT Z$ ; "READ" ; K$
762 FOR V=0 TO 2
764 FOR I=1 TO N
765 INPUT A$(V, I)
766 NEXT I
767 NEXT V
788 FOR I=1 TO N
790 INPUT A(I)
792 NEXT I
795 PRINT Z$ ; "CLOSE" ; K$
797 GET Y$
798 RETURN
```

Appendix H Further Reading

BASIC

Listed below is a short selection of the great many books about BASIC. Look at as many as you can and try to find one that suits your own needs.

Each of these books, with one exception, can be used as an introductory text. The exception is the one by Lien already mentioned on page 17. This is an encyclopedia of the BASIC language and is a most useful reference book.

Alcock, D. *Illustrating BASIC.* Cambridge: Cambridge University Press, 1977.

Bishop, P. *Computer Programming in BASIC.* Walton-on-Thames, Surrey: Nelson, 1979.

Coan, J.S. *Advanced BASIC: Applications and Problems.* Rochelle Park, N.J.: Hayden Book Company, Inc., 1977.

Coan, J.S. *Basic BASIC: An Introduction to Computer Programming in BASIC.* Rochelle Park, N.J.: Hayden Book Company, Inc., 1978.

Deitel, H.M. *Introduction to Computer Programming with the BASIC Language.* Englewood Cliffs, N.J.: Prentice-Hall, 1978.

Dwyer, T.A. and Crutchfield, M.A. *BASIC and the Personal Computer.* London: Addison Wesley, 1978.

Eagle, M.R. *An Introduction to BASIC.* London: Bell and Hyman, 1976.

Farina, M.V. *Programming in BASIC, the Time-sharing Language.* Englewood Cliffs, N.J.: Prentice-Hall, 1968.

Hubin, W.N. *BASIC Programming for Scientists and Engineers.* Englewood Cliffs, N.J.: Prentice-Hall, 1978.

Lien, D.A. *The BASIC Handbook: An Encyclopedia of the BASIC Computer Language.* San Diego, Ca.: Compusoft Pulishing, 1979.

Monro, D.M. *Interactive Computing with BASIC, a First Course.* London: Edward Arnold, 1978.

Scott, P.E. *Programming in BASIC: a Beginners' Course,* London: Hodder and Stoughton, 1975.

APPLE AND GENERAL

This second list of books is more general and contains books about Apple or about small computers in general.

Apple Computer Inc., *The Applesoft Tutorial.* Cupertino, California, 1979. (This is a good introduction to some aspects of Applesoft BASIC.)

Apple Computer Inc., *Applesoft BASIC Programming Reference Manual.* Cupertino, California, 1978. (A detailed reference manual of all Applesoft words and commands.)

Apple Computer Inc., *Apple* 2 *BASIC Programming Manual.* Cupertino, California, 1978. (An introduction to Integer Basic.)

Apple Computer Inc., *DOS Version* 3.2. Cupertino, California, 1979. (This is about DOS 3.2.)

Apple Computer Inc., *The DOS Manual.* Cupertino, California, 1980. (This is about DOS 3.3.)

Apple Computer Inc., *Apple* 2 *Reference Manual.* Cupertino, California, 1979. (A detailed reference book to all aspects of the Apple's physical make-up, the monitor and memory organization.)

Bradbeer, R., *The Personal Computer Book.* Farnborough, Hants.: Input Two-nine, 1980. (This is a good general introduction to small computers with lots of useful addresses and lists.)

Inman, D. and K. *Apple Machine Language.* Reston, Virginia: Reston Publishing Company, Inc., 1981.

Leventhal, L.A. 6502 *Assembly Language Programming.* Berkeley, Ca.: Osborne/McGraw Hill, 1979. (An introduction to writing machine-code on the microprocessor used in the Apple, i.e. the 6502.)

Lewis, T.G. *Pascal Programming for the Apple.* Reston, Virginia: Reston Publishing Company, Inc., 1981.

Waite, M. *Computer Graphics Primer.* Indianapolis, Indiana: Howard W. Sams & Co., Inc., 1979.

Zaks, R. *Programming the* 6502. Berkeley, California: Syken, 1980.

APPLE ASSOCIATIONS AND JOURNALS

(a) BASUG (British Apple Systems User Group) produces a newsletter which is available from PO Box 174, Watford, WD2 6NF, England. They also publish a journal called *Hard Core*. Contains an up-to-date list of user groups in United Kingdom.

(b) *Windfall* is a journal for Apple users, published monthly, available from Europa House, 68 Chester Road, Hazel Grove, Stockport, Cheshire SK7 5YB, England.

(c) *Apple Orchard* is published in the USA and is available from PO Box 1493, Beaverton, OR.97075, USA.

(d) International Apple Core is an organization made up of Apple computer user groups throughout the world. It publishes *Apple Orchard* (above), and can be contacted at PO Box 976, Daly City, California 94017, USA.

(e) A.P.P.L.E., 304 Main Ave. Sth., Suite 300, Renton, Wa. 98055, USA. The American user group. Publishes software and a journal.

Index

D

E

F

G

H

P

Q

R

S

T

U

V

W

X